THE
BUSINESS
GROWTH
HANDBOOK

THE
BUSINESS
GROWTH
HANDBOOK

Colin Barrow
Robert Brown
Liz Clarke

KOGAN
PAGE

First published in 1994
Reprinted 1995
Paperback edition published in 1997
Reprinted 1997

Kogan Page Limited
120 Pentonville Road
London N1 9JN

British Library Cataloguing in Publication Data

A CIP record of this book is available from the British Library.

ISBN 0 7494 0521 X (Hbk)   0 7494 1431 6 (Pbk)

Typeset by Photoprint, Torquay.
Printed in England by Clays Ltd, St Ives plc

Contents

Introduction

Recent years have seen a major resurgence of entrepreneurship throughout the developed world. Even in Eastern Europe and the former Soviet Union such skills are now greatly prized. In Britain alone the numbers of people running their own business grew from 1.9 million in 1979 to around 3.6m in 1995.

Now that such achievements are in place, surely we can relax and wait for the great benefits of a new and vibrant business age to descend? Full employment, shorter working hours, more leisure and above all greater wealth should be on the horizon, if not actually here. But all the empirical evidence points the other way. In the 1980s, driven by the monetarist policies of the Thatcher Government, monolithic state industries with obsolete technology and redundant workers were swept away in a great industrial purging. But many of the new entrepreneurs who sprang up in their place have fared little better. To be sure there are still stars in the firmament – Anita Roddick of the Body Shop and Alan Sugar of Amstrad for example. But many of the 1980s school of entrepreneurs have either failed to grow or, rather more seriously, they have failed to survive.

Research published in the autumn of 1990 presented strong evidence that only firms with fewer than 20 employees are net creators of jobs – or looking at it another way, small firms in Britain run out of steam at only 20 employees. This conclusion was drawn from the following stark statistics. Between 1985 and 1987 small firms employing between five and nineteen people created around 290,000 jobs compared with firms between 20 and 49 people who actually shed 80,000 jobs between them. In other words, in the latter group of firms growth had stalled. It is also becoming clear that Britain's recession of 1990–92 swept away more small firms as a proportion of the small firm population than previous recessions. However, it is also clear that recessions do not curb the enthusiasm to start up in business – both 1991 and 1992 saw record levels of new businesses, some 500,000 in each year.

The hypothesis that we at Cranfield subscribe to is that the major determinant of the relatively disappointing performance of small firms is essentially a failure to change from a one-man-band type of structure, to one based on team management and delegation. Most bankers and financiers cite weak management as the major reason they won't invest more in small firms, reinforcing this view.

The quality of management in small firms is another weak link. First, because there are so few managers and, second, because those that exist are rarely trained as managers. Unlike in the United States for example, the majority of UK entrepreneurs have no professional or other qualifications and only a small minority have either qualifications or man-management experience. They run their business on the basis of common sense. This may be effective so long as the scale of the firms' activities remains small enough for one person to control them all effectively, and no serious crisis overwhelms them.

Until now the chances are that you have managed your business, in the main, by successfully exploiting opportunities as and when they arise. Strategic planning will have played a relatively minor part in your thinking – if it played any part at all. After all, with an uncertain future opportunities can only be seen once they are on the horizon. Or can they?

Certainly, the elderly couple who scooped more than £6 million from the sale of a sixteenth-century bronze statue they had kept in their garden for 40 years had no commercial strategy in mind when they bought it. Even when they put it in the local sale, the 'opportunity' on their horizon was only the valuation price of between £1000 and £1800. The 'strategic' thinking was being done by a 23-year-old Sotheby's employee who, as part of her task, surveyed all local sales catalogues in her field of expertise. She went out to 'meet' the opportunity and netted her employer £620,000 in commission, and a further substantial six figure sum in free publicity.

This rather dramatic example illustrates the difference between luck that presents opportunities in a fairly random way, and strategy which seeks to make certain things happen in a focused and directed way. Left to chance alone, ventures follow only one natural law – the law of gravity. Developing a sound strategy is the method by which a business enterprise can defy gravity. The single most important reason why 75 per cent of all new businesses don't see their tenth birthday is because they never learn that lesson.

So how can you learn that lesson, and get out of the 'serendipity cycle' that sweeps small firms in and out like a particularly vicious tide? The American organisation researcher, L E Greiner, identified five distinctive phases in a company's growth pattern, and provided an insight into the changes in organisational structure, strategy and behaviour that needed to be achieved if they were to move on to the next phase of growth. By implication his research revealed that most firms never learn the lessons, or at any rate not in time. At best they bounce up and down against the frontiers of the phase they are in; at worst they fail and flounder.

Phase 1. Crisis of leadership
Phase 2. Crisis of autonomy
Phase 3. Crisis of control
Phase 4. Crisis of red tape
Phase 5. Crisis of ?

Over 300 companies have successfully completed the Growth Programme at Cranfield. Many have accomplished major strategic change brought about through the programme. Acquisitions (and divestments) abound, new products and services are launched, and new markets entered. This year, one of our earliest participants comes to the stock market, having grown from £3m to £50m sales since completing the Cranfield programme.

This book, based on our research and teaching at Cranfield, is intended to give you a clear insight into the characteristics of each phase of growth you are likely to experience, and a framework to help you manage your firm through the crises ahead. (The word crisis, incidentally, derives from the Chinese and translates literally as, 'dangerous opportunity'.)

Thanks are due to the participants on Cranfield Business Growth Programmes who, since 1987, have helped, albeit unwittingly, in preparing and testing this teaching material.

Colin Barrow, Robert Brown, Liz Clarke
Cranfield, May 1995

The Structure of This Book

The book is divided into three parts. Part 1 is concerned with establishing where your business is now – its current strengths and weaknesses. Part 2 looks at where you would like to take the business and the strategies you could pursue. Part 3 looks at how you will achieve your growth objectives – and helps you to document the transition by way of a new business plan.

In each part, the three principal management disciplines that all research in the small business sector confirms as being vital, are covered:

- People and Management;
- Financial Management and Control;
- Marketing Management.

Each chapter contains a wealth of examples and case studies to illustrate the points being made. Checklists and questionnaires are provided to help you put the ideas advanced into practice in your business immediately. At the end of each chapter there is an assignment task to help you review the issues raised in the light of your own experiences in your business. We firmly believe that all management theory is only useful insofar as you can apply it to profitable purpose in your business. The assignments will also be useful for instructors on other training programmes to steer their students through the course.

Part 1:

Where Are We Now?

The first six chapters are intended to help you establish the current position of your business. Just as a plan for a journey, for example, would be useless unless you had a clear idea of where you were starting out from, any business strategy needs a similar reference base.

Entrepreneurs have an almost irrepressible desire to move directly from spotting an opportunity to exploiting it – or attempting to do so. To continue the travel analogy, this is rather like seeing a road sign to an interesting destination and immediately following it, without first checking that you have sufficient fuel to complete the journey or that perhaps even more appropriate and exciting destinations are not just beyond the horizon. It's no great surprise, therefore, to find that a large proportion of management time is spent putting right yesterday's mistakes. Tom Frost, former chief executive of the National Westminster Bank, is on record as saying that mistakes account for between 25 and 40 per cent of the total cost in a service business. The following chapters pose the sort of questions you need to examine to establish your strengths and weaknesses, opportunities and threats across the key areas of your business and its current and potential markets.

In business school jargon, the activity of taking stock is known as the position audit.

Phase 1: Growth through creativity

Any business starting up does so because somebody (you!) has a good idea about providing a product or service for which they believe there is sound demand. If the idea is successful then the business can grow or evolve with equal success. The founder of the company is at the heart of everything. Assuming the business has been successful and shows steady growth – a description which fits only between 60 and 70 per cent of start-ups, the rest having already failed by this stage – there comes a time when the person who started the business with their creative ideas and personal, informal style of operation can no longer cope effectively. The person who provided all the drive, all the ideas and made all the decisions becomes overloaded with administrative detail and operational problems. Unless the founder can change the organisational structure of their firm and put in place a management team, any further growth will leave the business vulnerable – it will be incapable of becoming a substantial firm with a life independent from that of its founder. A cycle of one step forward and two steps back will probably begin, or else a gentle decline will set in. The end of this first growth phase, which can take anything from two or three years to a decade in extreme cases, is signalled by a *crisis of leadership*.

Table 1 will give you some idea of exactly how dangerous this opportunity is, as over 50 per cent of businesses that fail do so in less than five years – a further 25 per cent go in under 10 years.

Table 1 *Ages of 61,209 businesses that failed in 1987*

Age of business	All types	Manufacturing	Wholesale trade	Retail trade	Services
	%	%	%	%	%
1 year or less	10.0	7.8	7.7	12.0	14.9
2 years	12.4	13.0	12.5	15.9	12.7
3 years	11.4	11.3	11.3	13.7	11.2
4 years	9.4	9.9	9.5	10.1	8.9
5 years	7.5	7.0	8.4	7.6	7.8
Total 5 years or less	50.7	49.0	49.4	59.3	55.5
6 – 10 years	24.6	23.3	25.5	22.0	24.6
Over 10 years	24.7	27.7	25.1	18.7	19.9
Total	100.0	100.0	100.0	100.0	100.0

Phase 2: Growth through direction

A strong leader is required to pull the company through this crisis, a leader who is able to make tough decisions about priorities, and provide the clear, single-minded direction and sense of purpose needed to move the business forward.

Ideas the pioneer founder used to carry in his or her head now have to be formalised. Policies need to be evolved, teams built up and key people appointed with specific roles to play and objectives to achieve. The personal management style of the founder becomes secondary to making the business efficient. Sometimes the founder is not the right person to lead the organisation through this phase and, either through lack of management skills or temperament, may opt to give up or sell out.

Country Holidays

Philip Green, aged 37, an Ayrshire farmer's son has already made himself a sizeable fortune by building up and selling a company called Country Holidays before launching into the training business.

Country Holidays is basically an agency which lets country cottages to holiday makers. He launched it 12 years ago in Skipton and sold it in 1989 to the management for £14m, retaining a 10 per cent holding. 'Businesses have phases', he says. 'Country Holidays reached the stage where it needed steady system management rather than the flat out style of an entrepreneur'.

So Mr Green is now back in a two-roomed office in Skipton putting his entrepreneurial talents to work in building his new business. His selling tack is that most businesses need to improve their customer service and he can teach them how to do it.

A more immediately attractive service to some potential customers is Mr Green's offer to teach improved telephone selling skills. Also, like so many organisations from accountants to designers, he will do a little management consultancy for anyone who wants it.

Thus, he hopes to have built Train and Motivate to a turnover of £120,000 in this, its first year, with £250,000 next year and then a regular doubling each subsequent year. He has invested £80,000 of his capital in getting it started, and budgeted to lose £100,000 this year and to break even next.

But he admits that it is proving hard going. Initial mailing met with a good response. 'September was disaster, though' he says, with the lack of concern that only a degree of financial security can provide.

Success at this stage of growth depends on finding, motivating and keeping key staff – no mean task. The Cranfield Key Employee Study conducted in 1990 revealed that over 80 per cent of the proprietors of growing firms rated this a major problem, compared with around 50 per cent who were most concerned about finding customers and only 25 per cent who rated raising money or high interest rates as a top issue. Eventually, as the company grows and matures, the directive top-down management style starts to become counter-productive. Others working in the organisation acquire more expertise about their particular sphere of operations than the central director. Not surprisingly, they want a greater say in the strategy of the business. Such subordinates either struggle for power so that they can be heard, or become demotivated and leave. This is the *crisis of autonomy* and, if it is not recognised and managed, it will absorb so much energy and time that it will drag the company down. In the Cranfield study referred to above, three out of five of the growth companies surveyed reported the loss of key employees. Two-thirds of them experienced this loss within a year of making the appointment.

Proprietors usually put this defection of key employees down to better pay elsewhere. In this they are usually wrong. A MORI poll conducted in 1989 on 1000 employees for the Industrial Society asked people to identify the five most important things they looked for in a job:

- 66 per cent said having an interesting and enjoyable job;
- 52 per cent said job security;
- 41 per cent said feeling they had accomplished something worthwhile;
- 37 per cent said basic pay;
- 30 per cent regarded the chance to learn new skills as being of prime importance.

Interestingly enough, this study concluded that employers generally saw pay as the key factor in recruiting and retaining staff, and only 11 per cent thought job satisfaction was an important factor.

Phase 3: Growth through delegation

The solution to the crisis of autonomy is to recognise that more responsibility has to be delegated to more people in the company (see Table 2). The trouble is that most founders hang on to too many jobs in their firms, mostly out of a belief that nobody else can do the job as well as they. The reasons for this argument are legion and include the often expressed: it takes more time to explain the job than to do it myself; a mistake would be too costly; they lack the experience; and so on. There is probably an element of truth in all of these reasons, but until you

Table 2 *The stages of growth*

	Phase 1 *Entrepreneurial*	Phase 2 *Direction*	Phase 3 *Delegation*	Phase 4 *Co-ordination*	Phase 5 *Collaboration*
Structure	Informal	Functional Centralised Hierarchical Top down	Decentralised Bottom-up	Staff functions Introduced SBUs Decentralised Units merged into product groups	Matrix type structure
Systems	Immediate response to customer feedback	Standards Cost centres Budget Salary systems	Profit centres Bonuses Management by exception	Formal planning procedures Investment centres Tight expenditure controls	Simplified & integrated information systems
Styles/People	Individualistic Creative Entrepreneurial Ownership	Strongly directive Impersonal	Full delegation & autonomy	Watchdog	Team-orientated Interpersonal skills at a premium Innovative Educational bias
Strengths	Fun Market Response	Efficient	High management motivation	More efficient allocation of corporate & local resources	Greater spontaneity Flexible & behavioural approach
Crisis point	Crisis of leadership	Crisis of autonomy	Crisis of control	Crisis of red tape	?
Weaknesses	Founder often temperamentally unsuited to managing Boss overloaded	Unsuited Diversity Cumbersome Hierarchy Doesn't grow people	Top managers lose control as freedom breeds parochial attitudes	Bureaucratic divisions between line/staff, headquarters/ field etc.	Psychological saturation

learn how to *delegate decisions* rather than simply *dumping tasks*, your organisation will never reach full maturity.

Two problems arise at this stage. First, a number of the managers you appointed earlier on will simply not be up to the task of accepting their new responsibilities – not all people who can take direction can take part in a bottom-up planning process that is dependent on high quality inputs. So this means you are back in the recruiting game. You may be wise at this stage to stop relying on personal contacts or direct press advertising, as the majority of small firms do, and go for executive search through a consultancy using sound selection techniques. You probably thought this option too expensive at Phase 1 and possibly so at Phase 2, but by now you will have made enough mistakes in recruitment to know that it is a profession in its own right,and requires knowledge and skills you may not have. Furthermore, the indirect costs of getting the wrong people more than outweigh the cost of paying for an expert. One owner manager was a little startled, to say the least, when he discovered that doing the recruitment himself cost him over six times as much as using an agency – see Table 3.

A second point to be aware of is that every solution creates new problems. For example, delegating decisions to give people a strong sense of involvement will eventually lead to control problems – the *crisis of control*.

Finally, it's as well to remember that evolution and growth in business are not automatic. It's your job to know when the time for strategic change has come and exactly what that strategy should be.

Table 3 *The real cost of finding key staff*

	£
Cost of agency	
35% of salaries	8,750
No find, no fee	
(for £25,000 post)	
Cost of doing it yourself*	
Advertising	2,000
Following up contacts	2,500
5 weekends + 10 evenings (50 hours at £50 per hour)	
Time spent interviewing dross (20 hours at £50 per hour)	1,000
Lost profit because this all took six months instead of three	50,000
(Sales at £0.5million pa by 40% GM)	55,500

* The person in question lasted six weeks, made 15 verified calls, no orders, no quotes, had family problems and was trying to start up a business on the side.

FDS Market Research Group

Some business people may be prevailed upon to bring in specialist managers in fields such as finance or marketing because they recognise their own limitations in these areas. But few are willing to delegate wide-ranging responsibility for running their business to a professional outsider.

One of these rare exceptions is Janet Weitz, founder and chairman of FDS (Market Research) Group, a North London company with sales of £3.6m and a full-time work-force of 34 people. Three years ago, when turnover had reached £2m, Weitz decided to step back from the day-to-day running of her business and to bring in a managing director.

Weitz was concerned that outsiders would identify the company too closely with her and see it as a one-woman business. This could have acted as a brake on further growth. She was also keen to have a proper professional management in place for when the time came to float or sell the company.

The person Weitz turned to was David Dubow, a director of a larger rival market research company, MIL. Dubow joined FDS as managing director designate in May 1988 and a year later was confirmed as managing director. Now 38, Dubow says the move to FDS was an opportunity to gain independence and seniority at a younger age than appeared possible in his previous job.

He has also acquired a 20 per cent stake in the company. Weitz, who owns 69 per cent of the equity, has become chairman and now devotes her time to broader, strategic issues.

Coming to the intellectual and emotional decision to hand over the reins of a business she had run for 14 years was not easy, says Weitz. 'You can discuss it round a table and agree that it is right but it is difficult to let go. It is like your baby.'

Lengthy discussions with Dubow before he decided to join FDS and the year-long trial convinced her it was the right thing to do and that he shared her view of how the company should develop.

The time was right as well. 'I am in my mid-40s now', she says, 'I could never have let go in my mid-30s. I can remember when I would not let a piece of typing or a questionnaire go without checking it.'

At first Weitz and Dubow had not decided how long the trial period should last but a professional friend of Weitz's suggested they set a specific date. He also advised that Weitz move out of her office to make way for Dubow as a symbol of the change over. But Weitz liked her office too much and compromised by giving Dubow a larger office elsewhere in the building.

On the day that Dubow became managing director, Weitz arranged a formal handing over ceremony. 'We made a celebration of it and cracked open some bottles of champagne', Weitz recalls. Staff were understandably sceptical that Weitz would actually hand over power after all those years, says Dubow. 'But that faded fairly quickly. They could see that Janet and I got on and that we were saying the same thing in a different way.'

When Dubow came into the company he took a close look at its systems and methods of working before suggesting any changes. FDS was organised as an 'efficient small company' but some modifications were needed if it were to grow, he says.

Where Are We Now?

Previously, research executives operated on their own or in ad hoc groups. Dubow has created working groups with an executive in charge and more junior members to achieve greater continuity and a clearer line of command. He has also chased after more international business, an area where FDS was weak.

Weitz, for her part, has been able to concentrate on longer-term issues and on giving more time to industry-wide initiatives in areas such as carrying out research on the telephone and quality control. She was involved in the recent acquisition of a smaller research company and is considering diversifying FDS into political polling.

Both Weitz and Dubow have been pleased by their initial experience of her decision to share power – Weitz says she would find it very difficult to go back into the day-to-day management of the business – but such partnerships require careful management.

But even with good management teams in place further problems can occur. Once managers you can delegate to are in place, they will make their own decisions as well as the ones you delegate to them. In time the organisation will become increasingly fragmented and uncoordinated. This often becomes apparent in fairly dramatic ways, such as loss of profits, margin erosion, unplanned development and a lack of an overall strategy that everyone can commit to. Another crisis looms – the crisis of control.

Phase 4: Growth through co-ordination

During this phase the crisis of control is overcome by achieving the best of both the delegation and the direction phases. Decision-making (and power) is still delegated, but in a systematic and regulated way, with accountability becoming a byword for the first time. At this point the organisation begins to put in place strategic planning of some sort, to combine bottom-up and top-down planning methods. Systems and policies are developed to regulate the behaviour of managers at all levels. Communication is vital and a corporate culture takes shape giving new employees a feel for the way things are done in the company.

This growth phase usually ends in the *crisis of red tape*, where the clutter of rules and regulations that bind the company together results in missed opportunities. Bureaucracy rules and development and initiative are stifled. This crisis can be overcome, or even circumvented, by introducing innovative, non-bureaucratic planning procedures, or by sub-dividing the business into manageable units with their own separate missions and management. This is fine as long as you don't return these units back to Phase 1 type growth in a desperate bid to release creativity.

The Christal Group

Chris Jackson, founder and chairman of the Christal Group of Companies, a Newbury, Berkshire-based specialist transport group, took a decision to bring in a managing director from outside the company several years ago. Christal has since expanded strongly under Jackson, 46, and his managing director, Dennis Pye, but the combination of strong-willed entrepreneur and big-company-trained professional has not always been smooth. At one stage the group nearly foundered under the weight of big-company-style bureaucracy.

Jackson, a draughtsman by training, founded Christal Cabs in 1967 but later switched to provide a delivery service for computer parts. By the early 1980s Christal was struggling. Turnover had risen but, Jackson acknowledges, he was 'not very financially minded' and profits failed to keep pace. Jackson was relieved when he was made an offer by Lex Transport Services but the deal fell through when Lex decided to dispose of its transport operations.

Jackson had been impressed by Pye, who had made the initial approach on behalf of Lex, and asked him to become managing director, backed up by the offer of a 25 per cent stake in the business. Pye agreed to join and Jackson became chairman, taking a back seat and devoting more time to his family.

After a year, though, it was clear to Jackson that the switch to professional management methods was taking longer than he had hoped. A number of middle managers found Pye's insistence on prompt financial reporting and on planning difficult to take; they left.

'I realised that people needed me', says Jackson. He remained convinced that Christal needed what he calls Pye's more clinical approach. Pye prefers to call his style 'clear cut, objective', but he felt it needed leavening with a touch of entrepreneurial flair. 'Because of my professional training I weigh all the odds', comments Pye. 'The entrepreneur doesn't always do that. He has a gut feel that something is right.'

There have been disagreements, both acknowledge. 'One has to take a pragmatic view and look to the interests of the company', notes Pye. 'We have different skills which complement each other', says Jackson.

Having decided to take a more active role in the company again, Jackson found, like some of his middle managers before him, that it was difficult to fit into the new, more formal structure. 'I found myself out of place', he explains. 'I wasn't going through the right channels.'

This continued for a year or so until Jackson decided he needed to take an even closer hand in the planning of the business. At a board meeting in 1988 Jackson and Pye, together with the company's accountants, Coopers and Lybrand, and its bank manager, met to discuss their thoughts for the company's future.

Jackson took the formal title of marketing director as well as chairman (he has visiting cards made out in both titles) and threw himself into liaising with customers and improving the corporate image. As a former draughtsman he is working on a redesign of the vehicle fleet's livery.

Calling in a professional manager has not worked out exactly as Jackson had planned, but Christal has done well from the partnership. Profits have improved while turnover, which was £300,000 in 1981, has increased to £9m (half contributed by OTP, a recent acquisition which specialises in bespoke packaging for awkward loads).

Perhaps as important, Jackson has more faith in himself as manager. 'I had always been overawed by big company managers', he says. 'I always thought it must be easier to run a small company than a big one. Now I know it is just different.'

Phase 5: Collaboration

The way to circumvent red tape is to inculcate an attitude of collaboration throughout the organisation. This calls for much simplified and integrated information systems, and an emphasis on team-orientated activity.

Many successful Japanese and European firms now organise their work-forces into teams, where there used to be production lines. Volvo, for example, has a team responsible for making and assembling the whole of one car. This has the effect of making a group of people responsible for the whole of one major portion of a task, rather than having individuals responsible for small and sometimes rather meaningless parts of the process. In this way people can be encouraged to generate solutions rather than just pass problems on down the line.

A further emphasis at this stage of growth is on management education and personal development. This activity is viewed as a luxury in a new venture, and as a good investment in a mature venture.

Most of your businesses will lie somewhere between the crisis of leadership and the fourth stage of growth, using Greiner's model. It will be useful to keep some points in mind as you steer a course through these troubled and largely uncharted waters.

Tempting though it will be, don't be impatient try to skip phases. Each phase results in certain strengths and learning experiences that are essential for success in subsequent phases. When one owner manager was introduced to this way of looking at growth, the scales fell from his eyes. He had tried to delegate authority and involve his key managers in developing strategy almost from the time he launched the business. As a result, there was not a clear enough set of goals for them to aim for and they left one after another. The organisation nearly failed too. This was as a direct result of trying to move too quickly from Phase 1 to Phase 3, skipping Phase 2.

1

Your Mission

The mission statements and prime objectives both require examining at the beginning and at the end of the strategic review. If you already have or have had a mission and some key objectives, the analysis of strengths and weaknesses, threats and opportunities will allow you to measure performance and recognise how they should be modified or changed. If you have no mission or key objectives then that too will tell

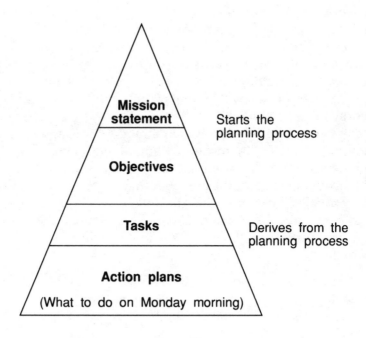

Figure 1.1 *The pyramid of goals*

Note: Mission statements and objectives are 'what' statements; tasks and action plans are 'how to' statements.

you something important. Without these your business will not have sufficient direction to pull you through the crisis in Phase 1 growth and into a more advanced growth phase.

Let's take mission statements and objectives first, as they are inevitably intertwined. These are direction statements, intended to focus your attention on the essentials that encapsulate your specific competence(s) in relation to the markets/customers you plan to serve.

First, the mission should be narrow enough to give direction and guidance to everyone in the business. This concentration is the key to business success because it is only by focusing on specific needs that a small business can differentiate itself from its larger competitors. Nothing kills off a new business faster than trying to do too many different things at the outset. Second, the mission should open up a large enough market to allow the business to grow and realise its potential.

Interestingly enough, one of the highest incidences of failure in small business is in the building trade. The very nature of this field seems to militate against being able to concentrate on any specific type of work, or on customer need. One successful new small builder defined his mission in the following sentence: 'We will concentrate on domestic house repair and renovation work, and as well as doing a good job we will meet the customers' two key needs: a quotation that is accurate, and starting and completion dates that are met.' When told this mission, most small builders laugh; they say it cannot be done – but then most go broke.

Ultimately, there has to be something unique about your business idea or yourself that makes people want to buy from you. That uniqueness may be confined to the fact that you are the only photocopying shop in the area, but that is enough to make you stand out (provided, of course, that the area has potential customers).

In summary, the mission statement should explain what business you are in or plan to enter. It should include some or all of the following:

- Market/customer needs – who are we 'satisfying'?
- With what product/service will we meet that need?
- What are our capabilities, both particular skills and knowledge, and resources?
- What market opportunities are there for our product or service, and what threats are there from competitors (and others)?
- What do we enjoy doing most?
- What do we want to achieve both now and in the future?

Above all, mission statements should be realistic, achievable – and brief.

Blooming Marvellous

Blooming Marvellous is a company formed by two young mothers in 1980. Both founders were interested in fashion and clothing, although neither had great first-hand experience in the field. They started making clothes for children, mothers such as themselves, and some general fashion garments. This kept the money rolling in for the first few years but, despite recruiting some good staff, the company failed to grow significantly.

After a brain-storming session the founders decided to concentrate their resources on the market that seemed to offer the greatest potential commensurate with both their skills and their personal desires. This led them to this mission statement, which provided the focal point for a burst of strong growth.

'Arising out of our experiences we intend to design, make and market a range of clothes for mothers-to-be that will make them feel they can still be fashionably dressed. We aim to serve a niche missed out by Mothercare, Marks and Spencer etc, and so be a significant force in the mail order "fashion for the mother-to-be" market.'

Drexel Burnham Lambert

Drexel Burnham Lambert's informal mission statement was rather more succinct: 'To be as big as Solomon Brothers so we can be as arrogant as they are and tell them to go stuff it.' (Drexels were founded in the early 1970s. By 1986 they were making post-tax profits of $450m but laid off 5,000 staff in 1990.)

More on missions

A manager with a small hosiery firm both impressed and irritated other participants at a training seminar by continually bubbling with enthusiasm about the company he worked for. Although it seemed, in the words of one course member, 'naive verging on the obnoxious', no one questioned his commitment. He clearly identified himself closely with the firm's aspirations.

This manager was not suffering from an acute case of business indoctrination. His dedication stemmed from a sense of mission; a rational and emotional belief in his company's products, services and business strategy.

Andrew Campbell, director of the London-based Ashridge Strategic Management Centre (ASMC), says: 'Many of the world's outstanding companies have employees with what we call "a sense of mission". These people believe that their company is special; they are proud of being part of it all.'

Campbell heads a research project into how managers can better understand and create a sense of mission in their organisations. He is convinced that firms increasingly need 'passionate' employees, and says: 'Many organisations have become depersonalised to the point where energy levels are low, cynicism is high and work fails to excite or fulfil employees. We find that committed staff perform many times more efficiently than apathetic ones.'

ASMC's work on mission has grown out of research during the past two years into the use and misuse of mission statements. These are used by business leaders to share issues such as the company's philosophy, commercial rationale and strategy with employees.

American research suggests that nearly half of the country's large companies have mission statements. ASMC's work suggests a similar figure in Britain.

After an exhaustive study of more than 100 statements from American, Japanese and European companies, the Centre concluded that these statements in themselves had little impact on business success. Much more important is whether a sense of mission already exists in the hearts and minds of employees. Employees not only need to have a clear understanding of what their company is trying to achieve but have to be emotionally committed to its aims before a meaningful statement can be written. If commitment is lacking, a mission statement is at best likely to be ignored and at worst treated with cynicism.

From these findings, ASMC has set out five principles to help managers trying to create a sense of mission:

- Leaders should pick a theme around which to develop the new mission. It should capture the company's future strategy and values, and should be easy to translate into behaviours and standards.
- Focus on action rather than words.
- Key standards and behaviours should clearly affirm the company's new direction.
- Be patient. Developing a new mission takes years.
- Build and sustain trust. This is often achieved by senior management being visible and open about the changes taking place.

'Leaders should not forget that although a sense of mission is an emotional force, it can be managed', Campbell says. 'It is an aspect of business which cannot be ignored. An organisation with a sense of mission has a strong advantage.'

Prime objectives

Objectives give some idea of how big you want the business to be. Your share of the market, in other words. It certainly is not easy to forecast sales, especially before you have even started on a new strategy, but if you do not set a goal at the start and simply wait to see how things develop, then one of two problems will occur. Either you will not sell enough to cover your fixed costs and so lose money and perhaps go out of business, or you will sell too much and run out of cash, in other words, you will overtrade. Obviously, before you can set a specific market share and sales objective you need to know the size and trends in your market.

The 'size' you want your business to be is more a matter of judgement than forecast – a judgement tempered by the resources you have available to achieve those objectives and, of course, some idea of what is and what is not reasonable and achievable. You will find the range of discretion over a size objective seriously constrained by the financial resources at your disposal – or realistically available from investors and lenders – and the scope of the market opportunity.

It will be useful to set near-term objectives covering the next 18 months or so, and a longer-term objective covering up to three or so years on. Your objectives may also include profit levels/margins and return on investment (see ratio analysis, Chapter 4, for an explanation).

You will also have a personal objective for the business which may include selling it on, taking it to the stock market, or going on the acquisition trail yourself. All three of these objectives have important implications for the business, but unless you intend to involve all your staff in these tasks, and by implication provide them with an appropriate motivation and reward system, it's best to keep these visions to yourself and your co-owners. However, the way to achieve maximum value in all such objectives is to move your business through to the third and fourth phases of growth as speedily as possible. If you still are the whole business, as most proprietors in Phases 1 and 2 of growth are, then you probably don't have the depth of management to get much value out of an acquisition (especially if it's a diversification). Anyone interested in buying your business would put in such a large 'earn-out' figure that it would hardly be worth selling; and the stock market would either not be interested, or place too low a valuation on your business.

ASSIGNMENT 1

Write your mission statement and principal objectives

1. Write your current mission statement if you have one, linking your product(s) or service to the customer/market needs it is aimed at.
2. What were your principal objectives when you started or took over your business? How well have you succeeded in achieving them?

We will return to missions and key objectives in more detail at the third stage of the strategic review, when we put together business plans (Chapter 17).

2

Opportunities and Threats

Having looked again at the reasons why you started the business (your first mission statement) and the objectives you set yourself (to survive, well done!), the next step in clearly understanding 'where we are now' is to look in some detail at:

- Your marketing environment
- Your customers and markets
- Your competitors

The purpose of each exercise, spelled out in checklists for you to complete in Assignment 2 at the end of this chapter, is to understand what has changed since you started and is likely to continue to change. What are the new opportunities and possible threats posed in this changing environment and what conclusions do you draw from them in terms of how you should respond?

The elements of the marketing process we will be following in Chapters 2, 3, 7, 8 and 15 are summarised in Figure 2.1. To illustrate each step a simple example is shown, taken from a study by academics Wong, Saunders and Doyle, contrasting 15 matched pairs of leading Japanese companies in the UK and their major British competitors.

Your marketing environment

Keeping yourself appraised of the marketing environment that created your business, and of subsequent developments in this environment, is of primary importance for you as leader of the business.

> *Robert Wright, in founding the Connectair air taxi business, saw a clear opportunity in the scaling down of activities by major airlines in the early 1980s. Economic recession caused cutbacks in staff and routes served. This opened the possibility for small feeder airlines to assist major airlines to maintain route coverage. Within two years the business was established, now benefiting from the improving economic climate. With the improved economy, however, threats developed from expansion plans of new entrants and major airlines, as well as the*

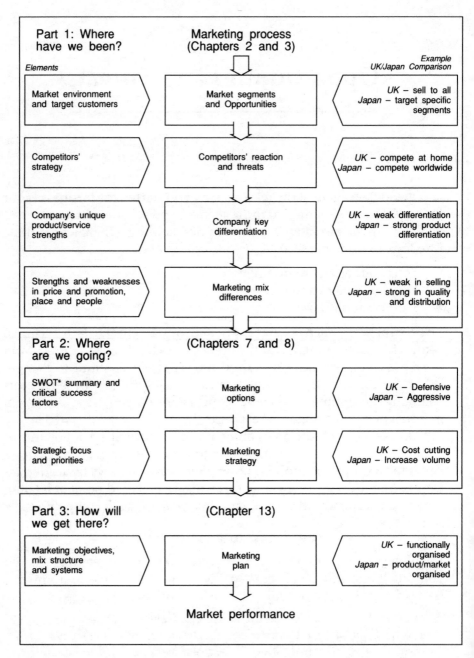

Figure 2.1 *Marketing strategy: Example comparing UK and Japan performance*

Source: After: Wong, Saunders & Doyle, Association of MBA's Journal, June 1989
*SWOT = strengths, weaknesses, opportunities, threats

substantial sums of capital needed to develop a sizeable airline business. Survival was assured but in the late 1980s the question was whether to invest more or to realise a considerable capital gain by selling out to a major competitor.

The Connectair example demonstrates that all businesses operate within definite economic cycles, often of around five years' duration, requiring responsive business strategies of alternate growth and retrenchment. Monitoring such cycles and being prepared to alter course is a sign of strength not weakness, and comes from a thorough reading of the usually well-publicised economic signals.

Robert Wright had also benefited from the deregulation measures favoured by the Conservative government of the period, flowing also from America, which encouraged the development of secondary competitive airlines. This emphasises the importance of your keeping abreast of legislation that can affect your market areas and of the longer-term implications from such changes (witness the extraordinary development in the US airline industry in recent years, 10 years on from deregulation).

Changes in technology have clearly had the profoundest effects on both the creators of the change and on players in their industry.

Pilkington Glass, after years and millions of pounds of expenditure, revolutionised the flat glass industry in the 1960s with its production of float glass; for the company the issue became, should it seek to dominate its industry by monopoly of the invention? For competitors, should their own R & D efforts be doubled? The imaginative solution by Pilkington (contrasting strongly with EMI's efforts to monopolise its medical scanner breakthrough) was to license the process to competitors, ensuring 25 years' revenue and growth stream for the inventor, and directing competitors to improve and add value (coatings, treatments) to the new process, rather than seeking to supplant it.

Technology changes not just the product and its cost-structure, but also its presentation (eg, plastic *vs* glass bottles), its distribution (eg, the 747 aeroplane bringing Third-World competitors or markets within reach) and even the way we promote the product (eg, computerised databases of customers providing one of the most useful direct marketing tools). Monitoring and adapting new technology, in its many guises, can clearly affect growth in your business.

Finally, there are the quite well known demographic and social changes going on around us which are often neglected by business. The greying of the population and the reduction in school-leavers, the growing concern about protecting the environment – how are these issues (see also Chapter 5) likely to affect your business? More importantly, how can they be seen as major opportunities to grow your business?

> *Body Shop grew not just by providing 'supplied to measure' quantities of natural beauty products, in returnable containers, but increasingly by the identification of the public with founder Anita Roddick's care for 'green' issues. Well publicised but genuinely concerned visits to the Amazon emphasised the group's claim to be protective of the environment and supported its affirmation that its products are natural. In-store promotions, emphasising protection of endangered animals, clearly appealed to Body Shop customers.*

Companies ignore such concerns at their peril, but their response must be genuine and of practical value. One car wash company promotes its environmental concern by stating it uses 'recycled water' but, as all water is recycled in our closed planetary system, this may not appear to be a genuine advance. As Mr Clean publicly explains, however, 'Drought Notices enforced by a number of local water companies have excluded car washes that use recycled water!' Environmental concern and efficiency clearly work hand in hand in this case.

You should now be ready to complete Checklist 1 of Assignment 2.

ASSIGNMENT 2

Checklist 1. The business environment (opportunities and threats)

1. In what ways will forecast changes in the general levels of national economic activity affect your business over the next three to five years?

2. Will changes in your local economy affect your business?

3. Will the changes brought about by the Single European Market in 1993 have implications for your business?

4. Have British Standards, European law and any other legal requirements which could relate either to your existing or planned product range, been considered?

5. Are there any other changes in legislation that will affect your business, eg consumer law, health and safety, and employee protection regulations etc?

6. Are there any significant changes in technology in your industry, that could affect the way you or your competitors will do business in the future?

7. How will demographic changes affect your business?

8. Are there any social trends, such as growing environmental awareness, animal rights issues, etc that have implications for your business?

Your customers and markets

Painstaking attention to the needs of their customers is how businesses are developed. Seeing your business through the customers' eyes means realising that customers want good pictures not good cameras; benefits to the customer must dictate the features of the product. Kenichi Ohmae of McKinsey provides a good example of this thinking:

> *A Japanese home appliance company was developing a new coffee percolator. Should it be redesigned to match General Electric's or Philips'? Attention changed to why do people drink coffee? Good taste was the answer. Lots of things affect taste: the beans, the temperature, the water. Of all factors, water quality made the greatest difference. The engineer's attention was redirected to providing features of a built-in dechlorinating function and a built-in coffee grinder. All the customer needed to do was to pour in water and beans; the machine did the rest.*

Now you have a product that provides a cup of coffee which tasted like the one you always had on holiday in France: good! The product engineers were not responding to competitive products, but to the essential customer needs. You must, therefore, regularly step back and ask what the customers' inherent needs are, to determine what the product is really about. Perrier saw its American customers adding lemon and orange squeezes to its mineral water; so the company introduced new product with built-in flavours and prices to match! Reckitt and Colman saw customers making their own mustard, by adding vinegar and liquid to dry mustard powder; the company finally mastered the process and the market by providing customers with what they really wanted – ready-mixed mustard.

Repeating the question, why do people buy from us, as your company develops, is essential; is the purchase decision rational or emotional, is it a planned decision or impulse purchase? Answers to these questions will help to dictate the features built into your products and services. With this customer focus, you are then making what you can *sell*, rather than selling what you can *make*.

One useful distinction to make in customer analysis is the difference between customers and consumers. Children may be the ultimate consumers for toys, but the buying decision may be made by the parent whose needs might include product features such as safety – quite different from the ultimate consumer's view! Close attention to the buying decision will help to focus much of your marketing effort:

> Autoglass started to provide a nationwide windscreen replacement service in the early 1970s. Reaching thousands of customers who had to make quick decisions in an accident situation seemed an impossible marketing task, however strong the company's depot coverage. Payment for the broken windscreen, however, was in most cases covered by comprehensive insurance policies. By approaching individual insurance companies and meeting their needs (guaranteed prices for guaranteed work), a manageable process of assisting drivers (needing instant replacement, on credit) could be developed, with recommendation slips being included with annual insurance reminders, suggesting that drivers contact Autoglass in emergencies.

The needs of the ultimate consumer and of customers linked in the buying process (including retailers, wholesalers in the distribution chain) have, therefore, all to be regularly reviewed.

Finally, and self-evidently, remember that customers change! Alan Melkman has provided a useful framework for classifying your existing customers (see Table 2.1). It may be a stimulus to action to broadly categorise your major customers by these stages. Clearly, relaunching the relationship by revisiting and re-analysing customer needs in the wedlock and deadlock stages, prior to otherwise inevitably losing business to competitive suppliers, may be the quickest way to rekindle sales! Checking on why customers have not re-ordered, against the frequency of your visits and personal contacts, is probably the other side of the same coin!

Table 2.1 *Customer dynamics*

Stage / Objective	Courtship	Engagement	Honeymoon	Wedlock	Deadlock
Customer attitude	Suspicious	Moderately suspicious	Trusting	Boring	Disenchanted
Supplier objective	Get first order	Get repeat order	Increase sales volume	Maintain sales	Sell in new products

Source: © Alan Melkman *How to Handle Major Customers Profitably*, 1979.

Building on your customer analysis by grouping customers who exhibit the same broad characteristics, you can construct market segments which, when combined, will make up your total market. Market segments can be constructed principally from:

(a) *Who buys*; customers can be grouped by age, sex and education, by income and occupation (eg 20 per cent of female office workers in the Victoria area now buy our bagels);

(b) *What is sold*; analysis of physical product sales by volume, price, outlet (eg hot-melt bagels represent 30 per cent of our Victoria Depot Sales, compared with 15 per cent in City Depot Sales).

The purpose of market segmentation is to provide a means of measuring your sales achievement, as well as a stimulus to further marketing thought and action to improve performances. By knowing, for example, that you have only achieved a 20 per cent penetration of office workers in the Victoria area, your marketing promotion activities can be fruitfully focused on improving this hit rate. Segments, therefore, have to be measurable (through desk research on published information, or field research among suppliers and customers) and reachable (to help you decide where to locate, how to advertise). Most importantly, regular information can be gathered to monitor whether your market segments are growing or declining.

Autoglass found it difficult at the outset to calculate the size of the UK replacement windscreen market. Figures on the total UK car population were, however, regularly published, showing a steady 3 per cent per annum growth. Windscreen manufacturers agreed that the replacement rate on toughened windscreens was approximately 3^1/$_2$ per cent per annum; slightly higher on laminated windscreens. Combining the replacement rate and car population gave *a replacement market of half a million windscreens, growing at above 3 per cent per annum as laminated windscreens were introduced. The market could be segmented by product (laminated and toughened), geography (Ministry of Transport figures on motor mileage by standard region), and by customer grouping (commercial fleet owners, company cars, insurance companies for private cars), giving Autoglass definable market groups and measurable market shares for focused marketing activity.*

Having achieved targeted market shares in windscreen product and customer groupings over 10 years (by a programme of new depots, building relations with commercial fleet owners, insurance groups and so on), Autoglass was subsequently able to expand its market by opening new segments (replacement sun-roofs and side windows) and geographical expansion (European acquisitions).

Estimating the size of your markets (through contact with manufacturers, industry associations, published government statistics on the economy and industry sectors) and being aware of the trends in market segments provide an indispensable framework for your major business decisions.

Keeping in touch with your customers and markets, enlisting the help of your customers to run your business, requires careful thought and systems. Restaurants which invite customer suggestions through contact addresses on the menus and deal quickly with complaints, invoices which require sales personnel to ask customers how they heard of the service, retailers who organise customer discussion panels – all of these are practical methods to ensure that customer satisfaction is at the centre of your business.

ASSIGNMENT 3

Checklist 2. Customers/markets (opportunities and threats)

1. What proportion of your sales do your five largest customers take up?

2. Do you know why your customers buy from you?

3. Can you distinguish between consumers and customers of your business's products/services and identify their individual needs?
   Consumers   *Customers*

4. Can you name and classify your major customers under the following categories?
   Courtship   *Engagement*   *Honeymoon*   *Wedlock*   *Deadlock*

5. List your major customers by how often you speak and visit them.
   Daily   *Once a week*   *Once a month*   *Less often*

6. How many customers did you lose last year? Name them and state why they stopped buying from you.

7. Have you segmented the market for your products/services? Do you know the size of each segment and your percentage share?

8. Which segment of the market did you enter first?

9. How many new market segments have you entered since launching your business?

10. What market segments are still open to you to exploit?

11. What are the growth prospects for each of these segments, and what is the size and annual average growth rate for your total market?

12. What systems do you use to measure and keep in contact with your customers and markets?

Your competitors

The starting point for competitor analysis is simply to identify those major competitors you admire (or fear) the most and which you intend to monitor on a regular basis.

Coldshield Windows identified Everest and Anglian Windows as the likely long-term leaders in the double glazing market. Although limited companies, their individual published accounts could not be separated from their controlling groups; their colour supplement advertisements and promotional activities, however, could be studied regularly. The Coldshield salesmen were asked to compare pricing and selling terms, particularly when attending Trade Exhibitions. Coldshield's advertising agency subscribed to MEAL data analysis giving monthly estimates of competitive advertising expenditures.

The objective of competitive analysis is to try to understand in detail how your competitors' products and services satisfy customer needs. A developer of private residential nursing homes, for example, knew that customers' confidence was built on numbers of qualified nursing staff, separate single rooms, purpose-built accommodation and on offering value for money. Therefore, before each new nursing home was developed, a thorough survey of competitors in each area was undertaken, to help determine the features to be built into the new development (see Table 2.2 for an example of the results of one such survey). Learning in the process that each nursing home had a lengthy waiting list of customers for rooms encouraged the developer to go ahead and match some of the better facilities available.

The thoroughness with which Japanese companies have bought, broken down and analysed western competitive products, and subsequently built matching and, in terms of customer needs, superior products, is well documented. The automotive industry, where product reliability was diagnosed to be more needed than chrome attachments, is a prime example. In the same way, by purchase and analysis of competitors' products and services, visiting exhibitions and studying advertisements, you should regularly compare your product offerings with competitors. Not all competitors are obvious: the lunch-time gin and tonic is frequently now substituted by the more fashionable iced Perrier in City bars. Reduced market share may not be the result, therefore, of the activities of a direct brand rival, but due to substitute product offerings.

The purpose behind the analysis is to thoroughly understand the key factors for success in your industry. Are competitors successful

Opportunities and Threats

Table 2.2 *Competitor analysis: Example comparing nursing homes*

Name of Home	Mngt	Nurses	Beds	Single	Time	Building	Price per week	Prom
The Laurels	Owner	22	32	Y	1	PB	£270	n/a
Aldbourne Nursing Home	Mangr	29	n/a	Y	1	PB	£350	10
Ashbury Lodge	Mangr	26	18	Y	2	C	£290	7
Ashgrove House	Owner	23	n/a	n/a	2	n/a	n/a	n/a
Bethany House Nursing Home	Owner	16	n/a	n/a	4	n/a	n/a	n/a
Park View	Mangr	15	15	Y	1	PB	£260	6
Station Court	Mangr	32	n/a	Y	2	PB	£300	10
Weymuss Lodge	Mangr	9	27	Y	2	PB	£275	6
Southdown	Mangr	10	14	N	1	C	£260	5
Total		182	106					

KEY:
Single = Single rooms (Yes or No)
Time = How long since registration in years
Building = Type of building (purpose built or conversion)
PB = Purpose built
Prom = Promotion (Rating of quality)
Mangr = Manager

due to features of their product or their after sales service? Is company image more important than payment terms? Professor Michael Porter, the Harvard expert on competitive analysis, sees competitive analysis as the way to make yourself different from your competitors. By identifying a competitor's strengths and weaknesses, understanding his position in your industry (price-leader or price-cutter?), what his goals are and how he might retaliate to your offerings, you gain knowledge of what you are competing with – making an important contribution to the marketing strategy you might pursue.

Perrier has built a 50 per cent market share in the UK bottled mineral water market in the last 10 years, using a humorous poster campaign (Eau-la-la!) to change a sleepy market sector into a vibrant one. Realising the importance of image to its health-conscious customer, Perrier had no hesitation in withdrawing all supplies from the market following a benzene scare at its bottling plant, prior to re-launching with new factory production. Realising also the difficulty of building further market share in the face of numerous new competitive British bottled waters, the company widened its competitive strategy by purchasing Buxton Mineral Waters, enabling the company to challenge domestic producers and reach parts of the market previously denied to it on chauvinistic grounds.

As the above example shows, competitors, like customers, also change all the time; hence the need for constant review. So how do you regularly keep track of your present and potential competitors? As noted in some of the examples above: buy and analyse their products and services, visit trade exhibitions, work with them, in trade associations, in pursuit of higher trade standards. This may not only serve the customers' needs better but also, by raising standards, build barriers to entry to new competitors in your market. The Glass and Glazing Trade Association, for instance, in addition to serving customers' needs by requiring members to adhere to strict British standards in terms of material, workmanship and insurance, only allows new members to join and use the GGF symbol after two years successful trading – quite a long time for some double-glazing companies! Stew Leonard, of the famous New England, In Search of Excellence store, actually organises staff visits, by specially ordered buses, to major competitor openings! Food for thought for you?

Please remember as you complete these checks: never knowingly underestimate your competitors. General Wavell underestimated the fighting ability of Japanese city dwellers in the jungles during World War 2 just as much as General Motors underestimated the Japanese motor industry's ability to produce quality cars. Make new mistakes in finding out about your customers and competitors, but do not repeat the old ones!

ASSIGNMENT 4

Checklist 3. Competitors (opportunities and threats)

1. Who are your principal direct and indirect competitors?

2. What do you know about their sales growth, profitability, selling methods etc? Could you rank them in order of success?

3. How do your major competitor's products and services satisfy customer needs?

4. How does your product or service compare with the competition with respect to:

	Yourself	Major competitor
Price		
Performance		
Packaging		
Safety		
Reliability		
Durability		
Quality		
Delivery		
After-sales service/Maintenance		
Guarantees		
Promotion/Advertising		
Image		
Payment terms		

5. So what exactly do you think makes your successful competitors successful?

6. What do you see as your main competitor's principal weaknesses?

7. Do you anticipate any new competitors coming into your market in the near future?

8. What barriers to entry exist, or could be erected, to prevent competitors entering your markets?

9. What changes have your major competitors made in the last 12 months in their competitive approaches?

10. How are you regularly tracking major competitors' activities?

3

Strengths and Weaknesses

Analysis of the external market should have provided a summary of the constantly changing opportunities and threats facing your business; analysis of your own company's internal strengths and weaknesses should summarise your ability to take advantage of, or at least, to cope with this environment. This analysis should be made under four headings:

- Products and services
- Pricing and distribution
- Advertising and promotion
- Sales and sales management

In each section you are endeavouring to take stock of how your business originally and currently matches up to the marketing environment.

Products and services

There are no such things as pure products or pure services; each product has a service element and each service a product element. In an increasingly competitive world the way in which some products are differentiated from each other, which is how your company initially succeeded, may be in their service terms.

Philips Whirlpool white goods are strictly comparable to competitors. Philips, however, provide distinctive service terms for customers and retailers. Customers, therefore, are allowed to replace any machine in the first 12 months which cannot be repaired; all parts are guaranteed for ten years. Additionally, Philips provide a 24-hour call care line for customers and will pay £12.50 if its repair engineers do not arrive within two days of a call. All retailers are provided with dealer support for advertising, finance for display stock and inventory, together with extended payment terms.

Strengths and Weaknesses

Service businesses can be more difficult to differentiate because services, being intangible, are often seen as a commodity and are certainly difficult to taste or test in advance! The customers even play a role in determining the quality and delivery of a service: in an English restaurant a complaint can lead at best to an improvement or, at worst, to a complete withdrawal of service! Marketing a service, therefore, requires strong, consistent branding. The company name is frequently the brand – 'I'm with the Woolwich' – and making the company name synonymous with good quality is making the service more tangible. At the end of the day, your company name and reputation may be the only difference between you and your competitors.

Being able to protect your company and brand names and to communicate them properly, is, therefore, an important aspect in marketing your product or service. Wally Olins of Wolff Olins, the corporate design specialists, has described the three main ways companies communicate their identity:

> *'Many small as well as major companies have a* monolithic identity; *IBM uses its company name on all its products, so that if they opened a supermarket it would be called IBM stores. General Motors, on the other hand, use an* endorsed identity, *whereby the group company name is used to reinforce local brand names: Vauxhall in England is promoted as being 'part of General Motors'. Finally, with* branded identity, *the name of the owning company is invisible, so that, eg Pearson's name is not used in the market-place to add support to Royal Doulton, Lazards or* The Economist. *Brand names as strong as these may not need extra support.'*

The early growth company probably follows the IBM example; so it is important to ensure that not only are your products patented, if this can be achieved (as Pilkington did with float glass), but also that your company name and later brand names are given trademark protection. (Trademarks protect 'what something's called'.) Common law can then be used to prevent competitors from passing off similar looking goods and services, trading on your product's reputation. Imitation may be the sincerest form of flattery, but it can be harmful to growth, particularly for a single product or service company. By protecting your product or name, you may be able to effectively prolong the natural life cycle of your product or service.

Knowing approximately at which stage of the life cycle your product or service is located is important, both in terms of your promotional plans (to sustain launch in early growth stages, by making people aware; or to prolong life in a mature, competitive market) and your strategic need to develop or acquire new, replacement products, as Figure 3.1 illustrates.

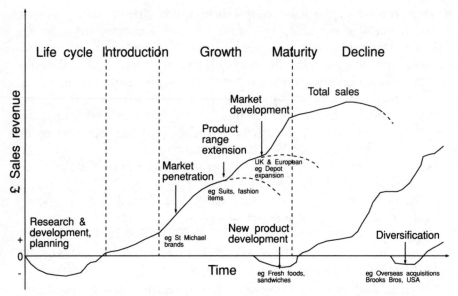

Figure 3.1 *Product/market strategy and the product life cycle (Illustrative example: Marks & Spencer)*

As the dotted curves in Figure 3.1 indicate, sales would naturally mature or decline without the new product or market segment initiatives. The more your company name or reputation is known, the longer it probably takes to carefully test market and research each new line addition, although acquisition can probably speed sales results.

For many products and services, product life cycles have been shortening under the impact of technology and speedier communications.

> *It took 25 years for sales of mechanical typewriters to fall below sales of electromechanical ones; then 15 years for electromechanical models to give way to electric ones. Within 7 years electric models had been overtaken by microprocessor controlled machines.*

Yet some products, with good brand names, logos and promotional support seem to last for ever: witness the recent revival of the Bisto Kid, while the fictional Betty Crocker (born in 1921) is alive and well in 1992, rejuvenated even, on the label of over 130 General Mills products.

Keeping your products and services fresh and alive, where technology permits and points the way, requires regular assessment on your part of the *features* built into your offerings (often inspired by your customer and competitor analysis) and the corresponding *benefits* derived by the customers from these elements. The process is outlined in Table 3.1.

Table 3.1 *Product features and corresponding customer benefits*

Your product **features**	What **benefits** do these **features** bring to customers?	Customer **benefits**	Benefits become product/service **promises** to promote to **customers**
Size Colour Weight Taste Feel Smell Others	Ask the question: 'What does it mean to me?'	Saves me time, money. Keeps me warm. Feel better, etc.	Save money, buy now! Sleep easier. Pay less taxes etc.

In the double-glazing industry, for example, manufacturers have worked hard to introduce Low-E coated glass, giving two pieces of glass the power of triple glazing, permitting salesmen to promote extra customer benefits in terms of money saving via lower heating bills and noise reduction by better sound insulation. Building in extra features (which for services might include staff training, accurate recording of complaints) may well, like identifying new market segments, enable you to prolong your product/service business life cycle by helping to keep your company different from the competition.

Declining product or service profitability is probably one of the tell-tale signs of life cycle maturity, as increasing competition or shrinking markets puts pressure on margins. Monitoring product profitability can be an important life cycle guide; yet market maturity may not be the problem if product or service quality has deteriorated after the early pioneering launch days. Visible and measurable signs of poor quality are easy to detect; they include errors, missed deadlines, and warranty costs. Not so visible, but equally important signs, include customer dissatisfaction, complaints and poor employee morale. Developing systems to monitor for these less-measurable indicators is important to enable you to spend more time on prevention (education and training) rather than the more costly problems of dealing with product/service failure (rework, repeat calls).

Monitoring and measuring company performance, therefore, can help you to keep your offerings better and different. A recent McKinsey survey has shown that 'companies lose two-thirds of their customers not because of product or unsatisfactory price, but simply through indifference to customer complaints. Well over 80 per cent of customers would repurchase if their complaints were quickly resolved'.

ASSIGNMENT 5

Checklist 4. Products and services (strengths and weaknesses)

1. Is your business still dependent on one product or service for over 80 per cent of profits?

2. Are your products and brand names protected (or able to be protected) through patents, copyright and the like?

3. Do you have a strong company/brand name, logo and slogan which works for your company and your customers?

4. How easy are your products or services to copy?

5. What proportion of your product/service range is in each phase of the life cycle?

6. When did you last launch a new product? Is developing and launching new products one of your business strengths?

7. How long did it take to move successfully from concept to test market and from test market to final customer?

8. Do your product/service benefits match customers' needs or are there gaps? List your product features and benefits, and compare them to customer needs.

Features   *Benefits*   *Customer needs*

9. How accurately can you assess the *profitability* of individual products (or groups of products)?

10. How do you measure customer satisfaction with the quality of your products and services?

Pricing and distribution (strengths and weaknesses)

The product, promotion and distribution aspects of your business can all be justified as creating value for the customer. But pricing, as Tom Nagle of Boston University has observed, is the time 'when you grab a chunk of that value and put it in your own pocket. It's a company's moment of self-interest and it cannot be portrayed as service to the customer'. It is also the biggest decision your company has to make and to keep constantly under review – and the one that has the biggest impact on company profitability.

In a new or existing business, undertake the favourite consultant's exercise of computing and comparing the impact on profits of a 5 per cent cut in your overheads, a 5 per cent increase in volume sales, a 5 per cent cut in materials purchased and a 5 per cent price increase. All these actions are usually considered to be within a manager's normal reach. Almost invariably, the 5 per cent price increase scores highest, as it passes straight to the net profit, bottom line. Even if volume falls, because of the effect price has on gross margin, it is usually more profitable to sell fewer items at a higher price; for example, at a constant gross margin of 30 per cent, with a 5 per cent increase, profits would be unchanged even if sales declined 14 per cent. Yet if prices were cut 5 per cent, an extra 20 per cent increase in sales would be needed to stand still.

Deciding what is a fair price is a problem which has taxed economic man ever since money was invented in the fifth century BC. It has been difficult because most useful items have a low value in exchange (eg water, before the advent of designer mineral water), while the least useful items, such as silk, have a high value in exchange. Value, like beauty, is often in the eye of the beholder; but this degree of subjectivity means that companies have a great deal of discretion in the area of pricing. A good quality product, priced too low, often does not have its quality recognised by the public. There is a strong belief in the link between price and quality – you get what you pay for – with the Japanese probably equating price with quality more than any other national group. When Brown-Forman, the distillers, tried to boost Jack

Daniel's sales by reducing the price of its premium brand, sales fell. On the other hand, how do you justify £50 for an ordinary bottle of champagne in a night-club?

Economists offer conflicting advice; from charging what the market will bear (hence night-club champagne) through marginal cost (what you pay for the last or least wanted item), to where your supply and demand curves intersect. Few growing companies are able to accurately draw their supply and demand curves; so, according to *Management Today*, over 80 per cent of UK companies price by reference to their costs, either using cost plus (which is materials plus a percentage, perhaps 50 per cent) or a cost multiplier (eg 3 times material costs).

While it is important to know your product or service costs, this is only one element in the pricing decision. You have clearly, in addition, to take into account the market place (particularly your competitors), the way you are positioning the product (luxury item, with strong branding for wealthy customers), and the life cycle stage of your product or market.

> *Mark Sanders, in designing and launching his innovative folding bicycle, the* Strida, *into the mature 100-year bicycle market recognised:*
>
> (a) *his manufacturer's capacity was strictly limited;*
>
> (b) *his target market was well-to-do, city commuters or life-style weekenders.*
>
> *An initial price of nearly £200 per model was well above established competitive models, but gave good margins to dealers in taking up the product and left room for manoeuvre later in the product life cycle when competition would react to the Strida's unusual features. Mark's initial skimming price strategy could then be replaced by a penetration strategy, aimed at building market share.*

Frequently, resistance to increasing prices, even in the face of inflationary cost rises, can come from your own team members, eager to blame price for performance lapses. In these instances it is important to make detailed price comparisons with competitors, using a scoring scheme such as the one in Table 3.2.

Such an analysis should help you either to improve your product or service, to justify your pricing stance, or at least to calm 'in-house' nerves to show that your prices are justified.

> *In Autoglass Ltd, the sternest critics of improved prices were a number of front-line depot managers, who feared their own bonus-related sales targets would be made impossible to achieve. Competitive analysis showed the company to be providing a unique 24-hour call-out service, on a nationwide basis, and gave the initially reluctant managers arguments to justify the increases to fleet customers.*

Strengths and Weaknesses

Table 3.2 *Pricing comparison with competitors*

	Worse −3 −2 −1	Same 0	Better +1 +2 +3
Product attributes			
Design			
Performance			
Packaging			
Presentation/appearance			
After-sales service			
Availability			
Delivery			
Colour/flavour/odour/touch			
Image			
Specification			
Payment terms			
Others			

Pricing and the distribution channels you operate are clearly closely related, particularly in terms of the trade or quantity discount structure you will need, to ensure your products or services are adequately represented in the market place. Prices, as noted above, are all too readily blamed for poor performance by management, when in fact poor distribution may be the key to low market share.

Dan Duncan, MD of the fast growing football magazine, When Saturday Comes *had been delighted when a specialist distributor had agreed to deliver the magazine to newsagents throughout the South-East. Previously sales had been organised by an army of volunteers on Saturday afternoons outside football grounds. As sales climbed, however, and as major retail outlets such as Menzies agreed to handle the magazine, Dan reluctantly realised the excellent regional distributor would have to be replaced by a major national distributor.*

If your product could potentially achieve a 50 per cent market share, but only reaches 25 per cent of the market through inadequate distribution channels where only 50 per cent of the public will buy it, it is not surprising that your maximum market share is only 6 per cent. No amount of extra promotional expenditure or price changes can alter the result. Equally, the way in which you distribute your products may be as significant as the products themselves.

> *Telford-based TWS, a window systems manufacturer, faced with static sales, commissioned a customer survey on the merits of its German window profile system. The major surprise of the survey was to discover that 80 per cent of actual and potential TWS customers did not have fork-lift trucks, the result being all deliveries had to be handled off, depriving the fabricating customer of 'window-making' time. The solution was to commission the product of a new delivery vehicle, complete with its own fork lift. 'Now it just takes 15 minutes instead of two hours to unload two stillages and we don't use the fabricator's manpower,' explained the MD of TWS.*

The beneficial impact on TWS sales by this improved delivery service is easily imagined! Even *how* you collect may also be a way of differentiating your business; Glen Fayolle, MD of Paper Safe, a security paper-shredding company, grew his customer base by supplying them with special plastic containers, designed to take valuable grade (to paper merchants) computer print-out paper.

Whether or not to invest in property, rather than in the working assets of your business, is often a painful decision for businesses in securing adequate distribution for products and services. The situation is aggravated in the UK where long leaseholds on property are common (20–25 years), compared with very short but renewable leases, for example, in Asia-Pacific (two-year leases are normal). The apparently low UK annual lease rent disguises the unbreakable capital commitment to payments over 25 years. Increasingly, prudent businessmen baulk at investment in 'safe' property, when money can be better invested in stock, which can perhaps be guaranteed to be turned over say 5 times per annum and earn 20 per cent each time. Businesses 'protected' by freehold property from the market environment (witness Dunn & Co the gentlemen's outfitters in 1991), may, in turn, not adapt in time to the challenges of that changing market place.

Finally, monitoring of your own company's (and competitors') product or service availability, clearly requires frequent visits, inspection and interrogation of distributors and customers alike. Sometimes the results, as for TWS above, can be surprising.

ASSIGNMENT 6

Checklist 5. Pricing and distribution (strengths and weaknesses)

1. What would be the effect on your profits of a 5 per cent increase or 5 per cent decrease in your major product/service price?

2. What is the formula you use to decide your prices?

3. Do you use different prices for a product/service depending on its life cycle? Give examples.

4. How do your prices compare with your major competitors'?

5. When did you last increase your prices and by what percentage?

6. How do you monitor your own and competitors' prices?

7. What discount structure do you offer to volume customers or middlemen?

8. Describe the distribution chain between you and the customer.

9. What property investment have you made to ensure easy availability to the customer of your goods and services?

10. Do your customers and target market segments have easy access to your goods and services? How do you monitor this?

Advertising and promotion (strengths and weaknesses)

Advertising

The economist J K Galbraith has commented on the power of advertising: 'In great measure, wants are now shaped by advertising . . . the individual product or service has little consequence.' Good advertising and promotion is a powerful way to differentiate products and services; advertising, frequently known as *above the line* expenditure, is, as Saatchi and Saatchi's Tim Bell has noted 'an expensive way for one person to talk to another'. It is about communicating effectively with your target customers; promotions, be they press releases, exhibition brochures, discount items, are frequently called *below the line* expenditure, as they are often not so visible as press and TV advertising. Both are expensive and aim to create a favourable image for your company.

Doing business without advertising, it has been said, 'is like winking at a girl in the dark. You know what you are doing but no one else does!' The most cost-effective advertising for your company is probably related to your main selling methods.

In double-glazing there are in the UK more than 2000 separate companies aiming to secure business. In principle, the product installation and services for each of these companies are basically very similar; yet Everest gradually emerged as 'fitting the best' because this is what their TV commercials have been telling us for a number of years. The commercials, frequently costing some 10–15 per cent of sales revenue, supported a large army of self-employed salesmen, many using cold-calling, door-to-door selling techniques, where recognition of company name and slogan facilitated their sales conversion efforts.

Yet major TV and newspaper expenditure of this sort is rarely within the financial capacity of most growing businesses and the benefits of such expenditure are frequently hard to quantify. The benefits of the huge advertising expenditure of companies privatised in the 1980s, such as BT and the gas and electricity suppliers, are difficult to assess considering their monopoly or near monopoly positions.

Promotion

The growing business has to focus more precisely on how to reach target customers at lowest cost; working for the most part with relatively small, fixed sums of money rather than elastic 'percentage of sales' type allocations. Frequently, below-the-line promotional expenditure may be larger than above-the-line items, as personal calling efforts require brochures in the hand, or relatively expensive exhibition stands, and since informing and persuading customers for relatively young life cycle products takes precedence over reinforcing advertising which may be necessary for more mature products. Whatever is the situation for the company, delivering the most cost-effective advertising or promotional activity is vital.

> *Autoglass asked each customer, when paying bills in their depots, how they had heard of the service. A form beside each till recorded each of the company's promotional activities: depot sign, Yellow Pages advertisement, insurance company recommendation, press adverts etc. In early years, Yellow Pages reference was by far the highest, so the company sought representation in all regional Yellow Pages. Later, when insurance company recommendations increased, expenditure on Yellow Pages coverage could be dramatically reduced. Equally, later experimentation with local radio could be monitored within days and weeks to judge its effectiveness.*

In this way, Autoglass could not only judge the effectiveness of budgeted advertising expenditure, but could also ensure that specific planned increases would be likely to increase sales. Working with an advertising agency may also be easier, for both parties, if the mechanism is in place to judge the results of their efforts and recommendations. Agencies paid by media rebate (10–15 per cent discounts on advertising spend) will, not surprisingly, rarely recommend reductions in media expenditure, hence the need for accurate information on response rates (costs per lead, conversion rate per lead) to judge advertising and agency effectiveness. Nonetheless, the achievements of an agency like Leo Burnett in turning a commodity (water) into a desirable designer product (Perrier), shows how the support of such agencies should not be underestimated.

Determining the most effective below-the-line promotional expenditure is just as important, given the higher expenditure most early growth companies are likely to have in this area. More money is actually spent on sales promotion techniques than on agency advertising. Yet both must work in harmony, as the objectives are the same: advertising campaigns are aimed at building long-term custom, while sales promotions are typically short-term activities to keep your company going. So, effective sales promotion can speed up stock movement, encourage repeat purchases, get bills paid on time, induce trial purchases. For example, your target customers may be the trade or even within your own organisation and you may be offering money (prizes, bonuses), goods (gifts, vouchers) or even services (free training, free services).

However, for the growing business, promotional opportunities that stimulate interest and awareness among new and existing purchasers, at lowest cost, are the most important. While discounting to move discontinued or other slow-moving lines may be necessary from time to time, the main positive promotional activities would include:

1. Ensuring all company small items are co-ordinated and effective (from business cards to Christmas cards).
2. Issuing regular press releases (public relations).
3. Participating in exhibitions (with new leaflets and brochures).
4. Experimenting with direct mail (databases) and telemarketing (direct response).

Business cards that are memorable (with perhaps a map on the back, for a hard-to-find restaurant) and commercial Christmas cards that are not blasphemous and help sales, may perhaps not seem worthy of a chief executive's attention, but they cost thousands of pounds and are perhaps the tip of the iceberg for your corporate identity programme. If they don't excite attention, perhaps your corporate communication package as a whole is unappealing.

What makes a good corporate Christmas card is highly subjective. The Financial Times *judged Ratners', the jewellers, card (Roy Lichtenstein cartoon of young lady on telephone saying, 'So this is what he meant by giving me a* Ring *for Christmas') to be the most memorable British card in 1990; the worst to have been Lancaster Kind, property consultants, announcing 'A babe is born', meaning themselves, the previous year. Clearly humour rather than blasphemy in reinforcing your company name and service is more likely to be favourably remembered!*

Recent research has also shown that 94 per cent of all press releases issued by companies are not printed. With UK editors receiving an average of 80–90 press releases per week, the rules that they must be newsworthy, topical, relevant, factual and informative, as well as free of 'puffy' jargon are not always being closely followed. The benefits of free publicity, however, should encourage companies to persevere and improve in this activity.

Paper-Safe, having been unsuccessful with press releases, approached Jamieson Farmer PR Ltd, who proposed that, as a large number of confidential waste disposal contracts are reviewed at year end, a product press release on the Paper-Safe disposal bins should be sent to 100 magazines for their November issue. The article was published in seven magazines, producing 41 sales leads.

Exhibitions
Exhibitions are not free. A tiny stand for four days in the Spring Gift

Exhibition at Birmingham NEC will cost at least £1500; for the Ideal Home Exhibition in Earls Court, you are looking at 10 times this amount. Lighting, display stands and manning costs will then more than double these costs. Yet similar outlays on newspaper advertisements are visible by customers for a few seconds on one day only, whereas with exhibitions you are at least guaranteed eye-to-eye contact with committed trade and retail buyers for as long as you can stimulate their interest. Because each exhibition is specific, both costs and sales benefits arising from it can be easily determined; each time you exhibit you have an opportunity to refocus your company by being forced to produce new exhibition leaflets, to rethink your personal selling messages and to re-listen to what your key customer groups tell you about your company!

Direct marketing

Finally, there are the exciting (or alarming) direct marketing media channels. Alarming for Europeans, who already believe we are deluged with junk mail, to discover that in the USA, 65 per cent of advertising expenditure is in direct mailing (20 per cent in UK in 1988) and, while UK citizens receive 29 direct mail items per annum, in the USA each person receives 300 items per annum. Is it worth it? Well, for the Post Office it is (representing a £7 billion market) and 62 per cent of UK recipients claimed to read their direct mail! Telemarketing is also growing rapidly, taking advantage of customer database lists provided by list brokers; so much so that 60 per cent of company purchasing managers receive a minimum of five calls a week. Again, is this effective?

> *Paper-Safe early sought the help of a telephone marketing company (UK Connect) to help launch their shredding service. Managing Director, Glen Fayolle, commented: 'We could have done the work ourselves, but they did it faster, contacting 270 companies in two weeks, where we could only contact a maximum of ten companies per week. They encouraged two companies which were interested in our services immediately, and the cost was easily offset by the number of positive leads fed immediately to our salesman'.*

ASSIGNMENT 7

Checklist 6. Advertising and promotion (strengths and weaknesses)

1. Have you determined the most cost-effective advertising media for your business? Please describe.

2. Do you work with an Advertising Agency to plan your advertising/promotion activities? How is the Agency remunerated? (Fixed fee or percentage media rebate?)

3. Do you budget annual sums or a percentage of sales for advertising and promotion? How much (£) per annum for advertising and how much (£) for below the line promotions?

4. What increase in sales spend do you expect to achieve for every extra pound spent on advertising?

5. What is your average cost per sales lead from advertising?

6. Which below-the-line promotional items create most business for you? Please describe.

7. Have you market tested a new promotional method recently, internally (own staff) or externally? Please describe.

8. When did you last issue a press release and with what effect?

9. Do you take part in exhibitions each year, if so, which and why?

10. Is direct mail or telemarketing effective in securing new customers for you?

Sales and sales management

Personal selling is the vital link in the communication process between company and customer; every growing organisation has to have someone responsible for this important first or last step, depending on your point of view, activity. Traditionally, the Sales Manager and the

Strengths and Weaknesses

Salesmen are the personable, likeable, smiling face of the organisation, the Mr Nice Guy in comparison with the Mr Mean in Accounts! Mr Mean, being not very likeable, is usually efficient in order to survive; Mr Nice, on the other hand, being well liked, has to be motivated and very well directed if his efforts are not to be totally diffused. Professor McDonald of CIT has noted:

> *Among European salesforces, there is an alarming lack of planning and professionalism. Sales people frequently have little idea of which products and which groups of customers to concentrate on, have too little knowledge about competitive activity, do not plan presentations well, rarely talk to customers in terms of benefits, make too little effort to close the sale and make many calls without any clear objective. Even worse, marketing management is rarely aware that this important and expensive element of the marketing mix is not being managed effectively.*

Many studies have shown that if the average salesman's salary is £12,000 per annum, the real cost to the company after travel, expenses and fringe benefits, is frequently double or even treble that, if sales support is added. At the same time, however, less than a third of the salesperson's working time is actually spent in front of the customer. Hence the need for responsible sales management able to:

1. Set and monitor sales target achievement;
2. Motivate, train and support the sales staff;
3. Recruit and organise competent staff.

Sales target setting, at the simplest level, may simply be in terms of ensuring minimum sales to recover the new salesperson's costs; for example a minimum £50,000 extra sales, at 50 per cent gross margin, to recover the average salesperson's real cost. It may also be in terms of unit sales volume, mix of products or even numbers of target customers to convert. Monitoring of sales achievement may not be simply in terms of these quantitative targets (to which may be added numbers of sales calls per day, letters written, exhibitions organised etc), but also in terms of qualitative achievement in terms of work planning and time spent in front of customers (see Figure 3.2).

Given such precise targets, the task of sales management in motivating and training sales personnel is made easier. Under-achievement may point to the need to evaluate salesmen call frequency and utilisation.

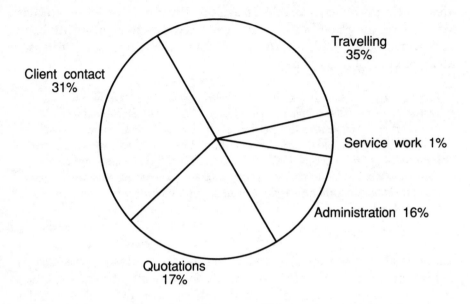

Figure 3.2 *Analysis of salesforce time*

JTM Business Consultants, in a customer survey, found that customers wanted the sales representative to call monthly, while their existing call pattern was fortnightly. This meant that salesforce time could be released to handle other work, such as new product introductions. Equally, another review found that the salesforce was calling on accounts too small to justify a call; it was decided to transfer small customers to the sales office and to use the telephone to make regular calls.

Sales targets should be mutually agreed between sales personnel and sales management, and motivation can be improved by judicious use of incentives. Analysts from Elton Mayo to McClelland have shown that all individuals have goals and aspirations and, if their needs are met, they will work harder. A remuneration plan, with bonus or commission related to performance, remains pre-eminent, however, and often needs to encourage teamwork as well as accomplishment of specific sales targets.

At specialist hi-fi chain Richer Sounds, branch managers get a cash bonus of 1 per cent of total profits and sales personnel half of this. Employees are rewarded not just on the basis of sales, but, as the quality of service is important, branches are also assessed monthly on numbers of customer complaints, how swiftly staff answered phones, punctuality, and efficiency in maintaining stocks of popular lines. Richer's package of staff incentives also includes the use of a country house near York and the loan of the boss's Rolls-Royce for a month.

Excessively complicated bonus schemes should, however, be avoided. Quite often, providing the sales force with information (eg sales by customer) and tools to make the selling task easier (from sales brochures to route planning) are as important as any incentives that can be created. Sales and product training need to be repeated regularly. In particular, businesses which pay a bonus of less than 10 per cent of basic salary might do better to spend their money on these aspects of salesforce relations.

Good and motivating compensation packages will clearly assist companies in recruiting and staffing the sales function. The number of sales staff required and their specific functions, derive from your listing of tasks required: opening new accounts, showing new products, servicing existing customers for orders and chasing up debts. Many of these functions can be handled by mail or telephone (repeat orders and debts); the number of personal sales personnel will depend on workload involved in visiting, selling to and administering (record cards) your customers. Increasingly, information technology can help to reduce this workload, eg customer ordering terminals, switching in to supplier stocking displays. Supplying customer database information to sales personnel can also reduce their administrative tasks. These developments are important for the growing business, where competing with major companies for good sales people is always difficult.

Finally, recruitment by the small growing business has traditionally been among family and friends, if for no other reason than these are likely to have been cheaper and keener than the all-too-expensive professional! Yet the informality of this process has to be generally replaced by more formal procedures (as we will see later in Chapter 14 – with job descriptions, formal interviews, telephone checking on referees etc), particularly when one realises that one misfit could destroy a small business while doing relatively little harm to ICI. At the same time it is important to remember that technical skills are usually less important than the fit of new sales personnel in your organisation. It is no sin *not* to employ people you do not like, however expert. Remember, however, that there is a role, even in a sales team, for a Mr or Ms Nasty. Don't let your customers, however, always be referred to as debtors! You may need to ensure this is not happening by regularly visiting customers with your sales staff.

ASSIGNMENT 8

Checklist 7. Sales and sales management (strengths and weaknesses)

1. *Who* is responsible for achieving the company's sales targets?

2. What *targets* is each salesperson set and how are these arrived at?
   Quantitative targets   Qualitative targets
                                                 (eg research competitors)

3. What *incentive* is there for them to achieve these targets?

4. What *support* do the salesforce have in terms of sales presentation packs, technical literature, back-up?

5. What *information* on results does each salesperson receive?

6. Have salespeople undergone specific sales *training* – and if so, when?

7. *How many* sales staff, agents, etc do you have and how are they organised? (By area, by products.)

8. How do you *recruit* your sales staff? Please describe the process.

9. What would happen to your sales if *either* you added an extra salesperson, *or* you lost one of your sales personnel?

10. When did you last go out with a salesperson (or wait on customers for a day)?

4

The Financial Position

The centrepiece of nearly all position audits on commercial organisations is an appraisal of the profit and loss account and the derived ratios. The case for it is simple. Typically, the figures are readily available and they are comparatively easy to handle. Identical questions can be put to a variety of organisations and the precision conveyed by a numerical answer assists interpretation and comparison. Here, if anywhere, management could become a science.

By contrast the non-quantitative information gathered using the checklists provided in earlier chapters is much more difficult and time consuming to obtain. The questions are less obvious, many may or may not apply to a particular organisation, they are liable to be misunderstood and they rely on at least a measure of subjective interpretation. As a result there is a tendency to concentrate on statistics and ratios, and to assume that these alone are the position audit.

But ratios, while providing a good backdrop, are by no means the whole picture.

Business objectives

There are universal methods of measuring what is happening in a business, but before we can measure anything we need some idea of what level or type of performance a business is wanting to achieve. All growing businesses have three fundamental objectives in common which allow us to see how well (or otherwise) they are doing.

Making a satisfactory return on investment

The first of these objectives is to make a satisfactory return (profit) on the money invested in the business.

It is hard to think of a sound argument against this aim. To be satisfactory the return must meet four criteria:

1. It must give a fair return to shareholders, bearing in mind the risk they are taking. If the venture is highly speculative and the profits are less than building society rates, your shareholders (yourself included) will not be happy.

2. You must make enough profit to allow the company to grow. If a business wants to expand sales it will need more working capital and eventually more space or equipment. The safest and surest source of money for this is internally generated profits, retained in the business – reserves. A business has three sources of new money: share capital or the owner's money; loan capital, put up by banks etc; retained profits, generated by the business.

3. The return must be good enough to attract new investors or lenders. If investors can get a greater return on their money in some other comparable business, then that is where they will put it.

4. The return must provide enough reserves to keep the real capital intact. This means that you must recognise the impact inflation has on the business. A business retaining enough profits each year to meet a 5 per cent growth in assets is actually contracting by 5 per cent if inflation is running at 10 per cent.

To control the business we have to examine carefully the various factors that affect return on investment.

Shareholders' and other lenders' funds are invested in the capital, both fixed and working, of the business, so this must be the area we relate to profitability. The example in Figure 4.1 shows the factors that directly influence the return on capital employed (Capital Employed = Investment: remember the Balance Sheet must balance).

	£		£	£
Sales	100,000	Fixed Assets	12,500	
– Cost of Sales	50,000	Working Capital		
= Gross Profit	50,000	Current Assets	23,100	
– Expenses	33,000	– Current Liabilities	6,690	
= Operating Profit	17,000			16,410
– Finance Charges and Tax	8,090			
Net Profit	8,910	Capital Employed		28,910
		= % return on capital		30.82%

Figure 4.1 *Factors that affect the return on capital employed (ROCE)*

You can see that Figure 4.1 is nothing more than a Profit and Loss Account on the left and the capital employed section of the Balance Sheet on the right. Any change that increases net profit (more sales, lower expenses, less tax etc), but does not increase the amount of capital employed, will increase the return on capital employed (ROCE) percentage. Any decrease in capital employed (lower stocks, fewer debtors etc), that does not lower profits, will also increase ROCE. Conversely, any change that increases capital employed without increasing profits in proportion will reduce ROCE.

We shall look in detail at all the important factors that affect ROCE later.

Maintaining a sound financial position

As well as making a satisfactory return, investors, creditors and employees expect the business to be protected from unnecessary risks. Clearly, all businesses are exposed to market risks: competitors, new products and price changes are all part of a healthy commercial environment. The sorts of unnecessary risk that investors and lenders are particularly concerned about are high financial risks, such as overtrading.

Cash flow problems are not the only threat to a business's financial position. Heavy borrowings can bring a big interest burden to a small business, especially when interest rates rise unexpectedly. This may be acceptable when sales and profits are good; however, when times are bad, bankers, unlike shareholders, cannot be asked to tighten their belts – they expect to be paid all the time. So the position audit is not just about profitability, but about survival capabilities and the practice of sound financial disciplines.

Achieving growth

Making profit and surviving are insufficient achievements in themselves to satisfy the ambitious entrepreneur – they want the business to grow too. But they don't just want the number of people they employ to get larger, or the sales turnover to rise, however nice they may be. They want the firm to become more efficient, gain economies of scale and to improve the quality of profits.

Ratios, the tools of analysis

All analysis of financial information requires comparisons. We have already seen that certain objectives are fundamental to all types of business. It is also true that there are three yardsticks against which business performance can be measured.

1. You can see how well you are meeting a personal goal. For example, you may want to double sales or add 25 per cent to profits. In a more formalised business this activity would be called budgeting, then comparisons would be made between actual results and the budget.

2. You might want to see how well you are doing this year compared with last, comparing performance against an historical standard. This is the way in which growth in sales or profits is often measured. There are two main limitations to this sort of comparison. One rarely affects a small business and one affects all sizes of business.

   If accounting methods change from year to year, perhaps in the way depreciation is dealt with, then you are not comparing like with like. Also the pounds in one year are not worth the same as the pounds in another, simply because inflation has changed their buying power, so a 10 per cent growth in sales when inflation is running at 15 per cent represents a real drop in sales volume.

3. You may want to see how well you are doing compared with someone else's business, perhaps a competitor, or someone in a similar line of business elsewhere, or an industry norm (see Table 4.1). This may provide useful pointers to where improvements can be made, or to new and more profitable business opportunities. For this type of analysis you need external information. Fortunately, the UK has an unrivalled wealth of readily available financial data on companies and industries.

Table 4.1 *How they check out*

| | | Tesco | | Sainsbury | |
	1990	Year *Increase/Decrease* %	1990	Year *Increase/Decrease* %
Group turnover (£m)	5,402	+ 64	7,257	+ 103
Pre-tax profit (£m)	362	+ 176	451	+ 134
Net margin	6.4%	+ 73	7.2%	+ 33
Dividend per share (p)	4.3	+ 123	6.1	+ 122
Earnings per share	16.36	+ 133	19.6	+ 119
Gearing	17%	–	40%	–
No of stores	379	– 4	354	+ 21
Selling area (M sq ft)	9,071	+ 21	6,386	+ 46
Av. store size (sq ft)	23,900	+ 26	22,110	+ 32
Sales per sq ft	£12.70	+ 39	£17.26	+ 16
Operating profit	334	+ 221	437	+ 130
UK market share	8.7%	+ 29.8	11.6%	+ 19.6

The main way in which all these business yardsticks are established is through the use of ratios. A ratio is simply something expressed as a proportion of something else, and it is intended to give an appreciation of what has happened. For example, a percentage is a particular type of ratio, where events are always compared with a base of 100.

We have already seen the return on capital employed (ROCE) ratio, which was expressed as a percentage. In our everyday lives we apply ratios to tell us how well, or otherwise, something is performing. One measure of a car's performance is in miles per gallon (petrol consumption). If the mpg rate drops, say, from 35 to 1 to 20 to 1, it tells us the car is long overdue for a service – or worse.

In the financial field the opportunity for calculating ratios is great, for computing useful ratios, not quite so great. Here we will concentrate on explaining the key ratios for a small business. Most you can calculate yourself, some you may need your bookkeeper or accountant to organise for you. All take a little time and may cost a little money, but they do tell you a lot about what is going on. Derek Bok, a president of Harvard University, summed this field up nicely in the following quotation: 'If you think knowledge is expensive, try ignorance.'

One main value of the position audit using ratios is that it points to questions that need answers. A large difference between what actually happened and what standard was set suggests that something may be wrong. The tools of analysis (the ratios) allow managers to choose, from the hundreds of questions that might be asked, the handful that are really worth answering. In a small or expanding business where time is at a premium, this quick preselection of key questions is vital.

Measures of growth

Growth is usually measured in three ways in emerging businesses. (The numbers in parentheses that follow each ratio title show their position in the summary of ratio tables on page 95.)

Sales growth (1)

This is the increase in sales year on year, in percentage terms. The accounts for a company called High Note (on page 76) which follow (see Figure 4.3) reveal a 30 per cent growth in sales (£100,000 rising to £130,000). Sales growth is a measure of increase in market power and gives you a feel for how fast an organisation is growing.

Table 4.2 shows how the fastest growing companies in the health care sector performed in this respect. Notice they are all small firms – no Glaxos here!

Table 4.2 *Greatest increases in turnover 1987 over 1986*

Company name	Turnover 1987 £000	Turnover increase 1986 £000	%
1. Rorer Pharmaceuticals Ltd	40,239	8,490	373.95
2. Regent Laboratories Ltd	8,620	3,146	173.99
3. Knoll Ltd	1,441	571	152.36
4. Cortecs Ltd	4,767	1,973	141.61
5. Lorex Pharmaceuticals Ltd	4,951	2,298	115.44
6. Consolidated Chemicals Ltd	1,140	575	98.26
7. Pharmacia Ltd	33,471	17,221	94.36
8. Fine Organics Ltd	17,448	9,700	79.87
9. Letap Pharmaceuticals Ltd	18,975	11,339	67.34
10. Immuno Ltd	5,540	3,401	62.89

Profit growth (2)

Is the increase in net profit after tax year on year, in percentage terms. For High Note the profit growth is 48 per cent (£8,910 rising to £13,200). Profit growth shows how much more money the business is generating for shareholders, which in turn could be ploughed back to finance further growth.

Headcount growth (3)

Is the percentage increase in the number of full-time or full-time equivalent employees, year on year. It needs to be accompanied by three further ratios to show whether or not you are getting good value from the extra people and not just a bigger overhead bill (see Table 4.3):

Sales per employee (4) (sales in £s ÷ number of employees)
Profit per employee (5) (net profit after tax ÷ number of employees)
Value added per employee (6) (net profit plus wages and salaries ÷ number of employees)

The wide variation in performance of the companies shown in Table 4.2, whose turnover ranged between £5.7 and £12.5m, give food for thought. Regent Labs have only generated half the sales per employee that Serona did in the year in question, and their return on capital employed was less than a fifth of the better performing company.

Table 4.3 *Headcount growth*

Company	Sales per employee £	Profit per employee £	Value added per employee £	ROCE
Regent Labs	51,928	1,644	9,590	6%
Swartz Pharma	95,567	820	12,432	14%
Serona Labs	101,509	2,578	15,684	33%
Servier Labs	96,310	1,264	17,480	27%

Measures of profitability

There are two main ways to measure a business's profitability. They are both important, but they reveal different things about the performance and perhaps even the strategy of the business. To know and understand what is happening you need information in both areas: return on capital employed and profit margins.

Return on capital employed (ROCE) (7)

The financial resources employed in a business are called capital. We have already seen that capital can come into a business from a number of different sources. These sources have one thing in common: they all want a return – a percentage interest – on the money they invest. There are a number of ways in which return on capital can be measured, but for a small business two are particularly important.

The ROCE ratio is calculated by expressing the profit before long-term loan interest and tax as a proportion of the total capital employed. So if you look at the High Note Profit and Loss Account (Figure 4.3), you can see that for year 1, the profit before tax is £14,850. To this we have to add the loan interest of £1250. If we did not do this we would be double counting our cost of loan capital by expecting a return on a loan which had already paid interest. This makes the profit figure £16,100. We also ignore tax charges, not because they are unimportant or insignificant, but simply because the level of tax is largely outside the control of the business, and it is the business's performance we are trying to measure.

Now look at the balance sheet. The capital employed is the sum of the owner's capital, the profit retained and the long-term loan, in this case £28,910 (£10,000 + £8,910 + £10,000). So the ROCE ratio for the first year is:

$$\frac{£16,100}{£28,910} = 0.56 \text{ which expressed as a percentage} = 56\%$$

The great strength of this ratio lies in the overall view it takes of the financial health of the whole business. If you look at the same ratio for the second year, you will see a small change. The ratio gives no clue as to why this has happened – it simply provides the starting point for an analysis of business performance, and an overall yardstick against which to compare absolute performance. A banker might look to this ratio to see if the business could support more long-term borrowing (though not in isolation, of course).

Return on shareholders' capital (ROSC) (8)

The second way a small business would calculate a return on capital is by looking at the profit available for shareholders. This is not the money actually paid out as dividends and so on, but is a measure of the increase in worth of the funds invested by shareholders.

In the case of High Note the net profit after tax is divided by the owner's capital plus the retained profits (these, although not distributed, belong to the shareholders). So in our example this would be the sum:

$$\frac{£\ 8,910}{£18,910} = 0.47 \text{ which expressed as a percentage} = 47\%$$

And for the second year this ratio would be 41 per cent.

If someone was considering investing in shares in this business, then this ratio would be of particular interest to them.

Once again the difference in the ratios is clear, but the reasons are not. This is only the starting point for a more detailed analysis.

Gearing and its effect on ROSC (9)

All businesses have access to two fundamentally different sorts of money. Equity, or owner's capital, including retained earnings, is money that is not a risk to the business. If no profits are made then the owner and other shareholders simply do not get dividends. They may not be pleased, but they cannot usually sue.

Debt capital is money borrowed by the business from outside sources; it puts the business at financial risk and is also risky for the lenders. In return for taking that risk they expect an interest payment every year, irrespective of the performance of the business.

The Financial Position

In our example this would be:

$$\frac{\text{Share Capital}}{\text{All Long-term Capital}} = \frac{18,910}{28,910} = 66.5\%$$

Finlay and Co

Arundbhai Patel, former Chairman, Finlay and Co:

'The capitalist system is one where you take risks, but only a few people in the world are prepared to take them. We bought Finlay's, a chain of newsagents and tobacconists, for £21.5m at the height of the retail boom in 1987. At one point we had a turnover of £50m a year and we were offered £60m for the chain of 282 shops. But we were heavily geared – and no business can generate more money just because interest rates are rising. We could not pay them, and so the banks sent in the receiver. We lost everything. It hurts to lose millions of pounds, you miss the cash, but one learns from the experience. I am a Hindu, and my religion is about a sense of duty to others. I believe if one does one's duty correctly, then one will go to Heaven. One is thankful to God even for failures.'

Heathcote Care Home for the Elderly

Clem Rogers of Heathcote Care Home for the Elderly:

'The whole thing has given me a partial nervous breakdown – everybody seems to think you are guilty if you try to run your own business. I had a home for very dependent elderly people, with a staff of 15 and 18 residents who paid £275 a week. I had a lot of borrowing, and last summer was difficult, because it was so warm and a number of residents died. We filled up again by the autumn, but I got £13,000 behind in interest payments to the bank with a business worth around £1m. It was a cash-flow situation, and the bank decided to foreclose. The home has carried on since the receiver took it over, with my impetus – my former matron runs it – but the debts were around £700,000. I now get £37.90 a week and £10 for employment training. I have lost my house and will also be in court, because my former wife is suing me for unpaid maintenance. My long-time partner has broken up with me over it all – I can see why people top themselves.'

Advent Communications –
A company with a healthy gearing ratio throughout its early growth

Small start-up winner Advent Communications owes its origins to its founders' reluctance to move to Chelmsford. They decided that the relocation package offered by GEC, their existing employer, was not going to be good enough.

In 1986 GEC decided to transfer a chunk of its Ministry of Defence work from its West London subsidiary GEC–McMichael to its Marconi Communications

71

operation in the Essex town. David Garrood, then 32, was divisional manager of a satellite communications operation he had set up within GEC–McMichael in 1983. He had built a £5m a year turnover and had a staff of 58. His most exciting product was a portable system for transmitting TV news pictures by satellite, allowing 'real-time' coverage from world trouble spots. It was used, for example, to cover the TWA hijack at Beirut Airport in June 1985.

There was no management buy-out or transfer of ownership, Garrood and two colleagues simply decided to set up on their own rather than move to Chelmsford. In the end, Garrood says, 'Marconi got the products, but not the people who had been developing them for two years. Basically, the team which ran GEC's sat-comms operation came here to Advent.'

Garrood and his partners knew they were going to need sizeable funds for their start-up. Their business plan, which they presented to a dozen venture capital outfits and to a number of private would-be backers, acknowledged that it would take about 18 months to develop products before they could start taking orders. 'We concluded that the most sensible way would be to have a solid capital base rather than attempt to do the job on smaller amounts of money', Garrood says.

Advent started trading in April 1986, though sales of completed products began only in August 1987. Profits for the year ending 31 July 1990 were up to £720,000 on sales of £4.5m. The target for 1992 is profits of £1m on sales of £6.5m.

3i provided £400,000 of financing – £150,000 in medium-term loans and £250,000 of equity. Ownership of the business was split 48 per cent to 3i and 52 per cent to the directors. Lloyd's Bank topped it up with a £50,000 overdraft facility (see Figure 4.3). Garrood had no qualms about surrendering equity in a business whose potential he felt had already been established inside GEC. 'We simply felt that 52 per cent of a £10m company was worth more than 95 per cent of a £1m company', he says.

| Finance | | Financial performance | | | | | | Expectations for 1992 | |
£000		£000	1986*	1987	1988	1989	1990		
400 (1986)	3i (150 loan, 250 equity)	Revenue	5	64	998	2,100	4,500	Revenue	£6,500
50 (1986)	Lloyds Bank (overdraft facility)	PBIT	(15)	(262)	69	387	745	PBT	£1,000
		PBT	(15)	(283)	45	366	720	Net Assets	£1,200
		Sh.funds	66	33	78	327	867	Employees	35
		Borrowings	NIL	171	169	190	155		

Key: * 4 months PBIT profit before interest and tax
       PBT   profit before tax

Figure 4.2 *A healthy balance sheet: Advent Communications*

As well as looking at the gearing, lenders will study the business's capacity to pay interest. They do this by using another ratio called times interest earned (10).

The Financial Position

This is calculated by dividing the operating profit by the loan interest. It shows how many times the loan interest is covered, and gives the lender some idea of the safety margin. The ratio for this example is given at the end of the tables on page 184. Once again rules are hard to make, but much less than 3× interest earned is unlikely to give lenders confidence. The × is shorthand for 'times' – a convention when using this and other ratios.

Gearing levels can also have strategic implications that affect a company's competitive stance.

Evans Medical

Evans Medical was founded in Worcester in 1809 and by 1961, when it was taken over by Glaxo, it was a large company by most standards. Within Glaxo it became the UK's largest manufacturer of generic drugs (less expensive versions of branded medicines on which the patents had expired). In 1985 Glazo hived off Evans in a management buy-out after deciding that generics fitted poorly with its increasingly successful patent drug business.

On its own Evans had a rough time. Generic drugs are a relatively stable market but, since they are essentially a commodity product, price competition can be vicious. Rivals were aware that Evans was vulnerable because of the debt involved in the buy-out so they sold parts of the business to stay afloat. By 1988 Evans had in response to this threat made profits of only £2.6m on capital of nearly £90m. Later that year Evans was taken over again, this time by a cash-rich small company looking for a big jump in the growth ladder.

Profit margins

Any analysis of a business must consider the current level of sales activity. If you look at High Note's Profit and Loss Accounts which follow (Figure 4.3), you will see that materials consumed in sales have jumped from £30,000 to £43,000, a rise of 43 per cent. However, a quick look at the change in sales activity will show that the situation is nothing like so dramatic. Materials as a proportion of sales have risen from 30 to 33 per cent (30,000/100,000 = 30% and 43,000/130,000 = 33%). Obviously, the more you sell the more you must make. To understand why there have been changes in the level of return on capital employed, we have to relate both profit and capital to sales activity. The ROCE equation can be expanded to look like this:

$$\frac{Profit}{Capital} = \frac{Profit}{Sales} \times \frac{Sales}{Capital}$$

That gives us two separate strands to examine, the profit strand and the capital strand. The first of these is usually called profit margins. The capital strand will be looked at later.

When we examine profit margins, all costs, expenses and the different types of profit are expressed as a percentage of sales. This ratio makes comparisons both possible and realistic.

An analysis of High Note's Profit and Loss Account (Figure 4.3) will show the following changes:

Area	Change	Some possible causes
Material Cost of Sales	Up from 30% to 33%	(a) Higher price paid (b) Change in product mix (c) Increased waste
Labour Cost of Sales	Down from 20% to 19%	(a) Reduction in wage rates (b) Increase in work rate (c) Change in product mix
Gross Profit	Down from 50% to 48%	(a) 3% increase in materials (b) 1% decrease in labour = net 2% decline in gross margin
Operating or Trading Profit	Up to 18.5% from 17%	A $3\frac{1}{2}$% improvement in expense ratios offset by a 2% decline in gross margin = net $1\frac{1}{2}$% improvement in trading profit
Net Profit before Tax	Up to 16.8% from 14.8%	Interest charges down from 2.1% of sales to 1.6%. Means another $\frac{1}{2}$% increase in net profit + $1\frac{1}{2}$% net increase in trading profit = 2%

Had we simply looked at the net profit margin, we would have seen a satisfactory increase, from 8.9 to 10.1 per cent. It is only by looking at each area in turn, the components of gross profit, operating or trading profit and net profit, that a useful analysis can be made. High Note's owner now has a small number of specific questions to ask in the search for reasons for changes in performance.

To summarise, the ratios of profitability that allow attention to be focused on specific areas are as follows.

Gross Profit percentage (11)

This is deducting the cost of sales from the sales, and expressing the result as a percentage of sales.

The Financial Position

In the High Note example, for year 1 this is:

£100,000 (Sales) − £50,000 (Cost of Sales) = £50,000 (Gross Profit)

then

£50,000 (Gross Profit − £100,000 (Sales) = 50 per cent.

This ratio gives an indication of relative manufacturing efficiency.

Operating or Trading Profit percentage (12)

This is calculated by deducting expenses from the gross profit, to arrive at the operating profit. This figure is then divided by sales and expressed as a percentage. For High Note in year 1, this is:

£50,000 (Gross Profit) − £33,000 (Expenses) = £17,000 (Operating Profit)

then

£17,000 (Operating Profit) ÷ £100,000 (Sales) = 17 per cent.

Net Profit before tax percentage (13)

In this case finance charges are deducted from operating profits to arrive at net profit before tax. This is then expressed as a percentage of sales.

For High Note, in year 1, this is:

£17,000 (Trading Profit) − £2,150 (Interest Charge) = £14,850 (Net Profit before Tax) ÷ 100,000 (Sales) = 14.85 per cent.
This ratio can also be calculated after tax.

	£	£	%	£	£	%
Sales		100,000	100		130,000	100
Cost of Sales						
Materials	30,000		30	43,000		33
Labour	20,000	50,000	20	25,000	68,000	19
Gross Profit		50,000	50		62,000	48
Expenses						
Rent, Rates etc	18,000			20,000		
Wages	12,000			13,000		
Advertising	3,000			3,000		
Expenses	–	33,000		2,000	38,000	
Operating or Trading Profit		17,000	17		24,000	18.5
Deduct Interest on:						
Overdraft	900					
Loan	1,250	2,150		1,250	2,050	
Net Profit before Tax		14,850	14.8		21,950	16.8
Tax Paid		5,940			8,750	
Net Profit after tax	8,910		8.9	13,200		10.1

Figure 4.3 *High Note's Profit and Loss Account for Years 1 and 2*

	£	£	£	£	£	£
Fixed Assets						
Furniture & Fixtures			12,500			28,110
Working Capital						
Current Assets						
Stock	10,000			12,000		
Debtors	13,000			13,000		
Cash	100	23,100		500	25,000	
Less Current Liabilities						
Overdraft	5,000			6,000		
Creditors	1,690	6,690		5,500	11,500	
Net Current Assets			16,410			14,000
Capital Employed			28,910			42,110
Financed by						
Owner's Capital	10,000			18,910		
Profit Retained	8,910		18,910	13,200		32,110
Long Term Loan			10,000			10,000
Total Capital Employed			28,910			42,110

Figure 4.4 *High Note's Balance Sheet for year ends 1 and 2*

The Financial Position

High profit margins are not always the passport to riches if their strategic implications are not clearly understood; Filofax is a classic example of this failure to recognise the relationship between profit and market attractiveness.

Filofax

Few companies rode the mid-1980s yuppie boom higher than Britain's Filofax, maker of the fashionable leather-encased personal organisers beloved of media trendies and financial whizzes. Filofaxes, invented for engineers, had been sold to British army officers, clergymen and the like since 1910, but only when they became a fashion fad did sales soar – from £681,000 in 1983 to £14.7m in 1989, and all without a single line of advertising. The formula was, however, flawed. While some customers were prepared to pay extra for the Filofax name, many simply wanted a good-quality ring-binder with diary, address book and information sheets. Because Filofax's profit margins were so high, and its products so costly, imitators could easily match the company's quality while beating its prices.

Losing market share is tolerable when your market is booming, but being a one-product company with a narrow customer base is a precarious way to live. Filofax's market stalled as soaring British interest rates (over half its sales are in Britain) made yuppies downwardly mobile. Worse, those who could still afford fads splashed out on new ones like electronic organisers and portable telephones. In the first half of 1989 Filofax's sales fell by a fifth, while its sparkling profits were transformed into a £554,000 pre-tax loss.

Working capital ratios (or liquidity)

The capital strand of the return on capital employed (ROCE) calculation has two main branches of its own.

$$\frac{\text{Profit}}{\text{Capital}} = \frac{\text{Profit}}{\text{Fixed Assets} + \text{Working Capital}}$$

The more dynamic of these is working capital, the day-to-day money used to finance the working of the business. It is important to monitor the relationship between sales and the various elements of working capital to see how effectively that capital is being used. But as the working capital is the difference between current assets and current liabilities, it is also important to monitor their relationship, both in total and in their component parts.

This is very often referred to as liquidity, or the business's ability to meet its current liabilities as they fall due. The most important ratios in this area are:

The current ratio (14)

A business's ability to meet its immediate liabilities can be estimated by relating its current assets to current liabilities. If for any reason current liabilities cannot be met, then the business is being exposed to an unnecessary level of financial risk. Suppliers may stop supplying or could even petition for bankruptcy if they are kept waiting too long for payment.

In the financial statements given for High Note, the first year's picture on the Balance Sheet shows £23,100 current assets to £6690 current liabilities (see Figure 4.4).

The Current Ratio $= \dfrac{\text{Current Assets}}{\text{Current Liabilities}}$

Therefore High Note's
current ratio $= \dfrac{23,100}{6,690} = 3.4$

This shows current liabilities to be covered 3.4 times, and the ratio is usually expressed in the form 3.4:1. In the second year this has come down to 2.2:1. At first glance this figure may look worse than the first year's position. Certainly, current liabilities have grown faster than current assets, but up to a point this is a desirable state of affairs, because it means that the business is having to find less money to finance working capital.

There is really only one rule about how high (or low) the current ratio should be. It should be as close to 1:1 as the safe conduct of the business will allow. This will not be the same for every type of business. A shop buying in finished goods on credit and selling them for cash could run safely at 1.3:1. A manufacturer, with raw material to store and customers to finance, may need over 2:1. This is because the period between paying cash out for raw materials and receiving cash in from customers is longer in a manufacturing business than in a retail business. It is a bit like the oil dip-stick on a car. There is a band within which the oil level should be. Levels above or below that band pose different problems. So for most businesses, less than 1.2:1 would probably be cutting things a bit fine. Over 1.8:1 would mean too much cash was being tied up in such items as stocks and debtors.

An unnecessarily high amount of working capital makes it harder for a business to make a good ROCE because it makes the bottom half of the sum bigger. Too low a working capital, below 1:1 for example, exposes the business to unacceptable financial risks, such as foreclosure by banks or creditors.

The Financial Position

The quick ratio or acid test (15)

The quick ratio is really a belt and braces figure. In this, only assets that can be realised quickly, such as debtors and cash in hand, are related to current liabilities.

$$\text{The Quick Ratio} = \frac{\text{Debtors} + \text{Cash}}{\text{Current Liabilities}}$$

For the High Note example, looking at year one only, we would exclude the £10,000 stock because, before it can be realised, we would need to find customers to sell to and collect in the cash. All this might take several months. High Note's quick ratio would be 13,100 (cash + debtors) + 6,690 (current liabilities): a perhaps too respectable 1.9:1. In the second year this has dropped to 1.2:1 (13,500 + 11,500).

Once again, general rules are very difficult to make, but a ratio of 0.8:1 would be acceptable for most types of business.

Credit control

Any small business selling on credit knows how quickly customers can eat into their cash. This is particularly true if the customers are big companies. Customers going bust can have a domino effect on their suppliers as the following two cases illustrate.

Levercrest

Husband and wife entrepreneurs Leslie and Anne Cluer know a lot about swings and roundabouts; their company, Levercrest, is a top supplier to Britain's playgrounds.

Levercrest was floated on the Unlisted Securities Market in 1990 via a placing through corporate finance boutique Guidehouse that valued the company at £5m and made the Cluers millionaires – at least on paper.

The company, which also makes park benches and rubbish bins, raised about £1.5m of fresh equity in its drive for expansion. It specialises in British Standard equipment and is hoping for greater sales at a time of mounting concern about the need for safer playground equipment. Levercrest wants to be the Body Shop of playground equipment, by supplying more of the equipment that takes the danger, but not the fun, out of playtime.

Cluer reckons lessons learnt when a previous venture making benches and cement products for schools went into voluntary liquidation in 1982 after a major client failed to pay will ensure a strict financial control. The liquidator said he was not to blame.

This year, Levercrest, which has been in profit since it was set up in the Cluers' garage in 1982, expects profits of about £700,000 on sales of about £5.5m.

Thompson Transport

It was the recession that finished us off. We founded the company in 1982, distributing mail-order goods like washing machines and freezers in West Glamorgan and Dyfed for a company in Southampton. My husband drove and I ran the office, and by 1989 we had ten employees and a turnover of £250,000. But then, as firms that were our regular clients went bust, we switched to dealing direct with factories; then the factories started going under as well – and we followed suit. We have debts of £150,000, and we'll have to sell the house to pay them off. I blame Mrs Thatcher for high interest rates and a lack of government – there ought to be minimum set rates for delivery routes. How could we compete with the bigger companies? They kept undercutting us.

Surprisingly enough, bad debts (those which are never paid) are rarely as serious a problem as slow payers. A survey by Intrum Justitia, the credit management and debt collection agency, in 1991, revealed that. The average credit period offered in Britain is 30 days but only one in 20 companies is paid within that time, with one in four receiving payment after 75 days. Companies with a turnover of less than £10m are more than twice as likely than larger companies to have payment periods exceeding 75 days. Three-quarters of businesses with turnovers of less than £2m found payments were taking longer than they had a year ago.

There are two techniques for monitoring debtors. The first is to prepare a schedule by age of debtor. Figure 4.5 gives some idea of how this might be done.

	2 months (or less) £	3 months £	4 months £	Over 4 months £	Total £
Brown & Co	1,000				
Jenkins & Son	1,000				
Andersons		3,000			
Smithers		2,500			
Thomkinsons			500		
Henry's			2,500		
Smart Inc				2,500	
	2,000	5,500	3,000	2,500	13,000

Figure 4.5 *High Note's debtors schedule – end of year 1*

This method has the great merit of focusing attention clearly on specific problem accounts. It may seem like hard work, but once you have got the system going it will pay dividends.

The second technique for monitoring debtors is using the ratio average collection period (16). This ratio is calculated by expressing debtors as a proportion of credit sales, and then relating that to the days in the period in question.

Average Collection Period $= \dfrac{\text{Debtors}}{\text{Sales}} \times 365$

Let us suppose that all High Note's sales are on credit and the periods in question are both 365-day years (no leap years). Then in year 1 the average collection period would be:

$\dfrac{£13,000 \text{ Debtors}}{£100,000 \text{ Sales}} \times 365 \text{ (days in period)} = 47 \text{ days}$

In year 2 the collection period is:

$\dfrac{£13,000 \text{ Debtors}}{£130,000 \text{ Sales}} \times 365 \text{ (days in period)} = 36 \text{ days}$

So in the second year High Note are collecting their cash from debtors 11 days sooner than in the first year. This is obviously a better position to be in, making their relative amount of debtors lower than in year 1. It is not making the absolute amount of debtors lower, and this illustrates another great strength of using ratios to monitor performance. High Note's sales have grown by 30 per cent from £100,000 to £130,000, and their debtors have remained at £13,000. At first glance then, their debtors are the same, neither better nor worse. But when you relate those debtors to the increased levels of sales, as this ratio does, then you can see that the position has improved.

This is a good position audit ratio, which has the great merit of being quickly translatable into a figure any businessperson can understand, showing how much it is costing to give credit. If, for example, High Note is paying 12 per cent for an overdraft, giving £13,000 credit for 36 days will cost £153.86 $\dfrac{(12\% \times £13,000 \times 36)}{365}$.

Average days' credit taken (17)

Of course, the credit world is not all one sided. Once a small business has established itself, it too will be taking credit. You can usually rely on your suppliers to keep you informed on your indebtedness – but only on an individual basis. It would be prudent to calculate how many days' credit, on average, are being taken from suppliers: a very similar sum to average collection period. The ratio is as follows:

Average Days' Credit = $\dfrac{\text{Creditors}}{\text{Purchases}} \times 365$

For High Note, in year 1, this sum would be (assuming all materials purchased this period):

$\dfrac{£\ 1,690\ \text{Creditors}}{£30,000\ \text{Purchases}} \times 365\ \text{(days in period)} = 21\ \text{days}$

In year 2 this ratio would be:

$\dfrac{£\ 5,500\ \text{Creditors}}{£43,000\ \text{Purchases}} \times 365\ \text{(days in period)} = 47\ \text{days}$

The difference in these ratios probably reflects High Note's greater creditworthiness in year 2. The longer the credit period you can take from your suppliers the better, provided that you still meet their terms of trade. They may, however, put you to the bottom of the list when supplies get scarce, or give you up altogether when they find a better customer.

Resource Administration

Resource Administration Group, a £4m turnover recruitment and property maintenance company with 22 employees, tightened up the terms and conditions of its purchase agreements as part of a general review of its sales and purchasing systems. It then went along to its larger suppliers to explain what it was doing.

'We had operated a very loose system before', explains Liam Forde, managing director. 'Now we set out formally that we won't take delivery unless the goods are of a suitable quality and delivered in a timely fashion.' A surprising outcome of this tightening-up was that some suppliers offered improved discount terms. 'Because we looked more professional, suppliers felt much safer in dealing with us and were prepared to offer us discounts.'

Resource Administration has also introduced a system of purchase order pads, one copy of which goes to accounts, so that tighter control can be kept of orders for items such as stationery. This system means that small orders can be combined to gain discounts or avoid paying delivery charges. It has been possible to achieve savings of £4000 from a single supplier since this system was introduced three months ago and savings of 5 per cent on an annual purchasing bill of £50,000 are expected.

More creditor controls

There are two other useful techniques to help the owner/manager keep track of these events. One is simply to relate days' credit given to days' credit taken. If they balance out then you are about even in the credit game.

In year 1, High Note gave 47 days' credit to their customers and took only 21 days from their suppliers, so they were a loser. In the second year they got ahead, giving only 36 days while taking 47.

The other technique is to age your creditors in exactly the same way as we did with the debtors. In this way it is possible to see at a glance which suppliers have been owed what sums of money, and for how long.

Stock control (18)

Any manufacturing, subcontracting or assembling business will have to buy in raw materials and work on them to produce finished goods. They will have to keep track of three sorts of stock: raw materials, work in progress, and finished goods. A retailing business will probably only be concerned with finished goods, and a service business may have no stocks at all.

If we assume that all High Note's stock is in finished goods, then the control ratio we can use is as follows:

Days' finished goods stock (18) =
$$\frac{\text{Finished Goods Stock}}{\text{Cost of Sales}^*} \times \text{Days in period}$$

For High Note in year 1 this would be:

$$\frac{10,000}{50,000} \times 365 = 73 \text{ Days}$$

In year 2 the ratio would be 64 days.

It is impossible to make any general rule about stock levels. Obviously, a business has to carry enough stock to meet customers' demand, and a retail business must have it on display or on hand. However, if High Note's supplier can always deliver within 14 days it would be unnecessary to carry 73 days' stock.

The same basic equation can be applied to both raw material and work-in-progress stock, but to reach raw material stock you should substitute raw materials consumed for cost of sales. Once again the strength of this ratio is that a business can quickly calculate how much it is costing to carry a given level of stock, in just the same way as customer credit costs were calculated earlier.

---

* Cost of sales is used because it accurately reflects the amount of stock. The sales figure includes other items such as profit margin. If you are looking at an external company it is possible that the only figure available will be that for sales. In this case it can be used as an approximation.

Trevor Millett, managing director of CJ's, a chain of 42 stores selling jeans and casual clothing, responded swiftly when he realised that 1990 was going to be a difficult year. Budgets were tightened, optimum staff levels reassessed and capital spending cut. But one area which Millett refused to trim was in the tills and computer systems which told him how quickly individual lines were selling and what his stock levels were. One of the main tasks of the sales manager Millett appointed at the beginning of the year is to keep an eye on stock levels.

'When a stock line is clearly not turning into money at sufficient speed we cut the price until it does', says Millett. Hooded tops, all the rage in April, were going out of fashion in June. Prices were cut and by late August, when other retailers also started discounting, Millett had almost cleared his stocks. When expensive items such as jackets sell better in certain stores than in others, Millett has no hesitation in switching stocks to the stores where demand is highest. Tight stock control ensures that the business has a positive cash flow and keeps its bank overdraft to a minimum. CJ's is the trading name of Peter Millett and Sons, a Hayes, Middlesex-based company with turnover of £12m and a work-force of 230.

Retailers should be able to see fairly quickly where stocks are building up because the evidence is on the shelves and the racks in the shop window. Excess stock levels are not always so obvious in businesses which involve a long manufacturing process but controlling levels of inventory is of vital importance to any business which wants to weather the recession. 'I have spent a good part of the past six months telling people to get their stocks down', comments Jon Moulton, managing partner of Schroder Ventures, a venture capital company. 'We closed a warehouse at one of our companies so they had nowhere to stock things. Companies must drive inventory out of their systems.' 'We have managed to save businesses by getting them to reduce stocks', says Allan Griffiths, head of the insolvency division of accountants Grant Thornton. 'If you can get rid of £250,000 from stocks of £500,000 you can relieve your cash flow problems. If you have cash in the bank you will survive the recession. If you don't you are in trouble.'

A common failing of large as well as small companies is to plan production levels to get the most out of their plant and equipment without taking into account the costs involved in holding stocks. There will be a direct cost in terms of borrowings to finance stocks while obsolete items may have to be sold at a discount and possibly even at below cost, warns Ivor Cohen, electronics industry adviser to APA, a venture capital firm.

In a recession many small business owners attempt to keep their work-force busy, producing for stock even if demand has fallen. 'If your output levels are too high you must start cutting back straight away', advises Allan Griffiths. 'If you go on building up stocks you will face a bigger cash drain. If you have to take the nasty medicine and reduce your work-force the sooner you do it the better.'

The Financial Position

Waterstone

Tim Waterstone started his eponymous book retail chain in 1982 after he had been sacked by W H Smith. Born in 1939, he read English at St Catherine's College, Cambridge, before becoming a marketing manager at Allied Breweries. He then worked for W H Smith, finally becoming chairman of the group's US subsidiary. With Waterstone's he proved that a good bookseller could be successful. Last year he struck a deal whereby W H Smith will buy Waterstone's in 1993 for a minimum £40m.

When Waterstone's got under way the average value of stock per square foot across all booksellers was under £40, and sales per square foot were under £140. One fed upon the other; with the trade becoming used to a stock presentation that was simply inadequate to satisfy the public – Waterstone reckoned then, and does still, that a decent general bookseller cannot do a proper job with fewer than 40,000 individual titles in stock at any one time. He told his backers that he would be stocking his shops at least twice the industry average. With stock at double the industry average at £80 per sq ft (more than £120 per sq ft now), Waterstone felt that sales of £300 per sq ft were easily achievable, and it is at this level that selling books (with controlled occupancy costs) becomes very profitable.

It really is strange that the situation had been allowed to degenerate to the level it had. In France particularly, but certainly in Germany as well, really good stockholding bookshops were trading all over the land ever since the post-war recovery. But when an industry starts to talk itself into a cycle of defeat, the momentum becomes irresistible. The myth of inevitable failure hung over everything the bookselling trade did and said. The perceived wisdom was that only W H Smith, operating very much in the middle and popular area, was viable. Nobody spent any money, and nobody opened any bookshops of any size. Even Dillons, purchased by Pentos in 1977, remained quiescent and dormant for ten years or so. The French and Germans could make money from bookselling, and the Americans – through B Dalton and Walden, and a number of lively regional chains – could move into a period of vigorous development, but here in Britain failure was the certainty, and the total dominance of the publisher over the retailer accepted as the natural course of events.

Cash control

The residual element in the control of working capital is cash or, if there is no cash left, the size of overdraft needed in a particular period.

Usually the amount of cash available to a small business is finite and specific, also the size of overdraft it can take, so stock levels, creditor and debtor policies, and other working capital elements are decided with these limits in mind.

Mulberry's clothes

*In 1970, on his twenty-first birthday, Roger Saul's parents gave him £500.
Instead of spending the money, their fashion-conscious son took his chance. He
used it to convert an old shed in the back garden of his parents' Somerset home
into a small workshop producing leather belts and bags. The Mulberry Company
was born. Eighteen years later, Mulberry has a large, purpose-built factory, 300
employees and world-wide sales of £30m. Mulberry's clothes and accessories are
sold in its own shops, franchises and 'shops within shops' in department stores.
Last September, in a move that smacked of taking coals to Newcastle, Saul opened
his first shop in Milan.*

*But financing Mulberry's growth has not been easy. Saul has changed bankers
many times over the years. 'Each time we found we got a good service for the first
two or three years but when we asked for more money the bankers suddenly said
"No". They said they couldn't see the firm continuing to grow. In other words,
they got cold feet.' Saul's reaction was simple: he went to a different bank.*

*The recession in 1980 hit Mulberry hard. Sales, particularly in the US,
plummeted and for the first time ever, it made a loss. 'Our problem was that we
had opened shops without realising the cash-flow implications', says Saul. 'We
were selling most retail, not wholesale, with the result that our money was tied up
until the goods were sold.' Saul went wholesale and started a franchise operation.
'We could open franchise shops without spending a penny of our own money', he
says.*

*Mulberry is still 100 per cent family-owned and Saul has no plans to bring it to
the stock market. 'People float companies either to raise money or to get out. We
want neither of those.'*

Circulation of working capital (19)

The primary ratio for controlling working capital is usually considered
to be the current ratio. This, however, is of more interest to outside
bodies, such as bankers and suppliers wanting to see how safe their
money is. The manager of a business is more interested in how well the
money tied up in working capital is being used.

Look at High Note's Balance Sheets for the last two years (Figure
4.4). You can see that net current assets, another name for working
capital, have shrunk from £16,410 to £14,000 – not too dramatic. Now
let us look at these figures in relation to the level of business activity in
each year.

$$\text{Circulation of Working Capital (19)} = \frac{\text{Sales}}{\text{Working Capital}}$$

For year 1 this is $\dfrac{1,000,000}{16,410} = 6\times$ and year 2 $\dfrac{130,000}{14,000} = 9\times$

The × is shorthand for 'times' – a convention when using this ratio.

So we can see that not only has High Note got less money tied up in working capital in the second year, it has also used it more efficiently. In other words, it has circulated it faster. Each pound of working capital now produces £9 of sales, as opposed to only £6 last year; and, as each pound of sales makes profits, the higher the sales the higher the profit.

Controlling fixed assets

A major problem that all new or expanding businesses face is exactly how much to have of such items as equipment, storage capacity and work space. New fixed assets tend to be acquired in large chunks and are sometimes more opportunistic than market-related in nature.

In any event, however, and for whatever reason acquired, once in the business it is important to make sure the asset is being used effectively. Controlling fixed assets splits down into two areas: looking at how effectively fixed assets are being used, and how to plan for new capital investments.

The fixed asset pyramid

Generally, the best way to measure how well existing fixed assets are being used is to see how many pounds' worth of sales each pound of fixed assets is generating.

Use of fixed assets (20)

The overall ratio is that of Sales ÷ Fixed Assets which gives a measure of this use of the fixed assets. Look back to the High Note accounts in Figure 4.3. The use of fixed asset ratio in that example is:

Year 1 $\dfrac{100,000}{12,500} = 8\times$ Year 2 $\dfrac{130,000}{28,110} = 4.6\times$

This means that each pound invested in fixed assets has generated £8 worth of sales in year 1 and only £4.60 in year 2.

This inefficient use of fixed assets has consumed all the benefit High Note gained from its improved use of working capital – and a little more. In fact, this is the main reason why the return on capital employed (ROCE) has declined in year 2. This may be a short-term problem which will be cured when expected new sales levels are reached: not at all unusual if, for example, a new piece of machinery was bought late in the second year.

Looking at the overall fixed asset picture is rather like looking at the circulation of working capital ratio only as a means of monitoring working capital. There we looked at stock control, debtors and creditors as well. Fixed assets use is looked at both in total and in its component parts. A pyramid of ratios stretches out below this prime ratio.

The fixed asset pyramid will look something like Figure 4.6, although the nature of the assets of a particular business may suggest others be included.

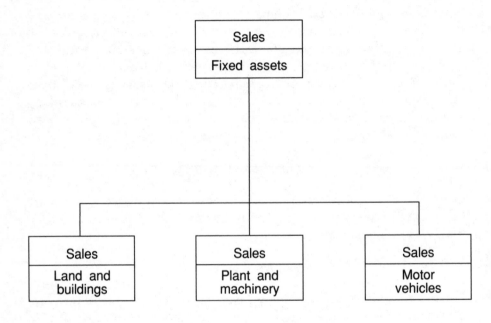

Figure 4.6 *The fixed asset pyramid*

For example, a shop will also be interested in sales per square foot of selling price.

More detail still

More sophisticated businesses also monitor the output of individual pieces of equipment. They look at down time (how long the equipment is out of commission), repair and maintenance costs, and the value of its output. If your business warrants it you can do this by simply expanding the pyramid as shown in Figure 4.7.

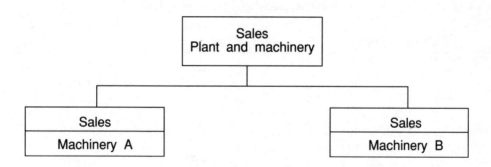

Figure 4.7 *Extension of fixed asset pyramid*

Averaging ratios

Ratios which involve the use of stock, debtors or creditors can be more accurately calculated by using the average of the opening and closing position. Seasonal factors or sales growth (contraction) will almost always make a single figure unrepresentative.

Look back to the High Note accounts (p 76). Here you can see an example where sales have grown by 30 per cent from £100,000 in the first year to £130,000 in the second. Obviously, neither the opening stock figure of £10,000, nor the closing stock of £12,000, is truly representative of what has happened in the intervening year. It seems much more likely that the average of the opening and closing stock figures is the best figure to use in calculating the stock control ratios shown earlier. So in this example, £11,000 ($\frac{£10,000 + £12,000}{2}$) would be the figure to use.

Other ratios

The ratios covered here are by no means the only ratios that can be usefully calculated. Each industry and trade will have special areas of its own. For example, advertising is a relatively large proportion of the cost of some cars, so that industry monitors comparative advertising spend. The ratio they use is 'pounds spent on advertising per car sold.' The figures for the UK car market in 1989 are given in Table 4.4.

Table 4.4 *Advertising per car sold in UK*

Make	£
Saab	401
Seat	321
Fiat	319
Citroen	294
Mazda	251
Renault	239
Audi-VW	197
Lada	183
Honda	167
Mercedes-Benz	165
Rover	112
Vauxhall	70
Ford	62

Market tests

This is the name given to stock market measures of performance. Four key ratios here are: Earnings per Share, Price Earnings Ratio, Yield, and Dividend Cover.

$$\text{Earnings per Share} = \frac{\text{Net Profit}}{\text{Shares Outstanding}}$$

The after tax profit made by a company divided by the number of ordinary shares it has issued.

$$\text{Price Earnings Ratio} = \frac{\text{Market Price per Share}}{\text{Earnings per Share}}$$

The market price of an ordinary share divided by the earnings per share. The PE Ratio expresses the market value placed on the expectation of future earnings, ie the number of years required to earn the price paid for the shares out of profits at the current rate.

$$\text{Yield} = \frac{\text{Dividends per Share}}{\text{Price per Share}}$$

The percentage return a shareholder gets on the 'opportunity' value of their investment.

$$\text{Dividend Cover} = \frac{\text{Net Income}}{\text{Dividend}}$$

The number of times the profit exceeds the dividend, the higher the ratio, the more retained profit to finance future growth.

Some problems in using ratios

Finding the information to calculate business ratios is often not the major problem. Being sure of what the ratios are really telling you almost always is. The most common problems lie in the four following areas.

Which way is right?

There is a natural feeling with financial ratios to think that high figures are good ones, and an upward trend represents the right direction. This theory is, to some extent, encouraged by the personal feeling of wealth that having a lot of cash engenders.

Unfortunately, there is no general rule on which way is right for financial ratios. In some cases a high figure is good, in others a low figure is best. Indeed, there are even circumstances in which ratios of the same value are not as good as each other.

Look at the two working capital statements in Figure 4.8.

	1		2	
Current Assets	£	£	£	£
Stock	10,000		22,990	
Debtors	13,000		100	
Cash	100	23,100	10	23,100
Less Current Liabilities				
Overdraft	5,000		90	
Creditors	1,690	6,690	6,600	6,690
Working Capital		16,410		16,410
Current Ratio		3.4:1		3.4:1

Figure 4.8 *Difficult comparisons*

The amount of working capital in each example is the same, £16,410, as are the current assets and current liabilities, at £23,100 and £6,690 respectively. It follows that any ratio using these factors would also be the same. For example, the current ratios in these two examples are both identical, 3.4:1, but in the first case there is a reasonable chance that some cash will come in from debtors, certainly enough to meet the modest creditor position. In the second example there is no possibility of useful amounts of cash coming in from trading, with debtors at only £100, while creditors at the relatively substantial figure of £6,600 will pose a real threat to financial stability. So in this case the current ratios are identical, but the situations being compared are not. In fact, as a general rule, a higher working capital ratio is regarded as a move in the wrong direction. The more money a business has tied up in working capital the more difficult it is to make a satisfactory return on capital employed, simply because the larger the denominator the lower the return on capital employed.

In some cases the right direction is more obvious. A high return on capital employed is usually better than a low one, but even this situation can be a danger signal, warning that higher risks are being taken. And not all high profit ratios are good: sometimes a higher profit margin can lead to reduced sales volume and so lead to a lower ROCE.

In general, business performance as measured by ratios is best thought of as lying within a range, liquidity (current ratio), for example, staying between 1.2:1 and 1.8:1. A change in either direction represents a cause for concern.

Accounting for inflation

Financial ratios all use pounds as the basis for comparison – historical pounds at that. That would not be so bad if all these pounds were from the same date in the past, but that is not so. Comparing one year with another may not be very meaningful unless we account for the change in value of the pound.

One way of overcoming this problem is to adjust for inflation, perhaps using an index, such as that for consumer prices. Such indices usually take 100 as their base at some time in the past, for example, 1975. Then an index value for each subsequent year is produced showing the relative movement in the item being indexed.

Tables 4.5 and 4.6 show how this could be done for High Note.

Table 4.5 *Comparing unadjusted ratios*

Year	Sales	Sales Growth	Percentage Growth (ie the ratio year on year)
	£	£	
1	100,000	–	–
2	130,000	30,000	30.0
3	145,000	15,000	11.5

These unadjusted figures show a substantial growth in sales in each of the past two years. Now if High Note's owner used a consumer price index for the appropriate period to adjust his figures, the years could be properly compared.

Let us assume that the indices for years 1, 2 and 3 were 104, 120 and 135 respectively. Year 3 is the most recent set of figures, and therefore the one we want to use as the base for comparison. So to convert the pounds from years 1 and 2 to current pounds, we use this sum:

$$\text{Current Pounds} = \frac{\text{Index for Current Year}}{\text{Index for Historic Year}} \times \text{Historic Pounds}$$

For year 1 sales now become: 135/104 × £100,000 = £129,808
For year 2 sales now become: 135/120 × £130,000 = £146,250
For year 3* sales now become: 135/135 × £145,000 = £145,000

*In other words, year 3 is virtually 'now'.

We can now construct an adjusted table, showing the real sales growth over the past three years (see Table 4.6).

Table 4.6 *Comparing adjusted ratios*

Year	Adjusted Sales £	Adjusted Sales Growth £	Adjusted Growth Ratios %
1	129,000	–	–
2	146,250	16,442	12.7
3	145,000	−1,250	−0.9

The real situation is nothing like as rosy as we first thought. The sales growth in year 2 is barely a third of the original estimate. In year 3, High Note did not grow at all – in fact it contracted slightly.

The principle of this technique can be applied to any financial ratio. The appropriate index will, to some extent, depend on the nature of the business in question. Information on current British indices is published regularly by the Statistics Office.

Apples and pears

There are particular problems in trying to compare one business's ratios with another. You would not expect a Mini to be able to cover a mile as quickly as a Jaguar. A small new business can achieve quite startling sales growth ratios in the early months and years. Expanding from £10,000 sales in the first six months to £50,000 in the second would not be unusual. To expect a mature business to achieve the same growth would be unrealistic. For ICI to grow from sales of £5 billion to £25 billion would imply wiping out every chemical company in the world. So some care must be taken to make sure that like is being compared with like, and allowances made for differing circumstances in the business being compared (or if the same business, the trading/economic environment of the years being compared).

It is also important to check that one business's idea of an account category, say current assets, is the same as the one you want to compare it with. The concepts and principles used to prepare accounts leave some scope for differences.

Seasonal factors

Many of the ratios that we have looked at make use of information in the Balance Sheet. Balance Sheets are prepared at one moment in time, and reflect the position at that moment – they may not represent the average situation. For example, seasonal factors can cause a business's sales to be particularly high once or twice a year. A Balance Sheet prepared just before one of these seasonal upturns might show very high stocks, bought in specially to meet this demand. Conversely, a look at the Balance just after the upturn might show very high cash and low stocks. If either of those stock figures were to be treated as an average it would give a false picture.

Ratios in forecasting

Ratios have another valuable use – they can be an aid to making future financial projections. For example, if you believe it prudent to hold the equivalent of a month's sales in stock, once you have made the sales forecast for future years, the projections for stock in the balance sheet follow automatically.

ASSIGNMENT 9
The financial audit

Carry out the financial audit, using ratios.

The tables that follow are to allow you to summarise the financial elements of the position audit, identify trends, throw up differences between your firm and your competitors (or the industry norm if you know it). You should also start to make some notes on the likely action required, or targets to set, for later in the strategic planning process.

For example, you may need some specific goals for the business plan – such as to improve your average collection period by X per cent.

You may find it more manageable if you first do the ratios on your firm and look at historic changes, and then do ratios for your competitors. Then compare and contrast your performance with that of competitors.

Financial audit: Summary of ratios

	2 Years Ago	Last Year	% Change	This Year	% Change	Main comp-etitors	% Difference from our performance	Action required[*]
1. *Percentage Sales Growth*								
2. *Percentage Profit Growth*								
3. *Headcount Growth*								
4. $\dfrac{Sales}{Number\ of\ Employees}$								
5. $\dfrac{Profit}{Number\ of\ Employees}$								
6. *Value added per employee (Profit + Wages/Salaries ÷ Number of Employees)*								
7. *ROCE* $\dfrac{Profit\ Before\ Interest\ \&\ Tax}{Capital\ Employed}$								
8. *ROSC* $\dfrac{Profit\ After\ Tax}{Share\ Capital\ \&\ Reserves}$								

[*]You don't have to wait to the bitter end to take steps to improve performance. So if, for example you see your sales per employee is way out of line with the norm in your industry, jot down any ideas for improvement as you go along.

	2 Years Ago	Last Year	% Change	This Year	% Change	Main competitors	% Difference from our performance	Action required*
9. Gearing: $\dfrac{\text{Share Capital \& Reserves}}{\text{All Long-term Capital}}$								
10. $\dfrac{\text{Operating Profit}}{\text{Loan Interest}}$								
11. $\dfrac{\text{Gross Profit}}{\text{Sales}}$								
12. $\dfrac{\text{Operating Profit}}{\text{Sales}}$								
13. $\dfrac{\text{Net Profit}}{\text{Sales}}$								
14. Current Ratio: $\dfrac{\text{Current Assets}}{\text{Current Liabilities}}$								
15. Quick Ratio: $\dfrac{\text{Debtors \& Cash}}{\text{Current Liabilities}}$								
16. Average Collection Period: $\dfrac{\text{Debtors} \times 365}{\text{Sales}}$								

	2 Years Ago	Last Year	% Change	This Year	% Change	Main comp-etitors	% Difference from our performance	Action required*
17. $\dfrac{Creditors}{Purchases} \times 365$								
18. $\dfrac{Stock}{Cost\ of\ Sales} \times 365$								
19. $\dfrac{Sales}{Working\ Capital}$								
20. $\dfrac{Sales}{Fixed\ Assets}$								
Other key ratios								
21.								
22.								
23.								
24.								

5

How to Diagnose your Organisation

In answering the question 'Where are we now?' any growing business will want to look not only at its market position and its financial status but also at the viability of its *organisation*.

The purpose of this exercise, which is spelt out in the checklists of Assignment 10, is to help you take a fresh look at your organisation in the light of:

- Organisation 'fit' with your changing business environment (identified in Assignment 2)
- Your organisational phase of growth (Greiner)
- Benchmarking against the best practice.

Assignment 10 also asks you to picture your organisation by suspending for a minute your logical left-brain thought processes and engaging the creative right-brain in literally drawing a picture of how you perceive your organisation as it is now. A picture is worth a thousand words and like all the assignments in this workbook, this exercise can also provide a fun way of involving your team in the thinking which will eventually come together in your business plan. So far a rich cache of organisation pictures has produced: islands without bridges, castaways in a stormy sea of shark competitors, ships with crew asleep and drunk downstairs, even a cosy, comfy country cottage. The messages can be strong!

Organisation 'fit' with the environment

In trying to diagnose whether you've got the right organisation in place there are unfortunately no clear rules about numbers of people, or management style or reporting relationships. It all depends on the business environment in which you operate. For example, if you're selling marketing services to the pharmaceutical industry and you rely on a professional, flexible salesforce, the last thing you want is a heavy, central organisation, which stops the local salesperson taking initiative with the customer. Then again, if you're selling battleships perhaps you do!

In fact there is no such thing as right organisation, there is only one which is appropriate to what you're trying to do with your business. Even then, as Greiner tells us, it won't stay right for long. The concept of fit says that your organisation is right if it fits the business environment in which you are operating and helps you achieve your strategy. Indeed without an effective organisation, you won't have a strategy!

ENVIRONMENT

STRATEGY

ORGANISATION

Here are some typical examples of fit and misfit of organisations with their changing environments:

- When ICL was selling large 'boxes' and the customer wanted user-friendly desk top systems there was an almost fatal misfit between strategy and environment.
- When ICL moved its strategy to selling solutions it found that the financial processes necessary for monitoring the sale of a few large boxes were no longer adequate for measuring many small sales – there was an organisation misfit to do with internal systems.
- When Robb Wilmot, MD of ICL in 1983, tried to move an organisation of 20,000 people towards his strategy for survival, he found an immensely frustrating misfit of resistance from his management team who hoped change would go away.
- When George Davies was removed from the Board of Next there was a well publicised management style misfit.
- When Sears Holdings tried to diversify into new markets it encountered a major structure misfit as its highly centralised 'supertanker' shape failed to allow a fast response to customers.

The sheer pace of environmental change in the 1990s is so fast that many businesses are being boiled alive. As Professor Charles Handy tells us, 'if you put a frog in a pan of cold water and gently bring it to the boil, it will sit there until it is boiled alive. The frog (and many organisations!) can't sense that the temperature of the water is changing.'

Sock Shop

Sophie Mirman, explaining the demise of Sock Shop, says:

> *'Of course we made mistakes. The biggest was our expansion into America. But we had an awful lot of bad luck at home: two hot summers, which depressed hosiery sales, combined with a series of train and tube strikes, which kept so many of our shops closed one day each week over several months. And on top of that, interest rates doubled to 15 per cent. Any one of these factors we could have coped with but not all of them together. And there was absolutely nothing we could do about any of them. I felt like a rabbit caught in headlights.'*

Like nostalgia, business ain't what it used to be. Every era has fads – in the 1960s it was mergers and acquisitions, in the 1970s diversification, and in the 1980s back to mergers and acquisitions. During the past few years, however, as a recent *Economist* article suggests, 'several business trends have started to emerge which look decidedly less faddish; some of them appear to be transforming the management map for good'.

The status quo will no longer be the best way forward. The economics of the market place are changing drastically. As markets change, so must managers. The odds are that tomorrow's bosses will have to be capable of managing highly decentralised businesses in a global market place. There are ever swifter changes in product technology, life cycles are shrinking, and information technology is transforming the way we do business.

To keep pace, western businesses are having to toss their old assumptions aside. Change is, after all, only another word for growth, but growth will no longer be achieved by doing 'more of the same'. These days competitors are as likely to be partners as they are rivals. Suppliers are being brought in to help design products. Every aspect of organisation – people, systems and structure – is changing. Companies are sweeping away sprawling headquarters and drastically cutting layers of management. The skyscraper shape of business is going for good. As it grows flatter the company of the future may well resemble the shamrock organisation envisaged by Charles Handy, its three leaves representing a central band of core workers, a secondary band of sub-contractors and a loose network of part-time and temporary workers. Vertical career paths are disappearing – managers will have to take the horizontal fast track. Firms will become greener and more interested in their business philosophy and ethics. A cross-disciplinary approach will be the key to business success in the future.

Your organisational phase of growth

Having identified in Assignment 2 the major external pressures on your business, you are in a good position to start diagnosing whether you have the right organisation for your present stage of growth. For example, one entrepreneurial company, successfully providing marketing services, when carrying out an environmental scan discovered just how volatile the market-place had become. They found that a government White Paper could cause them to lose the lot, that some customers were dissatisfied with the service, and that new competition was a much bigger threat than had been previously realised: 'They're coming after us'. The conclusion was that, 'We have been too inward looking and egocentric', and that the organisation had to become much more flexible and responsive, and much less complacent.

The Greiner model of the five phases of growth through which all businesses move is a very good basis for diagnosing where you are in the development cycle, and therefore what kind of organisation problems you can expect to meet. Most businesses will probably lie somewhere between the crisis of leadership and the fourth stage of growth. Each growth phase brings its own organisation challenge: Phase 2 the challenge of putting in necessary systems and procedures while finding, motivating and keeping key staff; Phase 3 the challenge of letting go, replacing a top down management style with delegation and team building; Phase 4, addressing an increasingly fragmented organisation through co-ordination, control and corporate culture.

Innovex

In 1992, as Barrie Haigh surveyed the management team he had built up at Innovex, he had good reason to congratulate himself. In 10 years he had built up the business to a £22 million turnover employing 600 people and specialising in providing medical representation and marketing services to blue chip pharmaceutical companies. Let's see how he got there.

Innovex started as a typical Phase 1 owner/founder organisation. The founder was a first-rate and enormously energetic entrepreneur whose physical and mental energies were absorbed with the customers. 'Success was down to a very few people, primarily the chairman.' Communication among employees was frequent and informal and usually around the billiard table. Long hours of work were rewarded by an involved, happy atmosphere. The approach to customers was action orientated and the feedback instant. There was a 'passionate attempt to avoid politics' and a disdain of internal management.

All this wonderful creative, exciting buzz was essential for the company to get off the ground. But therein lies the problem. As the company grew in size and age, more efficiency was needed in managing money and resources, new employees didn't always know what was going on, more people made informal communication more difficult to achieve. The company found itself burdened by unwanted management responsibilities which it reluctantly saw as necessary but didn't regard as fun. Instead of everyone being happy hunters the business needed the farmers of a Phase 2 organisation. Here is how people described their organisation as they approached the crisis of leadership:

> *'We're self-centred rather than customer centred.'*
> *'We're happy amateurs.'*
> *'We're not businessmen, totally top line sales driven.'*
> *'We're unplanned and confused.'*
> *'It's organised chaos, you sink or swim.'*
> *'We let ourselves down on detail.'*

In this case, the chairman weathered the crisis of leadership, survived the first phase and went on to install the functional organisation, accounting systems, and direction needed for Phase 2 growth. The business moved out of its quaint offices into a streamlined and prestigious building, the organisation grew enormously in number of employees and turnover, the customer reputation sparkled. The problems were over . . . or were they? Just as every young business is permanently hungry for money, so it seems a fact of life that every past success leads to future problems. The list of once-lionised business heroes who haven't been able to move on from their past successes is endless.

So our company's success in Phase 2 growth creates the seeds which make a second revolution and crisis inevitable. The chairman, as he saw his organisation become more diverse and complex, had less inclination to manage it all himself. After all, his skills were as the entrepreneurial/outward face of his organisation. He began to see the organisation as cumbersome and centralised, with the customers no longer understanding who did what. Even worse, because of the personal power and charisma of the chairman, the lower level managers were not accustomed to making decisions for themselves. Yet at the same time they were demanding more responsibility: 'If we are managers, then let us alone.' The crisis of autonomy had arrived.

Many, many companies founder during this stage. There is a desperate paradox. The man at the top must let go; he must move from meddler to strategist. Not only may this change in role make him personally feel extremely uncomfortable as he relinquishes power, but he frequently finds that there is no one to relinquish power to! There is a vacuum; lower levels of management want power but their history hasn't taught them how to use it. The top man must withdraw, delegate and build a management team but at the same time, as the owner/founder of the business, he may need to continue to reinforce the special vision and company culture which he, largely alone, has painfully built over the years.

> *Barrie Haigh took himself off on a Cranfield programme, restructured the company into profit centres with much greater responsibility, formalised communication and instituted both an innovative reward package and a programme of management development to start building the strength of his management team. The company is now sailing the smoother waters of Phase 3, growth through delegation. It is extraordinarily successful in the market-place and has created a marvellous environment – very much a people organisation, vibrant and exciting, a place where outsiders all want a job.*

> *However, the entire management team would now be the first to say that the only certainty in their organisation is that whatever is right for them now will be wrong in the future. They are already anticipating the next challenge of growth and the next set of rapids, or crisis which will spell both threat and opportunity to their business.*

Benchmarking against best practice

In putting your stethoscope to the heart of the business in order to diagnose organisational health, we have so far suggested two approaches:

- To assess how far your organisation 'fits' the external pressures from your business environment.
- To understand your own history and at what stage of development your business is (measured against Greiner's five phases of growth).

There is a third approach which is to look around for best practice in the corporate world, against which to benchmark your organisation. This, of course, is the approach sold in books such as *In Search of Excellence* which provides case studies and a blueprint of what successful companies are doing. In combination with our earlier approaches, this can give you some clues, or at least reinforce that you're heading in the right direction!

There are probably as many blueprints as there are management bestsellers. You're free to pick out your own from any airport book stall! However, there do seem to be common themes emerging which offer some clues about the shape of things to come. We have found the following seven points to be useful and practical in helping to grow businesses into effective organisations:

Characteristics of effective organisations
Personal list for the masters of change

1. Tune in to your company's environment
2. Create and communicate a clear vision
3. Build a strong culture/pride in the organisation
4. Empower people: make everyone a hero
5. Establish flexible organisation structures
6. Build coalitions and heighten teamwork
7. Create reward systems that share credit and recognition

We include a brief word on each below.

1. Tune into your company's environment. This theme summarises the need to stay in touch with your customers, competitors and other external pressures for change and to try to design your organisation around changing business requirements.

Sometimes when you carry out a quick radar scan of your external environment you will find that the terrifying blip on the screen turns out to be a seagull rather than a supertanker. But if it's the other way round, it's perhaps better anticipated!

2. Create and communicate a clear vision. It is increasingly being said that the one job of the leader is to inspire others with his own sense of a vision for the future.

'I have a dream' said Martin Luther King. It is visions which put the passion and the power into dry old mission statements. This vision creates momentum, it pulls people through the uncomfortable process of change by offering the picture of a better world. It gives people something to identify with, a meaning and purpose – just as the vision of a holiday, of marriage, or of retirement helps us to get through the daily routine! Many leaders have their own personal vision of their business, but it tends to stay in their heads as a kind of private day-dream in the bath or while pruning the roses. Often the manager assumes that this vision will transmit itself into the skulls of his or her employees by some miraculous paranormal process. Nothing could be further from the truth! To have any value to the organisation, the vision must be owned and lived by *everyone in the organisation*, and for this to happen it has to be constantly stated, restated and reinforced. There is an archetypal story of the liftman taking the chairman to his penthouse executive suite and chatting in the meantime about the business. The chairman mentions a possible diversification; the liftman immediately presses the emergency button and stops the lift – 'Mr Chairman,' he said, 'this cannot happen: it is inconsistent with our vision of the business we're in.' Just so! The vision should guide people's behaviour at all times. Don't keep either your problems or your dreams to yourself. For example:

- Anita Roddick's Body Shop has a clearly articulated vision and set of values which every employee buys into. The recruitment process sells this vision, if you're not green you don't join.
- Steve Jobs had a clear vision for Apple and gained enormous commitment from employees in working towards it. He's now doing the same at Next.

3. Build a strong culture. Effective organisations develop shared values which reinforce their vision. For example, the shared values of an entrepreneurial Phase 1 organisation create an emphasis on fun, informality and customer responsiveness. It is shared values (or culture) which motivate managers to stay with a Phase 2 organisation as it puts on the strait-jacket of structure and systems. It is a strong culture which grows the commitment of Phase 3's growth through delegation, and it is a strong culture which provides the control and co-ordination of Phase 4. These values sum up 'the way we do things around here' and define the unique personality, almost the finger print, of the organisation. The culture is the genetic code which lets people know what is acceptable behaviour in terms of working practice, socialising, drinking habits and dress. Successful companies, big and small, tend to have strong cultures. If the product brand represents the external image, then culture represents the internal image or branding which turns promotional puff into solid reality:

> *Culture not product. Increasingly, companies are having to market their culture or brand image, not simply their products, in order to beat their competitors. BMW and Sony sell an image called 'quality'; Britain's Body Shop sells 'environmental friendliness'. But this will convince consumers only if the appropriate culture thrives throughout the company. Japanese managers have this driven home to them throughout their careers; western business schools still find the idea hard to teach. But teach it they must.*
>
> The Economist, 2 *March 1991*

- Jim Treybig, who founded Tandem Computers in 1974, has built a $1.6 billion turnover business with 10,000 employees. His company is famous for his 'beer busts', for an informal style, for a president who attends every induction programme, and for a selection process which is a gruelling inquisition, even if the post is for a stock clerk! The message is clear – you have to be good to work at Tandem.

- Johnson & Johnson have long held a credo which passed the ultimate test, it guided their behaviour through the potentially devastating cyanide pollution of their product Tylenol.
- McDonalds QSCV (Quality, Service, Convenience, Value).
- Toshiba have a self-selection video which spells out the commitment which gives the flavour of the factory – if you don't like it, 'you might want to think twice'.
- ICL have had since 1983 the 'ICL Way', a statement of seven core beliefs.

4. Empower people: make everyone a hero. The days of the leader as hero are gone. Too many case studies of dinosaur organisations in the UK show that needing change doesn't make it happen, nor, on its own, does a new CEO at the top of the organisation. You need to mobilise the support of your people behind the change. You need to help people focus their energies on the new ways. Growing businesses we see around are doing just this. They are doing it by:

- Tapping their own reserves of creativity and energy through brainstorming sessions to find better ways of doing things.
- Pushing responsibility down as low as possible.
- Creating open communication and involvement through weekly happy hours, peanut parties or informal lunches.
- Involving everyone in the vision and the future of the business.

5. Establish flexible organisation structures. The organisation structure of the past was like a New York skyscraper: very tall, lots of levels of hierarchy, a great distance between boss and subordinates, vertical rather than horizontal communication. The shape for the future is different, even the metaphors have changed! People are talking of organisations being like doughnuts or amoebas or shamrocks – the search is on for new and creative organisation shapes. Around entrepreneurial business organisations we see the following clear trends:

- Smaller, flatter shapes. Doing away with levels of management so that there is as little hierarchy as possible between chairman and newest recruit.
- Emphasis on team-working within small business units (aligned to customer needs) but also teamworking across the organisation

with other parts of the business which are both customers and suppliers.

- Less emphasis on the old span of control rule as the job of the manager becomes more that of orchestrating the team rather than directing and controlling it. Less difference between the boss and subordinates; both very much part of the team.
- Less concern with keeping everything inside the organisation and a more flexible boundary with the outside world, which includes sub-contracting the transport fleet, outworking, collaboration with competitors, joint supplier agreements.
- More temporary forms of structure which run parallel to the formal organisation, ie multi-functional/cross boundary project teams, quality circles, business units which are spun off.
- Flexible structures where there may be more than one parameter for dividing up activities and more than one boss, ie matrix type alignments along several dimensions at the same time – by country, UK; by vertical line of business, retail or manufacturing; and sometimes by function as well, marketing and finance.

6.   Build coalitions and heighten teamwork. The local business team is *the* unit, but increasingly businesses are making attempts to create a total corporate identity, for example sending production people out to meet customers, rotating job roles, holding regular problem-solving meetings across departments, meeting up regularly with customers and suppliers.

7.   Create reward systems that share credit and recognition. What gets measured gets produced. What gets rewarded gets produced again. As a small company moves through Greiner's phases of growth it will constantly need to change both what is rewarded and how rewards are made. For example in Phase 1, growth, the need is for customers, the rewards are likely to be immediate, sales related and perhaps commission based. In Phase 2, growth through direction, control-based systems are introduced and managers measured against their control of costs. In Phase 3, the move towards profit centre responsibility necessitates rewarding not sales, not cost control, but profit performance and the rewards may more sensibly be linked to some measure of corporate profit sharing. There is room for continuous ingenuity in seeking out different rewards: individual or group incentives, free tickets and gift certificates, profit sharing, promotion, excellence awards, new work assignments.

The rule is expect it (and reward it!) or forget it.

ASSIGNMENT 10

Diagnostic checklists

1. Draw a picture of how you see your organisation now (warts and all). Your picture should not be an organisation chart and should not include words. (What picture would your management team draw and is *their* perception in line with yours?)

2. Complete the Organisation Development Diagnostic below to locate where your business appears to be in relation to the Greiner growth phases. What are the organisation issues you are likely to be facing?

3. Benchmark your organisation against best practice (p 113) (the seven characteristics of effective organisation).

Organisational development diagnostic
(adapted from John Leppard, 1987)

Instructions for completion
1. The organisation development diagnostic consists of 60 descriptive statements. Your task is to work through this list and to identify those statements you believe to be accurate in describing your company.
2. Each time you come to an apt description you should tick it on the questionnaire. When you have looked through all 60 statements, please transfer the ticks to the score sheet, recording your choice on the score sheet by putting a tick in the box carrying the same number.
3. Add up your ticks and total them at the bottom. Around which vertical columns do your scores group? This would appear to be your diagnosis of your company's present stage of development. What are the inherent challenges you face?

Organisational development diagnostic questionnaire

1. ☐ The organisational structure is very informal.
2. ☐ Top management are finding themselves bombarded with many unwanted management responsibilities.
3. ☐ Management focus mainly on the efficiency of operations.
4. ☐ Staff lower down in the organisation possess more knowledge about, for example, markets, products, trends etc than top management.
5. ☐ The main management focus is to expand markets.
6. ☐ Top management feel they are losing control of the business.
7. ☐ The main management focus is co-ordination and consolidation.
8. ☐ There is a lack of confidence between line managers and specialist staff/head office and the field.
9. ☐ The main focus of management is on problem solving and innovation.
10. ☐ There is an over-emphasis on teamwork.
11. ☐ The top management style is very individualistic and entrepreneurial.
12. ☐ Top management takes too long in responding to queries and requests.
13. ☐ The organisational structure is centralised and functional, ie based on specialisms.
14. ☐ There is not enough freedom to act delegated to those capable of doing so.
15. ☐ The organisational structure is decentralised and individual divisions or departments have a high level of autonomy.
16. ☐ Many people at lower levels have too much freedom to run their own show.
17. ☐ Decentralised units have been merged into product groups.
18. ☐ Line managers resent heavy staff direction.
19. ☐ The organisational structure is a matrix of task or project teams.
20. ☐ There is a dependency on group-think to the extent that some managers are losing the confidence to make individual decisions.
21. ☐ The main control system is whether or not the sales targets are met.
22. ☐ Top management does not provide enough direction.
23. ☐ Top management style tends to be directive.
24. ☐ Management tends to be over-directive and could easily delegate more.
25. ☐ The top management style is delegative.
26. ☐ The organisation has probably become too decentralised, breeding parochial attitudes.

27. ☐ The top management style is to be a watchdog.
28. ☐ We seem to have lost the ability to respond to new situations or solve problems quickly.
29. ☐ The top management style is highly consultative, meeting together frequently on problem issues.
30. ☐ We are directing too much energy into the functions of our internal teams and tending to overlook what is happening in the outside world.
31. ☐ Long hours are rewarded by modest salaries but with the promise of ownership benefits in the future.
32. ☐ Top management isn't as visible as it ought to be.
33. ☐ The main control systems seem to be concerned with standards and costs.
34. ☐ Flexibility suffers because those who could take decisions have to wait for management to agree.
35. ☐ The main control seems to be in the form of profit centre reporting.
36. ☐ Power seems to have shifted away from top management.
37. ☐ Each product group is an investment centre with extensive planning controls.
38. ☐ Everyone is criticising the bureaucratic paper system that has evolved.
39. ☐ The main control system is for work groups to evaluate their own performance through real-time information systems integrated into daily work.
40. ☐ There is almost too much personal feedback about behaviour at meetings etc.
41. ☐ The management focus is mainly on making and selling.
42. ☐ Top management are very harassed, conflicts between them are growing.
43. ☐ The main way managers are rewarded is by salary and merit increases.
44. ☐ People are demotivated (even leaving) because they do not have enough personal autonomy in their jobs.
45. ☐ The way managers are rewarded is by individual bonuses.
46. ☐ More co-ordination of operations is needed if things are to improve.
47. ☐ The way managers are rewarded is through profit sharing and stock options.
48. ☐ Fun and excitement seem to be lacking in the company.
49. ☐ Rewards are geared more to team performance than to individual achievement.

50. ☐ The constant high expectation for creativity in the organisation is stressful.
51. ☐ Top management are close to customers and have a good understanding of what the market requires.
52. ☐ Top managers do not seem able to introduce the new business techniques which are necessary.
53. ☐ To get on in this company, lower managers do not question decisions made by their seniors.
54. ☐ Staff have their performance appraisals from bosses who have little understanding about the subordinate's job and work problems.
55. ☐ People are told what is expected of them and then allowed to get on with their jobs as they see fit. It's management by exception.
56. ☐ Senior managers are continually checking up to make sure that jobs are completed – they tend to overdo this.
57. ☐ There are many head office personnel who initiate company work programmes to review and control line managers.
58. ☐ Too many people are working to the book.
59. ☐ Interpersonal conflicts are brought into the open and, on the whole, managed in a non-destructive way.
60. ☐ Trying to be always spontaneous and open in relationships at work is proving stressful.

Organisational Phases of Growth
The five phases of growth (after Greiner)

Phase 1 Growth through creativity	1 Crisis of leadership	Phase 2 Growth through direction	2 Crisis of autonomy	Phase 3 Growth through delegation	3 Crisis of control	Phase 4 Growth through coordination	4 Crisis of red tape	Phase 5 Growth through collaboration	5 Crisis of ?
1	2	3	4	5	6	7	8	9	10
11	12	13	14	15	16	17	18	19	20
21	22	23	24	25	26	27	28	29	30
31	32	33	34	35	36	37	38	39	40
41	42	43	44	45	46	47	48	49	50
51	52	53	54	55	56	57	58	59	60

Organisational development diagnostic: score sheet

How to Diagnose your Organisation

Benchmark against best practice

	Characteristics of effective organisations	Tick		
		Needs attention	OK	Good
1.	*Tune in to company's environment* How outward looking is your business in monitoring and understanding changing trends of customers, competitors, marketplace, technology, legislation?			
2.	*Create and communicate a clear vision* Do you have a vision of the kind of business you are trying to create? Does everyone in the organisation know about and feel committed to your company philosophy?			
3.	*Build a strong culture/pride* What's your internal brand image? What values is the business built around and how much do all employees feel a sense of pride in, and identification with, the organisation?			
4.	*Empower people* How far do your people feel a sense of ownership of problems? Do they take necessary action without being told to?			
5.	*Establish flexible organisation structures* How far beyond the formal organisation chart do you go? For example, in setting up project teams, quality circles, informal get-togethers?			
6.	*Build teamwork* To what extent do people identify with their immediate team rather than the total business?			
7.	*Appropriate reward systems* Are you measuring the really important performance criteria and rewarding people for the right behaviour?			

6

Assessing People, Structure and Systems

Following earlier work in picturing and benchmarking your organisation we can now examine the heart of the organisation in more depth: its people, its structure and its systems. This exercise aims at enabling you, in Assignments 11 and 12, to carry out a comprehensive analysis of your current organisation capability as a way of assessing whether you have the resources in place to achieve your plans for business growth.

The model we will use for analysis purposes is given in Figure 6.1 and you will find a worked example, along with checklists of questions (Figure 6.9), at the end of this chapter.

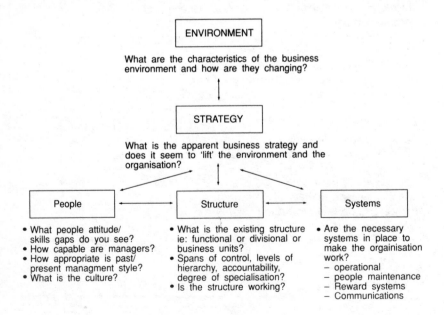

Figure 6.1 *Organising for change*

So far we have been looking outward at the fit between the total organisation and the business environment in which you are trying to survive (see Figure 6.2).

Figure 6.2 *The fit between organisation and environment*

It's now time to look inside the polo mint at the structure, systems and people of your organisation and how they fit not only with the external challenges but also one with another.

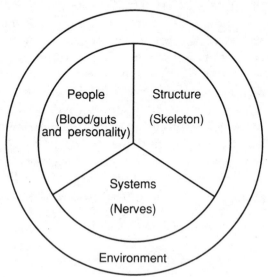

Figure 6.3 *People, systems and structure fit*

In its construction a business organisation is similar to an individual human being. Just like us, the organisation has a skeleton, a nervous system and some blood and guts. The skeleton of the organisation is its structure or shape – the thing which gives it form and indicates its potential for growth. Just as the starfish doesn't have the skeleton to grow into an elephant, so a vertical skyscraper-type business cannot behave like a small informal network business.

The nervous system of your business is represented by its processes and infrastructure, from the sales invoicing system to how people communicate with one another, from budgeting to appraisal. Systems form the linkages, the connections between one bit of the business and another.

The blood and guts, the messy bits of your business, are provided, as you suspected, by the people in it, who as individuals and as teams, contribute to the unique personality of your business entity. If, for example, you are diversifying into new market niches you may choose a business centre structure and profit sharing type systems. However, you will be in trouble if your people come from one function only, (ie sales or finance) and are incapable of knowing how to operate as general managers.

Our model suggests that as the environment changes so the organisation, in one bound, shifts to accommodate the new reality. Unfortunately, this is never the case. Even with enormous environmental changes (like the impact of Japanese competition on the Swiss watch industry) it can take a very long time before the organisation is prepared to recognise the unpleasant writing on the wall. Even when it does, different bits of the organisation will respond at different speeds – and therefore get out of sync. For example, your structure is almost always a reflection of what you needed in the past rather than now. Even when you change the structure you will find you also need to revamp the appraisal system, your method of tracking performance, or your management training. Running your own business is very like the feat of the circus performer trying to keep a great many plates spinning on sticks at the same time – one plate is always in a state of terminal wobble and in need of an urgent tweak!

We'll now examine what tweaking you may need to do to keep your people, systems and structure plates spinning smoothly and safely.

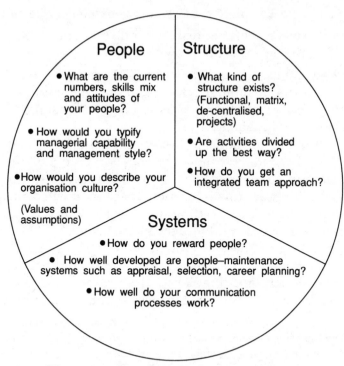

Figure 6.4 *Assessing organisation capability*

Assessing people capability

It is useful to look at people capability under three headings for:

- Skills and attitudes
- Management capability and style
- Culture.

Skills and attitudes

In his book *Teaching the Elephant to Dance*, Jim Belasco says: 'Regardless of the intentions expressed in the strategic plan, where you put your key people and money is the direction in which your organisation is going to move.' This means getting the right number of people with the right skills and attitudes in the right jobs. It means investing your resources in your new tomorrow. Even if you have the resources in place now, Greiner tells us that you won't for very long! Of course, when you do identify a misfit, for example the need for marketing skills, there will always be a time lag in acquiring those skills. Whether you train, recruit from outside or even make redundant, it all takes time and must be planned for.

117

Skills mix is the first place to start. Ask yourself the question,

Q.   'Will existing skills be adequate or do these need to be built up before the business can grow?'

There are several ways you can slice the skills cake: one is to look at it function by function, another is to look at the different levels of your organisation and yet another is to assess how many square pegs you feel you have in round holes.

If you look at the functional mix of skills it is inevitable that you will find shortages as the business grows. For example, the typical business start up in Greiner's Phase 1 is rich in sales skills. However, as it moves into Phase 2, growth through direction, it will demand skills to do with accounting and setting up basic systems – very different from the entrepreneurial profile of the Phase 1 employee! Again, as the business moves into Phase 3, growth through delegation, it is quite probable that there will be a need for some kind of personnel function, maybe professional marketing skills and, above all, management skills needed to run small parts of the business as autonomous units.

> *Twelve years ago, Bruce Elliot set up Elliot Brothers Audio Sounds Ltd. They are in a very interesting business sector, specialist engineers selling services to install radio stations and recording studios. The turnover is now £1.5m and Bruce employs 25 people. Bruce is well aware of the skills mix issues of moving from Phase 1 through Phase 2. In Phase 1 tremendous commitment of time and energy was needed from all staff in setting up prestigious recording facilities for the pop star clients. Bruce, not unnaturally, tended to recruit in his own image. As he sat in his shorts on a hot summer day puffing unashamedly on a cigar, he described his recruitment profile as being 'male, ex public school and rugby playing'. However, as he endeavours to set up the initial systems for Phase 2, growing through direction, Bruce has found that when it comes to setting up a new filing system, he and most of his recruits have already left for the pub!*

It's the same story for Marks and Spencer; their very success in recruiting particular skills in the past became an albatross around the neck of development. M & S have recognised this and are actively seeking to recruit rebels, people who won't fit in with their previous stereotypes. Similarly when Citibank in the States moved for market share in an environment of very passive financial institutions, it sought to employ a very different kind of animal as CEO – a guitar playing PhD!

It's also worth taking a slice diagonally through your organisation in order to identify any skills vacuums or even blockages.

> *Agrafax, a successful PR agency established for 14 years with 38 employees and a turnover of around £1.5m diagnosed that it was in danger of 'major cardiac*

arrest' caused by blockages in the flow of people into and through the organisation. Chairman Mike Evans explains:

'The people within are a high calibre, talented bunch but there are signs of stress, of blood pressure rising. Recruitment difficulties (in Shropshire) are restricting the flow of new blood into the organisation and the young blood, who are all very highly motivated, are putting pressure on for more autonomy, less restriction from above, more say in strategy, more initiative and greater reward.'

Traditionally, in large hierarchic organisations, it has been the supervisor/middle manager levels who have been blockages, like lumps of cotton wool draining away the life blood of the organisation. In a younger business it may be that the blockages are higher up. It's worth asking yourself whether it's even possible that you are the blockage and should remove yourself, or whether the Board of Directors you set up eight years ago now has the right characteristics and calibre for future growth. As the business grows, relationships inevitably change, sometimes painfully. As one MD explains:

'I'm identifying some casualties of growth; for example, when I set up the business George was my only co-director and we enjoyed a very immediate and special relationship. Now I have a board of directors and a young management team, George is off to one side. He doesn't like it and I'm not sure he can cope.'

Finally, as above, it may be better to face up to the square pegs in the round holes which are, after all, an inevitable consequence of growth. Very often people left in such positions – marooned at high tide – are uncomfortable and quite well aware that they are not performing. Facing the problem may be a relief to both parties.

As well as assessing skills mix, you will find it valuable to take a barometer to the attitudes and morale of your employees. Asking yourself the following questions may help pin-point whether you have a problem:

Q. 'What is my employee turnover rate? How does it compare with my competitors/last year?'

Q. 'Are levels of sickness/absenteeism high or low?'

Q. 'Do I know why people are leaving?'

A useful diagnostic tool which will give you a direct answer to the last question is provided by the exit interview. The exit interview means arranging for anyone leaving the company to be questioned by an impartial person who can establish the reasons why. For example, is that person leaving for more money, because of a better opportunity, or because he feels frustrated? Most people in these circumstances are quite happy to talk freely and you can learn a great deal. Attitude surveys, particularly if you carry them out year on year, will benchmark levels of employee morale and highlight problem areas.

Management capability and style

In looking at where your organisation is now, ask yourself the following questions:

Q.   'Do I have sufficient managers to run my business well?'
Q.   'How much growth could they handle without becoming overstretched?'
Q.   'Is there anyone who can run the business in my absence?'
Q.   'If one of my key managers left could someone fill his place?'
Q.   'How do I go about recruiting key managers?'
Q.   'How much can I delegate?'

Example 1

When Mike Evans, Chairman of Agrafax, asked himself these questions he identified significant gaps. Until recently the business had been small enough for most people to be working pretty much as loners. Where they managed, they managed accounts, rather than people. However, as the business grows in size there will be a strong requirement for good man-management. Mike has identified the management animal of the future as someone who is not only a technical specialist and a good communicator, but also a business person and motivator of people. As one of his directors explains, 'We have come through gangling adolescence and reached our twenty-first birthday.'

Example 2

As Barrie Haigh assessed the management team he had built up at Innovex he saw people who were highly intelligent, young, lively, capable, articulate and best of all highly motivated. The level of job satisfaction was remarkable. Yet Barrie saw little reason for complacency. He saw that as Innovex continued its phenomenal rate of growth, lack of depth of management potential could easily become the major constraint on growth. One hundred per cent of managers felt that they had as much as they could cope with at that moment and would be quite happy to stay in their present jobs for a further one to three years. Lack of obvious successors, both to himself and to his MD, had 'become a major issue'. His conclusion was 'we needed more depth of management throughout – and quickly.'

Take a look not only at the management capability of yourself and your team but also at your management style. As the old saying goes, 'It's not what you do but the way that you do it.'

Q.   What typifies the style of yourself and your managers?

One Yorkshireman described his immediate boss as 'having the charisma of a slug'. Or do you lean towards the Attila the Hun style typified by Harold Geneen of ITT in his philosophy, 'Express criticism, withhold praise and instil job insecurity'. The management style of the founder can sometimes be a major block on growth into Phase 2 and beyond. Nor should you believe that you are frozen into one way of behaving. With a conscious effort even management leopards can change their spots.

> *John Hornsey, a young and abrasive technical director, moved south from Yorkshire to attempt the turn around of a threatened engineering factory. He succeeded brilliantly in solving the problems which had built up over the years. In the process, by his own admission, he came close to committing murder; telephone directories and occasionally the telephone itself were uprooted. John was perceived, not unnaturally given his style and the rescue job he was attempting, as a fire-eating monster. No one saw the human behind the gruff exterior. At that time it didn't matter. However, as the factory moved into a period of growth and expansion, John recognised that he and the management team needed to make a conscious effort to change towards a more consensus style of management. People didn't feel empowered and they weren't about to stick their necks out when the blood still ran from the walls. John stood up in front of the total workforce of 300+ and said, 'We are going to have a different management style, we are going to change.' He introduced an attitude survey to take the temperature of the water and committed himself, in advance of the survey, to live by its results. This he and the management team have done, introducing exceptionally effective team briefings, management walk about and other consultative mechanisms. It took time for the work-force to be convinced, but now they think him the best boss they ever had.*

Culture

When you put together all the day-to-day ways in which you and your managers behave you get *culture*. How the receptionist greets a visitor, whether managers are visible to staff, where managers eat and with whom, who goes or doesn't go to the pub, what people wear: all these things and many more provide the signals which people read as 'the way we do things round here'.

Q.   How would you and your managers describe your business culture?

The sum of your culture can provide a nutritious jelly as in the case of one small company which describes itself as 'demonstrably different from our competitors – we have a real enthusiasm, great atmosphere, dynamic and professionally run' or the culture can be treacle, the inertia which will stop your business from changing and growing – because 'We've always done things that way'. Years after the death of Walt Disney, for example, his top management apparently met every new proposal with the comment, 'Walt wouldn't like it'.

One of the frequently used and productive ways of assessing culture is to get a group of your managers to brainstorm a list of words or impressions which sum up the characteristics of your business under the two headings of 'Where have we been?' and 'Where are we now?' The results can be illuminating.

No prizes for guessing the name of this company!

What we used to be like	What we are now
• Penny a week • 'Man from the . . .' • Mum and Dad's insurance company • Old fashioned • Staid • Downmarket	• Changing • Diversifying • Big (biggest) • Becoming up to date • Still too deferential

Or this.

Historic	Now
• Best pilots • Military attitudes • Rigid hierarchy • Introverted – no grasp of the market • Decision by committee	• 'Putting people first' training programme • Customer first • No more military titles CEO no longer called 'CX' • New rewards system • Are top leaders in business or politics?

(Answers at the end of this chapter.)

Or you could assess your culture and try to place it in one of the following boxes (see Figure 6.5). Whichever box you end up in doesn't mean you can't change your culture. For example, the famous Abbey National Building Society has deliberately been trying to move from a 'process' culture towards a 'work hard, play hard' culture, more suited to a highly competitive and decentralised marketplace.

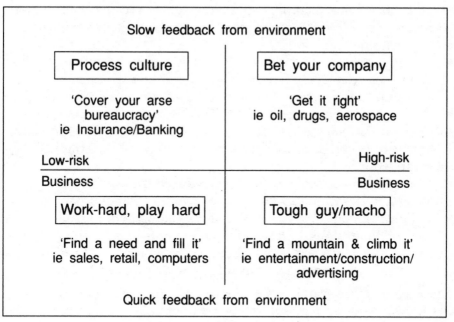

Figure 6.5 *Four pure cultural types*
Source: *Managing Change and Making It Stick*, Roger Plant

Assessing structure capability

Structure is the skeleton of organisation. It tells you how work is divided up, who does what, and how the different roles relate one to another. Structure is more than 'the organisation chart of today'!

Structure is not just what you put on a piece of paper with boxes and lines, it's the reality of who makes the decisions, how you design individual jobs and who brings teams together.

While your business can increase in size without changing its structure, Greiner suggests that the structure of your business will necessarily change at different stages of development. Is your structure a straitjacket for the people who work within it? Does your structure reflect the problems you're trying to solve now or is it an inappropriate inheritance from the past? Managers are constantly restructuring their companies, sometimes for some very good reasons, for example:

- ICL moved to a structure of business centres in order to align itself better with the market place (ie the retail business centre which has very successfully sold POS terminals to national supermarket chains).

- A factory manufacturing components has created a customer service department to signal its new concern with getting closer to the customers.
- An advertising agency decided that it had its resources in the wrong place. Staff functions such as graphics, print purchasing and accounting were put back into the line under business heads.
- A company producing dyestuffs flirted with a matrix structure but decided that such a structure demanded far more flexibility and maturity from its managers than they could demonstrate. They scrapped it.
- Glaxo Pharmaceuticals UK Ltd has reduced the levels of hierarchy in its factories from eight to four, to achieve a flatter organisation.
- A European oil company now operates along two, possibly three matrix dimensions. It has individual country management (UK, France, etc), vertical lines of business which run through all countries (ie commercial transport), and a European Head Office.

Those managers in search of the ideal organisation structure – the Holy Grail – will be disappointed. In answer to the question, 'What is the right structure?' comes the reply, 'It all depends'. It all depends on the business environment you're operating in and how uncertain it is. It all depends on what kind of business you are historically and what kind of people you employ. The only statement we can make with any certainty of being right is that, whatever structure you have in place now, it won't be the one you need in the future. So before we start examining matrix structures, or business centres, or centralised structures, it is worth asking yourself the following questions:

Q. 'What stage of development is my business at now?' (Greiner's Phases, 1, 2, 3, 4, 5)

Q. 'How is my business currently controlled?' (profit centres/budgets/corporate plans)

Q. 'How would I describe my present structure?' (informal, functional, centralised, divisional, matrix).

We will start to address these questions under headings for:

- How to divide things up
- Type of structure – advantages/disadvantages
- How to pull things together again.

How to divide things up

When most people talk about business structure they mean: how are activities divided up into groups and functions, individual roles and responsibilities; how big is the span of control; who is the boss of whom.

In terms of defining individual roles and responsibilities, the discipline of writing a job description is very useful for clarifying the job and helping recruitment.

Q. 'Does everyone have a job description and do they know exactly what is expected of them?'

Historically there has been a tendency to break jobs down into their component parts and specialise. At its worst extreme this has resulted in the archetypal production line job of putting the handles on a car door. The costs of over-specialisation include insularity, inflexibility, lack of team orientation and possibly poor motivation. Job enrichment has been a response to over-specialisation, in its attempt to build back into jobs a craftsman-type pride in having authority, doing a whole job, and working as a team. What is your own assessment – do you need more generalists or specialists, or both?

The evidence is that if you're an innovative organisation coping with rapid change and growth then you will do better to have broader and fewer job classifications which allow greater mobility and flexibility. For example, it's said that part of the inertia factor of General Motors in comparison to Toyota is that GM has 11 times as many job classifications as Toyota.

How do you group activities within your business? Ask yourself:

Q. 'Are the various tasks in my business divided up in the best way?'

The most commonly used dimensions are probably those exemplified by Figure 6.6

The traditional principle is to group together like activities. Unfortunately, these groupings tend not to stay static as new market requirements force new kinds of responses. What therefore results is a rapid, complicated overlay of different types of structure. This can be very messy and can also involve making some difficult decisions, for example:

- Should quality control be centralised or put into specific business units?
- Should the sales function remain centralised?
- How should business units relate one with another?
- What should the role of the Head Office be?
- What exactly are the decision-making line functions and what are the purely advisory staff functions?

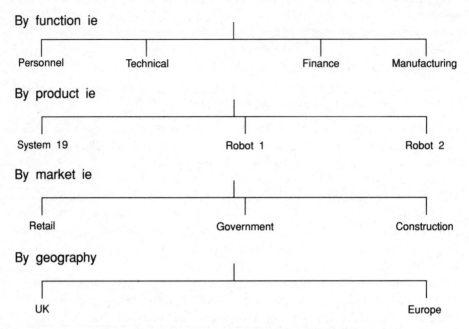

Figure 6.6 *Typically used organisational dimensions*

Finally, there are the old chestnuts – the rules to do with span of control. Urwick has a lot to answer for! In the 1920s he established a rule of thumb which said that no manager should have more than a maximum of five or six direct reports. This reinforces the one man, one boss principle and allows for clarity and strong control by the manager. However, there is a very big price tag. Obviously, the narrower the span of control, the more levels of hierarchy must exist. The more levels of hierarchy there are, the more difficult it is to get sensible communication up and down the organisation: 'Send reinforcements we're going to advance' very soon becomes 'Send 3/4d we're going to a dance'.

It is said that if an organisation has five levels of management and the president communicates a message from the top, then the percentage of information recalled by each level will be as follows:

Level 1   63 per cent
Level 3   40 per cent
Level 5   20 per cent

Small wonder that an engineering firm of 250 employees, with seven levels of hierarchy, reported communication problems!

The advice circulating around most businesses in the 1990s is 'cut out as many levels as you can and go for a flatter organisation'. Or as Metal Box described in a memo of 1985:

'There will be no intervening layers of management between the executive group and the accountable heads of the separate businesses.'

Some businesses are being asked to 'cut out levels of management without increasing the span of control'. This can be something of a conjuring trick.

Certainly there needs to be some limit to the number of direct reports. Obviously, one cannot conscientiously carry out an infinite number of appraisals. However, as the role of manager changes from policeman/controller to conductor/orchestrator, the issue is much less important than managers think.

Types of structure: advantages/disadvantages

Greiner's model is a useful way of reminding ourselves that there is no one right answer. Neither matrix, nor business centre (son of SBUs: strategic business units) is the universal answer – it's a case of horses for courses. Let's rapidly recap Greiner's development cycle. In Phase 1, the business is small, entrepreneurial, outward looking and its structure minimal and informal. During Phase 2, the need for strong direction around formal systems and standards argues for a functional structure where manufacturing is separated from marketing, and marketing from sales, where a hierarchy of titles and specialised positions is built up. However, as the organisation becomes larger and more diverse this centralised structure becomes cumbersome and actually restricts the business from moving quickly into new markets (as was seen in the case of Sears Holdings in the States).

Thus the demand for greater autonomy leads to more delegation and a decentralised organisation structure. In this decentralised structure, greater responsibility is given to business unit managers, profit centres are established and top executives at the Head Office try to restrain themselves to manage by exception.

The new decentralised structure works until there is a crisis of control – when the top executives at HQ start to panic and feel that they are losing control over field operations. Decentralised units are merged into product groups, the Head Office re-staffs itself with specialist advisers, but the daily operating decisions remain decentralised. However, a lack of confidence gradually builds up between line and staff, and between Headquarters and the field – a

Type of structure	Identifying features	Advantages	Disadvantages
Informal	• Business start-up • Few people • Highly committed • Little need for structure	• Fun • Market orientated • Responsive	• Can be disorganised • Attention to detail lacking • Few systems in place
Functional/ centralised	• Functions are separated one from the other • Vertical hierarchy • Clear accountabilities • Strong HQ • Cost centres	• Clarity of role • Specialisation by function • Systematic	• Unresponsive to business/market change • Communications up/down and across suffer • Compartmentalisation and empire building
Decentralised business units	• Focus on business accountability • Unique business mission • Business manager calls the shots • HQ manages by exception	• Motivates managers • Responsive to customers • Flexible	• 'Robber Barons' may go out of control • Problems of integration of different strategies • Problems of HQ control
Product groups	• Daily operating decisions remain decentralised • HQ takes a more active and specialist role in co-ordinating plans and investment strategy	• HQ people are more comfortable • A global response to markets and competition may be more possible • Strategies are integrated	• Cumbersome red tape • 'Us' and 'Them' builds up between field and HQ • Conflicts arise
Matrix	• Dual chain of command: two bosses (everyone had a mother and a father) • 'Business Results' manager on one axis and a 'Resource Manager' on the other hold equal power	• New and exciting; can build in flexibility • Allows organisation to respond to two sectors simultaneously (ie market and technology) • Suited to uncertainty and complexity	• Difficult for managers to get used to • Tendency towards anarchy • Power struggles inevitable • Severe 'groupitis' can occur • Role ambiguity inevitable

Figure 6.7 *No right structures, only appropriate ones*

crisis of red tape is looming, towards which the response is probably a move towards a matrix structure of teams and functions across the organisation.

Clearly it all depends where you're at, and the summary chart (Figure 6.7) is intended only to be used to check that the structure you are about to introduce is not going to create more problems than it will solve. There is plenty of room for creative thinking in devising new and flexible structures which work for *you* (project teams, quality circles, temporary groupings etc).

How to put things together again

The problem with organisations is that they are like Humpty Dumpty; having divided them up into little bits in the interests of efficiency, it is often very difficult to put them together again in such a way that they will actually work. So for differentiation gone mad read this delightful spoof McKinsey report on Royal Festival Hall.

McKinsey report on the Royal Festival Hall concert
The four horn players are seriously under-employed and their number should be reduced. In fact, if their workload was shared out among the other players they could be dispensed with altogether.

The 12 first and second violins were observed to be all playing the same notes. This duplication of effort should not be tolerated and the group could be cut drastically. If the sound becomes too thin it could easily be amplified electronically to whatever level is desired.

The playing of semiquavers was seen to be a considerable, and in our view unwarranted, effort. It could even lead to a demand for payment at piece-work rates. If short notes such as quavers and semiquavers were grouped together, by rationalising the score, into more economic units, a less qualified work force, and even students, could be engaged without the loss of efficiency.

In some passages there is far too much repetition, and we recommend a thorough reprocessing of the material. For example, it serves no useful purpose for the oboe to repeat passages which have already been fully dealt with by the violins. If all such superfluous passages were eliminated, the concert, which at present lasts up to two hours, could be adequately completed in approximately 20 minutes. The unproductive interval could then be dispensed with.

The conductor does not fully grasp today's concepts of management science as applied to orchestral activities, and he is apprehensive that artistic standards might decline. In this unlikely event, there would be compensating financial savings, since audiences, who are only, after all, a major distraction to the smooth functioning of the operation, would decline. Although improbable, this would merely call for parts of the concert hall to be shut off, thereby bringing added cost savings in electricity, personnel, ticket printing, etc, on the one hand, and an essential improvement of acoustics by reduction of the background noises.

At the worst, the whole enterprise could be shut down, with consequent major economies in artist fees . . . and we could then all retire to the bar.

The experts now say that it is integration rather than dividing things up (differentiation) which is the key organisation challenge of the 1990s. Indeed, it is inevitable that as your business gets older and bigger and moves up the Greiner growth curve, every time you reorganise you create another set of boundaries between parts of the organisation: barriers between the first and the second floor/between male and female/between secretaries and managers/between line and staff/between field and head office/between sales and marketing/ between UK and European.

No wonder we all need as much help as we can get in co-ordinating activities. Ask yourself:

Q. 'How is integration achieved at present?'

Traditionally, integration was achieved through the manager at the top of the hierarchy personally co-ordinating and controlling. As the business grows more complex and diverse this becomes more and more difficult. The solutions lie somewhere in the area of team-work.

When you look at your organisation:

Q. 'Do people work individually or in teams?'

There are some clues. Corporate vision which is shared by everyone integrates (as in the consultancy group McKinsey). A strong set of shared values or culture integrates (like McDonalds). Informal net-works help to integrate (Tandem beer-busts – get togethers every-where in the world at 4pm every Friday afternoon). Project teams across disciplines build integration; job rotation and mobility also help to integrate.

The essence of the challenge is to create team identity at both a local level and also at a corporate level. Teamworking is the shape of the future.

When Mike Arama, chairman of a chain of 15 petrol stations was looking for a new accountant, he felt it was not only vital that the candidate should have good technical skills, but that he should fit in with the existing close knit team. The psychometric test Arama chose to use was the Belbin Self-Perception Inventory. It was developed by Dr Meredith Belbin in conjunction with the Henley Management Centre to give individuals a simple means of assessing their best team roles. Dr Belbin's research led him to identify eight dominant types of team behaviour. The full Belbin Interplace System is available from: Belbin Associates, 52 Burleigh Street, Cambridge, telephone 0223 60895.

Assessing systems capability

Systems are the nerves of the organisation, the processes and connections which can switch the organisation on – or stop anything happening at all! Organisation systems are generally considered boring, but the truth is they can be very powerful levers for change. Systems can be sexy!

You will already have looked at many of your day-to-day operating systems to do with sales forecasting, budgeting and invoicing etc. We now ask you to do the same with regard to your people systems. We'll consider people systems under three headings:

- Reward systems
- People maintenance systems
- Communications.

Reward systems

Earlier on we rather crudely stated that 'What gets measured, gets produced. What gets rewarded gets produced again'. Getting your reward systems right will be crucial to moving your business in the direction you want. Unfortunately, it is not a case of plugging in to one sort of reward system (for example, bonuses or share options) and expecting that to work forever. As you go through different phases of growth, the behaviour you will be looking for will change and so must the way you reward it. This is an area requiring constant monitoring and as much imagination as you can apply in devising many types of rewards.

Q.   'How do you currently reward people for achieving goals?'

Let's look at two small businesses who are moving from Greiner's Phase 2, growth through direction, into Phase 3, growth through delegation. What are the issues concerning how they reward behaviour?

Flexiform is moving fast towards creating a general manager culture where the people rewarded will be those who can manage their people and grow their business team. The chairman has put a lot of effort into reward systems and they are now generally regarded as OK. There is a good bonus system in which all share and it works well. But as money is a short-term motivator, many people would like to see little and often rewards. Rewards could be more immediate, perhaps quarterly rather than annually. Managers see value in having the freedom to give small, unexpected rewards to their people. The company is good at the little signs of recognition which mean a lot – the bunch of flowers, blowing a hooter when a new client is signed up and the occasional dinner out. They recently paid out very happily a large cash sum for the best slogan to encapsulate their mission statement. As one manager says, 'It certainly made everyone at least read it.'

Farmtext, on the other hand, is just hitting the rapids. Everyone is used to working every hour that God sends – but now the promises of jam tomorrow are starting to wear thin. Managers at all levels are voicing a strong concern that the rewards do not match the demands made of them. It's felt that there comes a time when you can't take liberties with people, cancel holidays and work weekends. One younger manager sums it up: 'Recognition of our efforts is the message, we fuel growth, we're all dead keen to grow the business! What's the reward?' There isn't a lot of money about, but the problem is a real one if the business is to retain its best people. The management team is looking hard at putting together the right package: it's not just basic pay, nor promotion prospects, but also status and recognition, and above all some form of profit sharing and ownership.

As you test out your reward systems, ask yourself what it is that you're expecting from people, and is this what is being produced and being rewarded? It's very easy to find that you are expecting one thing (ie profitable growth) and rewarding another (sales targets). Don't be frightened of discriminating between good and bad performance; accountability for results must go with growth. How imaginative are you being in rewarding your people? Are you for example:

- Paying enough?
- Linking rewards to performance?
- Giving cash bonuses, including instant ones?
- Rewarding team performance as well as individual effort?
- Putting people's pictures on bulletin boards and in newspapers?
- Making excellence awards?
- Rewarding those who know and use your vision?
- Giving free tickets to the theatre/match/concert?
- Giving gift certificates?
- Promoting technical and managerial stars?
- Badges (like the IBM 'Golden Banana' award)?
- Giving good people autonomy?
- Giving different work assignments, job rotation?

- Saying 'thank you'?
- Sending people to business schools?
- Having celebrations?
- Giving a share of the business?

People maintenance systems

We know that people are the key; that means it pays to keep them healthy. Personnel policies can seem set in concrete, but changing them as you grow is absolutely possible and essential if you are going to stay fit. This means taking a good look at your recruitment policies, your induction programme, your training, who you're promoting and how you appraise people:

Q. 'How do I go about recruiting for key positions. Am I satisfied with the results?'

Q. 'How much training do I give all staff, myself included?'

Q. 'On what criteria do I promote people?'

Q. 'Do I regularly appraise all staff performance in a way they find helpful?'

You can bet that at least one of these 'plates' is wobbling dangerously and about to fall off its stick. Just as the perfect life style is a myth, so you'll never get the perfect package of personnel systems. When you take a look at what you've got you'll probably find it's very like the curate's egg – only good in parts. Here are some examples of the good and bad bits of the systems we've recently come across:

Farmtext is growing into new markets. It needs new skills in the area of finance, marketing and perhaps personnel. These skills don't exist internally, they will have to recruit from outside. But they're experiencing a lot of difficulty recruiting, not only because they are in a country area and not only because they are looking for specialist skills. They just don't know how to do it. They need job descriptions and person specifications, they need clearer job criteria, they need to match the job and the person instead of taking whatever they can get, they need to increase their batting average in making good people decisions. They need a framework for a selection profile and an interview process.

Induction is a golden opportunity for making a good and lasting impression. Innovex runs an orientation programme for all its new recruits. It demonstrates that they and the company are something special. It tells the Innovex vision. The chairman pours the tea and teaches on every programme – that's how important it is and how special is their culture.

Training everyone on an ongoing basis is something Innovex believes in. This year their managers will all go through a core programme of management training and will add on any elective they need. A minimum of 8–12 days training a year will be the rule. The chairman takes himself off to business schools. All the secretaries and administrative staff will have video and in-house training on being appraised, on word processing skills, on basic finance. The trained will become the trainers.

Appraisal is the keystone to management performance. If you haven't got a system, get one; if you've got one, review it. As in the case of many young companies, John Green of Green Systems has found that his appraisal system has become archaic and is no longer consistent with where he is taking the business. Interviews are rushed, linked to salary reviews; the process is of tick boxes and no comments; and appraisal is against qualities not results. It's a one way tell, not a two way dialogue. Nothing much happens afterwards. The new appraisal scheme will reflect the new needs of the business. It will hold people accountable against business objectives, it will reward those who reflect the Green Systems vision and values, it will be a full two way conversation where both parties have their own agenda, it will result in action and training and career development – it will build the managers of the future.

Communications

Finally, a seemingly innocuous question:

Q. 'How good are your internal communications?'

Once you're past the euphoria of Phase 1 growth we suspect that your answer is likely to be, 'not very'. Communication problems are a classic consequence of growth. In the early days you don't need anything very formal, you are probably a small team, openly involved in sharing information and playing bar billiards together.

The troubles come as you get bigger and people no longer come together on such a regular basis, new people have joined who don't have the same shared history, and none of you have time for meetings. Cracks begin to appear in the communication downwards, in communications across from one department to another and in the extent to which anyone listens to the ideas coming up through the organisation.

The state of your communications is a good barometer of your corporate health. Once this goes, look out for fragmentation, Us and Them type behaviour, lack of team identity, frustration about goals, patchy information flow, politicking and cliques. It's a paradox that even informal communications (once you're past a certain size) need formalising. Communications never happen unless there are the disciplines and mechanisms to *make* them happen.

Assessing People, Structure and Systems

Are you satisfied that you have in place at least some of the following, very simple mechanisms:

- Cascade briefing groups downwards on a regular basis.
- Management by walk about (MBWA).
- Informal get togethers (eg Tandem beer busts).
- Regular management meetings.
- Twice yearly 'State of the Nation' get togethers for the whole team.
- Quality circles or cross boundary think-tanks – problem-solving meetings.
- Presentations by one department to another.
- Social occasions: Christmas parties, away days, theatre outings, visits to the pub.
- A weekly happy hour meeting of all staff.
- Somewhere to eat where people can relax and mix.

People		
	Skills and attitudes	• Will existing skills be adequate or do these need to be built up before the business can grow? • What is the labour turnover rate compared with competitors/last year? • Are levels of sickness/absenteeism high or low? • Do I know why my people are leaving?
	Management capability and style	• Do I have sufficient managers to run my business well? • How much growth could they handle without becoming over-stretched? • Is there anyone who can run the business in my absence? • If a key manager left is there someone to fill his place? • How much can I delegate? • What is my personal management style and that of my managers?
	Culture	• How would my managers and myself describe the organisation culture?
Structure	What kind of structure exists?	• At what stage of growth (Greiner) is my business? • How is my business currently controlled? • How would I describe my present structure?
	How to divide things up	• Does everyone have a job description and know what is expected of them? • Are the various tasks divided up and grouped in the best way?
	How to integrate	• How is integration achieved at present? • Do people work individually or in teams?
Systems	Reward systems	• How do I currently reward people for achieving goals?
	People maintenance systems	• How do I recruit for key positions? • How much training do I give all staff (myself included)? • On what criteria do I promote people? • Do I regularly appraise staff performance?
	Communications	• How good are internal communications?

Figure 6.8 *Checklist of questions for organisation audit*

Organisation analysis (worked example)

John Elliot set up Ebac Ltd 20 years ago in Bishop Auckland, selling domestic and industrial dehumidifiers and bespoke air conditioning. The business grew vertically into manufacture and product design. The business grew rapidly in the 1980s in both turnover and profit, with annual sales and profits exceeding £10m and £1m respectively. Despite or possibly because of these good figures, the company was heading out of control, culminating in two years of losses totalling over £1.5m. But the worst thing is that when profits disappear so do the bankers. The cash shortage was much worse than the loss of profits. John says that there can be no doubt that the problems were all self-inflicted, even though they could have been lessened by a longer-term perspective from the banking fraternity. John goes on to say that there is, however, a benefit in the apparent inability of bankers to relate to business! Businessmen must fully explain their plans which means they must think them out, in advance. To do this a structure is required.

Following is John Elliot's initial analysis of the organisation capability of Ebac Ltd (Figure 6.9).

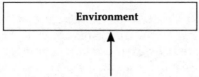

The business environment is changing in a way which will polarise the difference between small entrepreneurial businesses which can respond to changing demands, and large businesses with their economies of scale and momentum.

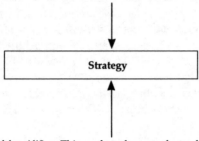

- *Domestic dehumidifiers:* This market-place may be too big for us. However, we are market leaders so, despite apparent bad fit, still warrant consideration for specialised new products.
- *Industrial dehumidifiers:* Very good fit for our size and skills and, therefore, most likely to give long-term profitable growth.
- *Rail air conditioning:* Good fit but limited growth potential means poor margins but likely to discourage new entries.
- *Manufacturing:* This is probably our greatest natural strength and our current programme of improvement will strengthen it further.

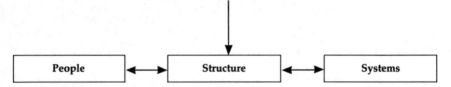

- *Attitude/skills gaps* lack of accountability
- *Managers* may lack commitment, don't understand real costs
- *Management style* too tolerant, better at short-term problem solving than devising long-term solutions
- The *culture* is 'get it started and sort out problems as they arise'. No thinking ahead

- *Existing structure* is functional, ie sales and manufacturing are separate units since they require different visions, and one leader cannot deal with two visions
- *Dividing things up:* Some staff are expected to operate outside their span of control, accountability not always clear, specialisation of roles needs encouraging
- *Is the structure working?* Not well enough

- *Operational:* we need to create a culture of continuous improvement and focus on value-added functions
- *People maintenance:* increased involvement and development within their span of operation
- *Reward systems:* consider team bonuses?
- *Communications:* continue developing communication skills at all levels

Figure 6.9 *Organisation analysis: John Elliot's example*

Assessing People, Structure and Systems
ASSIGNMENT 11

Assessing your current capabilities

Environment
(Key external challenges from Assignment 2)

1.

2.

3.

4.

Strategy
(What are the major directions in which you
are trying to move the business?)

1.

2.

3.

People	Structure	Systems
(current characteristics of skills and attitudes, management capability, style and culture)	(how do you divide things up, what about teamwork?)	(the essence of your existing reward, people maintenance and communication procedures)
1.	1.	1.
2.	2.	2.
3.	3.	3.
4.	4.	4.
5.	5.	5.
6.	6.	6.

ASSIGNMENT 12

Preparing an agenda for organisational change

Fits or misfits: your agenda for change

Going back through the present characteristics of your organisation (outlined in Assignment 11) add a tick √ or a cross X to represent whether each of these features are 'fits' or 'misfits' with the challenges you face. The misfits should give you your organisational agenda for change and should indicate where your primary challenges lie. Please outline each of these as you would in preparing a brief for a consultant. Four items are probably as much as you can realistically handle. What lever for change will you need to pull (ie primarily people, or systems, or structure)?

Item 1

Item 2

Item 3

Item 4

Answers to culture questions (p.122) are:

1. Prudential Assurance Company Ltd
and
2. British Airways

Part 2:

Where Are We Going?

If you have worked through the assignments at the end of each of the previous six chapters, you should by now have a good feel for your current strengths and weaknesses. The financial and people resources available to support future strategies should be apparent.

In Part 1, the position audit to determine the key factors in 'where have we been', you have been looking again at your product/service's external market and competitive environment. For each business you have been encouraged to define the target customer segments you need to serve, as this is at the heart of successful modern marketing. Wong, Saunders and Doyle's Anglo/Japanese study found that:

> *Sadly, 47 per cent of British firms (as against 13 per cent of Japanese) acknowledged they were unclear about the principal customer categories and their special requirements. With comments like 'We do not see the market as being made up of specific segments. Our market is made up of the whole industry. Anyone in the market can be our customer'. Not surprisingly, the British competitors were increasingly pushed to the sidelines of their market, comprising largely lower-potential segments as opposed to the high-potential or up-market sectors targeted by the Japanese.*

Equally, in the competitive environment, Japanese companies have shown themselves to be as much competitors in export markets as at home, in stark contrast to their more 'stay at home' British counterparts. While a strong home base in indispensable, the opening of European markets following 1992, and the new opportunities and competitive threats this will pose for British companies, means serious consideration must be given to the actions required by the new environment. British companies have led in company acquisitions in Europe in recent years, but is this the most cost-effective way to deal with the situation for your business?

> *Amberley Plc, for example, a British owned and USM listed company specialising in rising damp treatment, overcame language, legal employment and promotional problems in France in the early 1980s to successfully extend its depot network and direct selling methods across Europe. By sustained internal growth it has achieved profitable operations in three major continental countries and only now is considering acquisitions, most probably in the UK, by backward integration with companies supplying chemicals for its damp-proofing treatment.*

Within your own business unit's internal strengths and weakness audit, the main objective has been to clarify again the key product or service differentiation which led to the establishment of the business, and which needs to be constantly refreshed if its product life cycle is not to come to a premature end.

> *Many British companies, according to Wong, Saunders and Doyle, were weak at differentiating their products from competition or possessed little competitive advantage. Only 20 per cent of British companies claimed they were 'good at product differentiation' compared to 53 per cent of the Japanese. On measures of R & D, design, process development and volume production capabilities, the British competitors consistently emerged the weaker.*

Yet if Perrier can turn a commodity, water, into a well-differentiated brand by clever use of each element of the marketing mix, this ought to make us sceptical of those who claim differentiation cannot be achieved. To make it worse, the Perrier product was largely developed by an Englishman, Lord Northcliffe, before it was acquired by Gustave Leven in 1946!

> *Perrier is presented as a top quality product (hence total withdrawal and subsequent re-launch after 1990 benzene scare), with product differentiation (distinct green bottle, bubbles, twists of lemon/lime), high pricing to match quality and to provide margins to justify distinctive promotions, varying from country to country (humour in England), and is distributed world-wide from its single, magical, source: 'La Source', near Nimes, in south-west France. The whole 'marketing mix' is clearly being focused on health conscious, wealthy and younger target consumers.*

Similarly, many Japanese companies have succeeded by adherence to the basics of the marketing mix: making good quality products (which they were not famous for even 25 years ago, proving that it is a process which can be learnt), continually extending their range to meet the changing preferences of their customers, and investing in their distribution channels (stocks, technical training, dealer support for promotional spending).

All these lessons from Part 1 now need to be summarised in Part 2, Chapters 7 and 8, to help us clearly decide 'where we are going'; ie, for each of our business units what our marketing options are and what our marketing strategy should be. At the same time we will review our financial options, and the management and people issues that will influence our strategic choices.

7.

Marketing Options

Your marketing options come, in the first place, from your audit of your business strengths/weaknesses and opportunities/threats (SWOT analysis). A SWOT should be prepared for each of your business/product activities and should be:

1. a summary of the key elements in your business (Assignments 2–8);
2. brief, concise and interesting, without being too abbreviated;
3. focused on the real issues facing your company;
4. action orientated, so that positive proposals can be envisaged.

Each strength should be something you can build upon; each weakness, something that seriously needs to be corrected, as the following example from Autoglass suggests (Figure 7.1).

SWOT analysis

	Strengths	Weaknesses
1. *Customers*	We have a unique position with UK insurance companies	We are weak in the garage repair sector
2. *Product*	We provide a unique 24-hour, 7 days a week service to motorists	We lose some customers because answerphone system not alive
3. *Place*	We have strong depot representation in South	We are weak in depot representation in North
4. *Promotion*	Insurance companies give us good coverage to all insured motorists	We do not have representation in all Yellow Pages throughout country
5. *Price*	Our prices, with our fast service, are competitive with garages	We are a price follower not leader
6. *Finance*	Our Southern depots are earning a minimum 25% return on assets	Our new start-up depots in Midlands are losing money
7. *Operations*	We have well-motivated managers through profit sharing scheme	Employee turnover is high because of irregular hours

Figure 7.1 *SWOT analysis 1: strengths and weaknesses (Autoglass Windscreen Repairs Ltd)*

In the same way, your summary of opportunities and threats should give you the confidence, and in some cases the justification, to plan future marketing actions, as the following environment analysis for Autoglass (see Figure 7.2).

	Opportunities	Threats
8. *Market*	Growing steadily at real 3% pa	Slow market growth does not favour rapid expansion
9. *Political*	Government favours changing MOT regulations to include windscreen inspection	Entry into EC is encouraging cheaper windscreen imports from France, disrupting our traditional UK suppliers
10. *Technology*	Energy crisis encourages motor manufacturers to fit lighter bonded laminated windscreens (favours specialist fitters)	Switch by motorists to laminated windscreens threatens to make our stocks of toughened windscreens obsolete
11. *Competition*	Shows no signs of becoming organised enough to approach insurance companies	Our market share would be threatened if car accessory company (eg Kwik-Fit) diversified into windscreens

Figure 7.2 *SWOT analysis 2: opportunities and threats (Autoglass Windscreen Repairs Ltd)*

If the SWOT analysis has been carefully drawn, marketing actions and options can be developed (see Figure 7.3).

SWOT action plan

SWOT ref (Figure 7.1)	Action	Target date	Who actions
SWOT 3 Improve depot coverage in North of England	Investigate opening 2 new depots in main population centres, Manchester and Leeds		PJB/RJB
	• Contact estate agents	Nov 90	PB/RB
	• Visit suitable sites	Dec 90	
	• Cost and prepare plans	Jan 91	
	• Select and train staff	Jan 91	
	• Open 2 depots	Mar 91	
SWOT 7 Reduce employee turnover by recruiting YT staff and providing suitable training	Approach Training Centre, Birmingham to: • Draw up approved training programme		PS/CB
	• Obtain Training Centre approval	Oct 90 Nov 90	
	• Fit out one Depot (Neasden) as training centre; cost and approve		
	• Recruit suitable applicants	Nov 90 Jan 91	
	• Post trainees to 2 new Depots	Mar 90	

Figure 7.3 *SWOT action plan (Autoglass Windscreen Repairs Ltd)*

Marketing Options

Critical success factors

The financial costs and benefits of these options clearly need to be determined, in terms of both revenue and capital needs (Chapter 9). Before this, however, to focus attention on the marketing priorities facing your company, you should endeavour to finalise your marketing options analysis by determining and ranking the critical success factors which are vital for your company's success (see Figure 7.4).

Competition position / Critical Success Factor (CSF)	Importance of CSF (%)	Your own business Autoglass	Main Competitors (0–10) Windshield Enterprises	Bridgewater Glass	Associated Windscreens
CSF 1 Achieve improved depot coverage to meet insurance co's national requirements	50	7	5	4	7
CSF 2 Control windscreen and glass stocks to limit capital investment	25	6	7 (aided by Laddow)	5	7 (aided by C Pugh)
CSF 3 Develop competent staff for new depots, by setting up Training Dept	15	4	3	3	3
CSF 4 Achieve national recognition while controlling promotional expenditure	10	7	5	3	5
Total	100	24	20	15	22

Figure 7.4 *Critical Success Factors (Autoglass Windscreen Repairs Ltd and competitors)*

By weighting each factor out of 100, and scoring your own company's current achievement and that of your competitors out of 10, even though this may be subjective, you should develop a clearer understanding of the priorities each marketing option entails.

One problem with a quite open subjective assessment of your own and competitors' performance on Key Success Factors, is that companies frequently rate themselves ahead of, or at least equal to, main competitors (as Figure 7.4 shows for Autoglass). Care should be taken through market research with customers, for example, to see if they agree with both your assessment of the key success factors and how your company and competitors compare in these areas.

ASSIGNMENT 13

SWOT analysis

Using the information gained in going through the marketing position audit, summarise the *key* market/business strengths and weaknesses of your business and the *principal* opportunities and threats you see ahead of you.

If you operate in a number of very different markets you will need to do a separate SWOT analysis for each business.

SWOT analysis 1, Own company compared to competition (see Figure 7.1)

	Strengths	**Weaknesses**
1. *Customers/Market segments*		
2. *Product/Service*		
3. *Place* (Distribution)		
4. *Promotion* (Advertising)		
5. *Price*		
6. *Finance*		
7. *Operations* (Sales)		

SWOT analysis 2, *Key* opportunities and threats existing in current environment (see Figure 7.2)

	Opportunities	Threats

8. *Total Market*

9. *Political/ Government environment*

10. *Technology*

11. *Competition*

Critical success factors 3

From your SWOT analysis, establish priorities for action by *highlighting* what are the critical success factors for your business, and rank your current achievement on these factors versus your major competitors (see the Autoglass example in Figure 7.4).

Competition position / Critical Success Factor (CSF)	Importance of CSF (% weighting)	Your own business	Main competitors		
			(1)	(2)	(3)
CSF 1					
CSF 2					
CSF 3					
CSF 4					
Total	100				

Weight each factor out of 100; score your business and each competitor out of 10. Typically CSF 1 should be around 50 per cent, being the main way in which your business will stand or fall in your market sector. Check that customers agree with your assessment.

8.

Marketing Strategy: Focus and Priorities

SWOT and key success factor analysis is the essential first step in determining your marketing options. The next step is to apply some strategic analysis to your products/services and markets. It would not be sensible, for example, to invest heavily in products nearing the end of their life cycle; there are several useful tools which can be used to help develop a good strategic perspective. One is the Boston matrix, developed by the Boston Consulting Group in the early 1970s.

This suggests that a company's products should be classified according to their ability to generate or consume cash, against two dimensions of market growth rate and market share. This process is summarised in Figure 8.1.

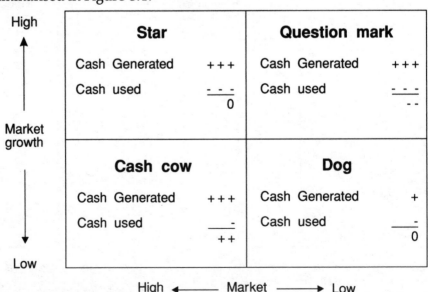

Figure 8.1 *The Boston matrix*

The concept behind this 'product portfolio' approach is, of course, to seek to use cash generated by 'Cash cows' to invest in 'Stars' and a selected number of 'Question marks', while considering dis-investment for 'Dogs'. Cash flow is used, rather than profits, as it is the real determinant of a company's ability to develop its products/services. Investment is directed in favour of achieving market share or growth while maximising cash flow, as shown in Figure 8.2.

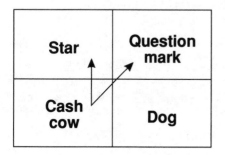 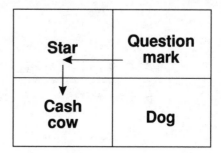

Figure 8.2 *Matrix suggests investment direction*

Some companies have used business strengths instead of market share, and market attractiveness instead of market growth; the strategic investment concept is the same, divesting from the dog area and investing in stars, and selectively in the other two boxes. You should endeavour to rank your products in this way, plotting them on the matrix, using circles to denote the approximate size of sales of each business unit. The direction in which these circles should be moving, should influence your strategic investment decisions. Remember, however, that the analysis is only directional and that market and company circumstances can change quite rapidly.

Doulton Glass, for example, saw its product portfolio change quite dramatically in three short years, 1979–82. Its double glazing (DG) activity, from being a fast growing Star, with increasing investment and depot network, became in 18 months a Dog as market growth halted and market share was lost in a bitter, competitive discounting war. Disinvestment of DG became imperative to staunch cash out-flow and to permit selective new investment out of Cash cow Glass Merchanting (M) into the Question mark products, Safety Glass (SG) and Automotive (A), where market growth was being stimulated by safer glazing regulations and market share could be achieved by acquisition of small competitors (see Figure 8.3).

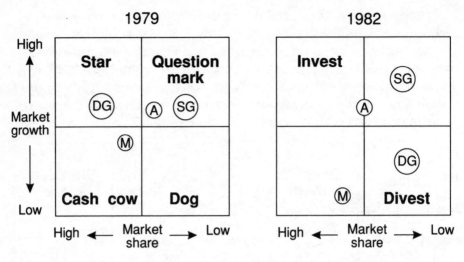

Figure 8.3 *Product position in matrix changes overtime*

Another helpful tool is the checklist shown in the marketing strategy chart (Figure 8.4).

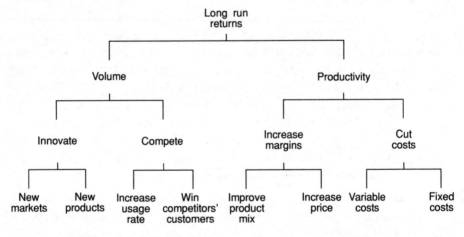

Figure 8.4 *Marketing strategy: the strategic options summary*

The chart illustrates the two major strategic options to pursue for each business unit:

1. Improve productivity;
2. Increase volume.

These directions are not mutually exclusive, but each has a different strategic focus.

Improve productivity

Improving productivity is a constant requirement for a growth-minded business, not simply an activity during periods of economic recession (when it is still, nonetheless, important – much better than adopting the 'turtle position' ie 'pulling in your head and your hands and getting off the highway!'). Productivity needs to be improved by acting on both your costs and your margins.

Cutting costs

Costs need to be constantly controlled and balanced against the needs for good quality and good service. In particular you need to separate and act on your variable and your fixed costs:

- *Variable cost* cutting is always in evidence in recession; witness the automotive and banking staff cuts in the early 1990s. Some employers aim to keep flexibility

  For example, Fiat in Italy chose to lay off 65,000 car workers (half its work-force) for one week per month, to cut production levels by 40,000 vehicles. Fiat saw no point in permanent job cuts when the future (Gulf War influenced) was so hazy.

Other companies sought actual pay cuts rather than redundancies, together with tight control on expensive overtime. Focusing attention on the 20 per cent of items that make up 80 per cent of your costs will probably yield biggest results.

- *Fixed cost* reductions, similarly, should not include scrapping investments in technology that could bring economies and extra nimbleness in the future (like flexible-manufacturing facilities, where, for example, Peugeot has invested in product lines that can turn out two models at once). Many firms, following Japanese practice, increase their use of sub-contractors to help offset increased risk.

  Marks and Spencer have grown dramatically in recent years by doing just this, but equally share some of the risk with suppliers, ensuring loyalty to the firm when better conditions prevail.

Equally, alliances between firms, aimed to reduce fixed cost investments, can be advantageous. In the soft drinks industry, Perrier provide distribution for Pepsi in France, while Bulmers reciprocated for Perrier in England, avoiding the need for extra investment in warehousing and transport.

Increasing margins

Increasing margins may be the result of the variable cost control actions noted above or through better buying (quantity discounts, payment term discounts), or by increased investment. It can also result from external market appraisal leading to changes in your product mix sales or even from increased prices.

- *Product mix* analysis requires that your accounts give you accurate costs and gross margins for each of your product/service lines.

  Autoglass Ltd, for example, at a time of depressed sales, recognised the extra margin from fitting laminated compared with toughened windscreens. An incentive scheme for fitters, combined with display aids for customers emphasising the extra benefits of laminated vs toughened, saw an increased proportion of laminated sales in a static market, and a marked improvement in gross margins.

- *Increasing price* is always difficult; you know what to do when cutting prices to stimulate demand: you make a lot of noise and publicity! Some people think that increasing price should be the opposite, being silently passed through to suppliers and customers alike. This is rarely the way to generate long-term loyalty! Better companies seek to combine increases with improvements in service or product offerings. Even the Post Office when increasing prices by 1p, frequently seeks to announce improved services, for example the reintroduction of Sunday collections. Equally, warning suppliers of planned increases may enable you to reduce slow moving stock and build longer-term customer/supplier loyalty.

Increase volume

A systematic approach to building sales volume was early devised in the form of a matrix by Igor Ansoff as shown in Figure 8.5.

In terms of risk, developing new products for new markets is clearly the most difficult strategy; by keeping one of the variables constant, either an existing product or an existing market, you are clearly ensuring, in military terms, that 'you are keeping one foot on the ground' and reducing risk. The lowest risk is in competing more strongly with existing products and existing markets; the two strands of strategy in terms of priority are therefore:

- to compete more strongly;
- to innovate, with new products and new markets.

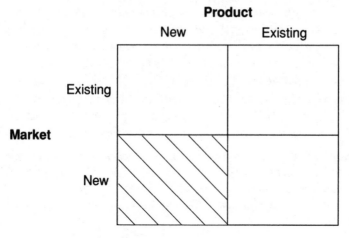

Figure 8.5 *Growth matrix*

Compete

Competing more strongly with existing products within existing markets may be less glamorous than launching new products into exotic markets, but usually ensures better returns. What is required is to sell more to existing customers – to increase their usage rate – then to capture customers from competitors.

- *Increased usage rate* is possible because customers have a life cycle curve just like products, winning their early business (courtship) does not mean that you are their only supplier. Winning more of their business (wedding) is clearly a priority.

  Equinox Furniture Design, for example, being a UK producer supplied UK retailers with small 'top-up' orders, as overseas suppliers insisted on minimum orders of at least a dozen items. Equinox decided to offer customers an incentive to place minimum orders of five of each product. This virtually doubled their 'sell-in' to many existing customers, while still leaving them competitive with overseas suppliers, in terms of size of minimum order.

Equally, deadlock and divorce can loom with existing customers if you do not actively seek to maintain the marriage relationship; setting up computer links to facilitate direct customer ordering, carrying out joint promotions, or simply sharing information may be the way to build customer loyalty and sales. None of these actions require the expensive promotional costs for attracting new customers, which is why increasing usage rate has to be the most attractive method to build sales volume.

- *Winning competitors' customers* again means following a low risk strategy of working with existing products in existing markets. Gaining entry to a competitor's customer is never easy, unless they are in the wedlock–divorce stage. To know this requires constant market intelligence, to reveal when a competitor's quality is down, deliveries are late or a trusted sales person has left. Your attention should always be to focus on added value rather than price: there is no point in growing unprofitably.

  Equinox Furniture, for example, emphasised their production and small order delivery flexibility to gain entry to customers with foreign suppliers. Prices were not discounted. Only when they were accepted as a trusted supplier did the company seek to improve orders by offering minimum order incentives.

  As you seek to win competitors' customers you may also be seeking to convert the sizeable army of non-users of whatever you and your competitors sell. This usually involves seeking referrals from existing customers, sometimes by offering incentives, and can also involve buying mailing lists of customers with a similar socio-economic grouping as your present customers.

Innovate

Innovation, involving new products and new markets is clearly higher risk. But there are exceptions:

- *New markets* may mean simply taking existing proven products/ services into a new geographical area, as Amberly Plc successfully achieved by taking British rising damp cures and selling methods on to the Continent. The challenges involved coping with languages (recruitment), adapting promotional methods (using multinational advertising agencies) and expanding under control (good accounting systems).

  It may mean simply expanding the range of your existing products, as Ratners the jewellers have done, by providing price ranges and jewellery products suitable for secretaries to duchesses, together with geographical expansion (USA acquisition). In this situation businesses are basically expanding their 'core' businesses, the ones they know best. (Sir Graham Day, Chairman of Rover and Cadbury's once described a core business as 'one you can bet on'. Peters and Waterman describe it as 'sticking to your knitting'.)

- *New products* may equally mean simple line extensions of your existing core businesses.

> *Autoglass realised early that success in establishing a windscreen replacement business would still leave seasonal troughs in their fitting business. By expanding into side windows (vandal area) and glass sun-roofs (peaking in season of lowest windscreen replacement activity) the company was able to build a balanced product line, with good labour utilisation, concentrated none the less on 'automotive glass'. Even glass polishes and cleaning items provided a useful added contribution.*

You should clearly be seeking to extend your existing product lines and seeking new market segments for your existing business. Yet major successful companies, like Marks and Spencer with food now providing 40 per cent of their turnover or Sainsbury's with Homebase, are clearly able to launch new products and enter new markets, the most risky combination of all. How is this done? By hastening slowly and sometimes by acquisition, ie careful market testing in one's own premises, listening to one's own customers and employees (such as Stu Leonard's Dairy in Peters and Waterman's classic example) and careful acquisition of proven earnings. Beware synergy, which should really be spelt *sin*ergy, unless you can actually quantify the extra value added – for example in better buying by quantity discounts, reduced price competition through acquiring significant market share – both of which Autoglass finally achieved in buying its major competitor, Windshield Enterprises. Careful test marketing has to be the key, as in new products/new markets Murphy's Law prevails: if a thing can go wrong, it will.

> *Lucius Cary, the successful owner of Venture Capital Report, invested £5000 seed-capital to help David Vint develop a prototype of his new wax-filled hot water bottle. The 'Huggie' as it was labelled, was designed to provide a safer alternative to the traditional hot water bottle. A good working prototype resulted in a further £100,000 investment in manufacturing facilities and although the Christmas launch went well, a large number of Huggies were returned as faulty. Many of the thermostats did not work properly, while the wax oil filling started to penetrate the skin of the bottle when stored for a time. With hindsight, Lucius admitted 'we were trying to break too much new ground'. The inventor, David, remains unabashed: 'If we had £200,000–£300,000 more, I think the product would be a world-wide best seller'. The assets of the business were bought from the liquidator by an industry competitor.*

The careful process of screening new ideas, developing the product, thoroughly test marketing prior to launch is both time-consuming and expensive. But much less expensive than jumping all those hurdles and rushing into the market. Hastening slowly but surely must be the key.

None of the above marketing strategic options may sound very exotic, particularly when compared with the predatory activities of a Hanson Trust!

> *Perhaps the most daring strategic change in Europe since the war by a single man was the way in which Antoine Ribaud transformed BSN from being one of Europe's leading flat glass manufacturers into a leading European branded food company! This extraordinary achievement, by an extraordinary man, came after his failure to take over the leading European flat glass manufacturer, St Gobain. Thwarted in this attempt, Antoine sold his low-yielding glass business to his major competitors and invested the enormous proceeds into the higher yielding branded food business.*

Extraordinary strategies and strategists do exist; for the growing business incremental options, such as we have outlined above, come first. When totally frustrated, however, as Antoine Ribaud was, or when all incremental options have been exhausted, you may need to completely re-think! If you divested all your businesses, what new diversification would you seek? Are the green pastures next door, really greener? Antoine Ribaud proved it could be done!

ASSIGNMENT 14

Strategic options

1. Try to position your products/services in the Boston Matrix below (see the example in Figure 8.1)

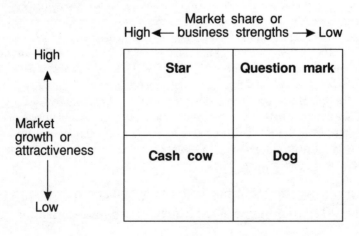

2. What are the directional implications from your products/services of the Boston Matrix analysis?

3. What opportunities are there for you to improve productivity in your business?

    (a) *Cutting costs:*

    (b) *Increasing margins:*

4. How can you increase volume in your business?

    (a) *Compete:*

    (b) *Innovate:*

5. What are your diversification or divestment possibilities?

    (a) *Diversification:*

    (b) *Divestment:*

9.

Choosing Between Alternatives

The analysis of strategic options

So much for developing strategy, now for the hard choice of which to pursue. If you have done a thorough job you should now have more options than either your management or financial resources could sensibly pursue – at the same time, at any rate. It is the comparison that will help you to choose the most desirable avenues.

Is the strategy compatible with your strengths?

As well as the greater risk associated with moving away from market penetration strategies, the further away you move from your own strengths, the less likely you are to succeed. The work done in preparing the position audit, and the marketing SWOT analysis can be summarised to help you reduce areas of subjective judgement to something resembling the quality that numeric comparisons can provide.

Let's suppose you make and market rugby shirts and you are considering whether to move away from supplying just the club/ supporters market, where you are strong at present, and to get into the fashion market for rugby type shirts as well. Here you will be up against quite different competitors and the criteria for success in the market-place will be different too.

The first step in making your decision is to review what you think are the critical factors for success (see CSFs, Chapter 7) – in other words what any company has to do right to succeed. For example, price might be important in the traditional rugby shirt market, but when it comes to the fashion market, image may be the deciding factor. Don't just rely on your opinion, ask customers in the market what they think too – both about the critical factors and about your rating against each factor.

You can research these factors either by questionnaire, or by face-to-face discussion with a reasonable number of customers and potential customers. Don't just rely on your salespeople's opinion; they always see price as the deciding factor. From Figure 9.1 you can see that you and, more importantly, your customers rank image as being the most important factor and price the least important, in this market.

Critical success factor	Weighting	Strengths and Weaknesses	
	%	Your rating (out of 10)	Your main competitor's rating (out of 10)
Product	20	X 9 = 1.8	X 7 = 1.4
Price	10	X 9 = 0.9	X 6 = 0.6
Promotion	20	X 2 = 0.4	X 9 = 1.8
Image	50	X 2 = 1.0	X 9 = 4.5
	100	4.10	8.30

Figure 9.1 *Critical success factors*

You can reflect this relative importance by giving each factor a weighting, with the total for all factors being 100 per cent. In this example your customers feel that half the consideration in their purchase decision is given over to the image of the rugby shirt, and price accounts for only 10 per cent. You now need to rate your company and your main competitors against each critical success factor. So for example, if your main strength lies in the product itself, for which you are well respected as a rugby shirt maker, you might rate this 9 out of 10, as you might also rate your keen competitive prices. Unfortunately, if you have virtually no promotional skills as all your sales are through rugby club membership lists and you have no fashion reputation, ratings on these factors might drop to only 2 out of 10.

Weighing all these factors up by rating yourself out of 10, you end up with a score of 4.10 compared with your competitor who has 8.30. (This is done by multiplying your rating out of 10 by the weighting factor expressed as a decimal: in Figure 9.1, for example, for product it's 0.2 X 9 = 1.8.) Your competitor has an inferior product, whose stitching wouldn't last a minute on the pitch and they are over-priced. Sadly they are wizards at promotion and are the envy of every fashion-conscious female! As these two factors combined make up 70 per cent of why people in this market buy, it gives your competitor an overwhelming advantage.

So much for strengths and weaknesses – it still needs to be seen if there is an opportunity worth pursuing. The first step here is to define what constitutes a desirable opportunity. Let's suppose your main aim is to break out of the low growth, low profitability commodity rugby shirt market and into a faster moving sector, then growth and profit would feature high on your shopping list of what factors make for an attractive market to move into.

Factor	Weighting % A	Scoring criteria 10	5	0	Score B	Result A × B
Market size	15	£50M	£5–49M	under £5M	10	1.50
Growth rate	25	15%	10–14%	under 10%	10	2.50
Competitiveness	20	Low	Medium	High	5	1.00
Profitability	35	Over 15%	10–15%	under 10%	5	1.75
Seasonality	5 100%	Low	Medium	High	7	0.35 7.10

Figure 9.2 *Market attractiveness*

Once again you could weigh the importance of each factor and get some scoring and these might then be weighted to account for 60 per cent (25 per cent growth rate + 35 per cent profitability) of your reasons for seeing a market as attractive.

Now you need to develop a set of scoring criteria for each factor. If the market was under £5 million in size, or delivered a profit below 10 per cent it would be fairly undesirable. This would be scored zero. A large market with over £50 million per annum sales and profit of over 15 per cent would be very attractive, and so would be scored 10. By multiplying the weighting in column A by the score in column B and dividing by 100 (to return the percentages in column A to decimals so you can use them in multiplication) we arrive at a market attractiveness factor of 7.1. This makes the fashion rugby shirt market an attractive market to go for, being well above the average of 5.0.

The final stage in the SWOT analysis is to put these results on a chart, plotting business strengths against market opportunity. Here you can see that while the market is attractive, your strengths as seen by the market don't really lie there. If you do want to enter that market then you need to tackle your image and improve your promotional skills.

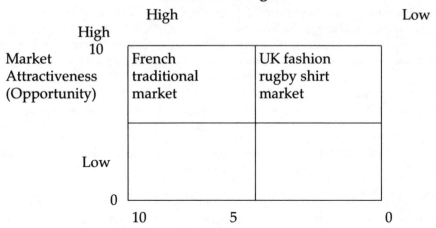

Figure 9.3 *The opportunity/strength matrix*

The real power of SWOT, however, is to help you choose between competing market options. Suppose that rather than go into the UK fashion market for rugby shirts, you also had the chance to go into the French traditional rugby shirt market (Figure 9.3). By going through a similar exercise for the French market segment you might come up with a strength factor of 8 and a market opportunity of 7. Not quite such an attractive option, but you have nearly twice as many strengths to exploit that opportunity.

You can follow this through to evaluate as many optional marketing strategies as you like. But you must remember to keep the Market Attractiveness criteria the same throughout. You may, and indeed probably must, vary the critical success factors for each different market you are examining. For example, exporting to France may have Britishness as a critical success factor in the rugby shirt market, which may not feature at all in the home market.

The final spin-off is that a SWOT analysis forces you to identify the critical factors for success in your market, by getting your customers to tell you what they think. And it makes you spell out what constitutes an attractive market opportunity in a way that should make your choices more rational, and easier to communicate to your management team. That has to be one whole lot more thorough than relying on a wet finger to test which way the wind is blowing.

Other considerations in choosing between competing growth strategies include the following.

Will it help you to achieve your prime objectives?

If your prime objective is to increase your return on investment from 10 per cent to 20 per cent then pursuing any strategy that doesn't return at least 20 per cent is going to make life very difficult for you.

> *Tandem Computers, who eventually made it to the Fortune 500, for a while pursued mutually exclusive strategies. They wanted to increase their ROI to 25 per cent and so use money efficiently, but would only pursue market strategies which resulted in quick cash paybacks. They succeeded in their marketing strategies, and piled in the cash until it filled up half their balance sheet. But as they could only get 12 per cent on the money market for their cash, the other half of their capital employed had to realise 38 per cent ROI to bring the average up. This in turn led them into more and more risky areas.*

So your new strategies must help you meet your objectives in terms of growth rate, market share, profitability etc.

Within your mission?

Having spent a lot of time developing a mission statement that everyone believes in, there is not much point in pursuing strategies that lie outside it. Remember, your mission is supposed to be narrow enough to give you focus and wide enough to give you scope for growth.

> *Blooming Marvellous, the UK designer maternity wear company, could be forgiven for revising their mission only if women gave up having babies, or once 500,000 out of the 700,000 women who have babies each year in the UK were in one (or two!) of their outfits.*

Otherwise stick to the knitting – at least until you are into Phase 4 growth with strong management, in depth.

Are acceptable levels of risk involved?

All new strategies involve taking risks. Risks can be loosely classified into those you have to take, those you don't have to take, those you can't afford not to take and those you can't afford to take.

The first type of risk basically describes the nature of the business you are in. If you're a bookmaker, it's no good worrying that your money is all on a horse! Some risks are not integral to the business and so you don't *have* to take them, for example the risk of currency changes, up or down, can be laid off by someone in international trade. It means your costs may be a little higher, and you won't win if currencies move in your favour, but you won't make expensive mistakes either. Whichever route you take, it will have virtually no effect on the customers' desire for your product or service.

There are other risks you cannot afford not to take. For example, if all your main competitors are spending heavily on new product development, or on improving their point of sale tills and sales analysis equipment, then by doing nothing you may be left too far behind to be competitive.

Finally, some strategies call for such a high resource commitment that if they don't succeed the whole company is prejudiced – the risks you can't afford to take. Ferranti, Tie Rack and the Midland Bank before them, saw their companies threatened when their American market development strategies turned sour.

Barriers to entry

Any new strategy can be significantly more attractive, if by pursuing it, you make it more difficult for new competitors to enter the market – or for existing companies to stay the course.

Tim Waterstone's strategy of seven-day, late-night trading and well-educated knowledgeable staff all on substantial bonus schemes, has transformed the UK bookselling market. W H Smith couldn't match this strategy – so they bought 51 per cent of the company, making Waterstone a multi-millionaire in the process. Sweet revenge for a man who was fired by the same company eight years earlier.

The time value of money

While reviewing your company's plans for the future you and your management team may come up with a number of exciting new business opportunities. The only trouble is that before they can be exploited you may have to invest in new equipment – and perhaps even some extra space.

It seems reasonable enough – after all, you have to speculate to accumulate. The key question is what is the right proportion of money to spend now, to receive a given amount of profit in future years.

Table 9.1 *Cash Flow of Investment*

Year	Cash out (a) £	Cash in (b) £	Net cash (b – a) £
0	50,000	–	(50,000)
1	5,000	15,000	10,000
2	5,000	15,000	10,000
3	12,500	37,500	25,000
4	12,500	37,500	25,000
5	5,000	15,000	10,000
			30,000

The example in Figure 9.1 illustrates a typical problem. The proposition is that you should invest £50,000 capital to make £80,000 over the next five years: a clear profit of £30,000, apparently a satisfactory situation as the return is 60 per cent [(30 ÷ 50) × 100]. The cash will come in and out as shown.

This is based on a £50,000 investment now, followed by some cash expenses and cash income in the future. In other words, a typical business buying in materials, adding value and selling mainly on monthly terms.

Present value

You may by this stage have a nagging feeling that the £10,000 coming in in five years' time is not worth quite the same as the identical amount coming in next year. And you would be right.

If you were offered a pound in a year's time you would instinctively value it lower than a pound today. The exact amount lower would depend on how much return you want for your money. So, for example, if you want to make 20 per cent profit, you would only pay about 80p now for each pound payable in a year. If the £1 on offer was coming in in two years' time you would value it even lower – and so on as time progressed.

The concept that explains this diminution of value with time is called Present Value. It is calculated by using a mathematical equation which fortunately you need never know, as tables are readily available (see Table 9.2) or the information is stored in most financial calculators (eg Hewlett Packard).

Table 9.2 *Present Value Table*

| Year | Percentage | | | |
	14	15	16	17
1	0.877193	0.869565	0.862069	0.854701
2	0.769468	0.756144	0.743163	0.730514
3	0.674972	0.657516	0.640658	0.624371
4	0.592080	0.571753	0.552291	0.533650
5	0.519369	0.497177	0.476113	0.456111

Table 9.2 is an extract which shows the present value of a pound received in one to five years' time, on the assumption you want to make between 14 and 17 per cent return on your investment.

Let's return to our example to see how present value works in practice. Let's assume that we want to make at least 17 per cent return on the investment we are to make. Accordingly we would select the present value factor at 17 per cent, from Table 9.2, and put the appropriate factor against each year of the life of the investment (see Table 9.3).

Table 9.3 *Present Value of Cash Flow of Investment*

Year	Net cash flow (a) £	Present value factor @ 17% (b)	Net present value (a × b) £
0	(50,000)	1.000	(50,000)
1	10,000	0.855	8,550
2	10,000	0.731	7,310
3	25,000	0.624	15,600
4	25,000	0.534	13,350
5	10,000	0.456	4,560
	Net present value		(630)

Take the present value factor for each year and multiply it by the net cash flow. (The net cash flow is arrived at in Table 9.1) This gives the net present value of the cash that this investment generates. In this case it comes to £49,370 (8,550 + 7,310 + 15,600 + 13,350 + 4,560), which is £630 less than the £50,000 we put in (Year 0 is now and £1 now has a present value of £1 – hence the factor 1.000). So if you had expected to make 17 per cent return on your investment, you would have been disappointed. You would have been even more upset if you were anticipating a mouth-watering 60 per cent, as first indications suggested.

The real rate of return

The present value concept tells us whether or not an investment is going to achieve a given rate of return. (You can arrive at that rate by looking at your past achievements, your competitors' performance, or by setting a challenging objective.) It won't, however, tell you what return you are actually going to get for your money – rather an important thing to know.

Going back to the example, all we know is that the Net Present Value is negative, as the target rate of return has not been achieved. To establish the exact rate of return we would need to recalculate the present values using a low enough percentage to make the net present value a positive sum. So if we were to plump for 14 per cent the figures would look like Table 9.4.

Table 9.4 *Present Value of Cash Flow of Investment, PVF at 14%*

Year	Net cash flow (a) £	Present value factor @ 14% (b)	Net present value (a × b) £
0	(50,000)	1.000	(50,000)
1	10,000	0.877	8,770
2	10,000	0.769	7,690
3	25,000	0.675	16,875
4	25,000	0.592	14,800
5	10,000	0.519	5,190
	Net present value (NPV)		3,325

Once again, by adding up the sum of the present value of cash flows from years 1 to 5, and deducting it from the cash going out at the start of the project, we arrive at the net present value (NPV). In this case it is a positive figure, so we know the project makes a return greater than 14 and less than 17 per cent – the two rates we have tried.

We can deduce the actual rate by doing the following sum:

Interpolating Equation

$$\text{The Internal Rate of Return (IRR)} = \text{Lowest Trial Rate} + \left[\frac{\text{Positive Cash Flow}}{\text{Range of Cash Flow}} \times \text{Difference between High and Low Rates} \right] \%$$

$$= 14 + \left[\frac{3,300}{3,996} \times 3 \right] = 14 + 2.47 = 16.47$$

Now that we have a slightly more meaningful piece of information on the proposed project profitability, we know it will make a real return on the money invested, of 16.47 per cent. We can then compare that with the other projects we may have in mind in exactly the same way as you could, for example, compare the 6 per cent return offered on a current bank account, with the 12 per cent on offer from a one year building society bond.

Nothing is certain

The danger with the net present value technique is that in producing very precise figures – 16.47 per cent for example – it can give you a false sense of security. You could be forgiven for believing that what you have forecast will actually happen in much the way that you expect.

No one can see five years into the future with any great degree of accuracy, although you can often get an idea of the type of events that might occur, and some order of their magnitude. For example, if you set out to buy and run a car, at the outset you would know its approximate cost within ± 10 per cent, its working life within a year or so and the running costs such as insurance, road tax, repairs, petrol etc, also to within 10 per cent. If, after doing all your sums, the car you would like is within your budget only if petrol costs don't rise more than 10 per cent per annum, or if you can be certain that it will last five years rather than the more likely four, then you are probably making a bad decision.

It is exactly the same with capital budgeting: you need to subject your figures to what is known in the trade as 'sensitivity analysis'. In other words, to find out how sensitive a particular project is to a particular likely event. Returning to our earlier example, suppose that 16 per cent was an acceptable return, but we wanted to see what the project could stand up to, we could re-run our calculations as follows.

Let's assume that the revenue flow is going to build up more slowly than we think, although over the life of the project the expenses and revenues will be the same, ie £50,000 out and £80,000 in (see Table 9.5).

Table 9.5 *Sensitivity Analysis*

Year	Net cash flow (a) £	Present value factor @ 16% (b)	Net present value (a × b) £
0	(50,000)	1.000	(50,000)
1	8,000	0.862	6,896
2	8,000	0.743	5,944
3	25,000	0.640	16,000
4	25,000	0.552	13,800
5	14,000	0.476	6,664
	Net present value		(696)

We can now see that this project is so sensitive to a 20 per cent (£8,000 vs £10,000) drop in profits in the first two years, that it would not make economic sense to invest. The big question now is how likely is your forecast to be 20 per cent out.

While some of the arithmetic in the above examples may have been cumbersome, the concept once grasped is simplicity itself. A pound to be received tomorrow is worth less than a pound today, simply because of what you could do with the money if you had it at your disposal now. So the only meaningful way to compare pounds out now with pounds in in the future, is to discount the value of those future sums in line with your profit expectations.

If you still budget for your capital expenditure, ignoring present value, then it is unlikely that many of your business investment decisions will make the profit you expect.

Diversification

The shaded box in Ansoff's Growth Matrix shown on page 155 is frequently the favourite choice of entrepreneurs seeking accelerated growth. However, diversification is the most risky strategy of all – and can in the most serious cases threaten the very survival of the business you seek to save.

Michael Peters and Partners

Michael Peters headed up the first design company to be floated on the Stock Exchange. He graduated from the London College of Printing before obtaining a masters degree in fine arts at Yale University. He returned to London to join Collet Dickenson Pearce as creative director of the design department. In 1970 he formed Michael Peters and Partners, a design consultancy specialising in corporate identity. It was floated in 1983, to give the company's 60 employees a stake in the business at a reasonable price. For two or three years the company was very much the darling of the stock market. It was only when Peters started to diversify that things went disastrously wrong, and the company had to call in the receivers. Now he is back to basics as chairman of Michael Peters Ltd.

Towards the end of 1985, Peters and his small management team went on what can best be described as a diversification binge. They moved into retail design, exhibitions, conference and event management, and even human resource management. For a business that was under-managed itself, that was pretty rich.

Some of the companies that Peters bought to anchor his diversification around were successful, but many were not. But things went disastrously wrong when they expanded into the United States, a market that has been the graveyard for many UK companies. At the end of the day trying to make the company's management team, which had been used to working in the brand and corporate identity business, manage activities it wasn't familiar with – some of them 3500 miles away – was a recipe for disaster.

After the receivership, they are back to running their core business as plain Michael Peters Ltd. In Peters' own words; 'We are once again back to basics, working with those clients who have always worked with us in our core brand and corporate identity business. That's what made us famous in the first place, and that's where we made our money. It has been a very painful experience, but I've learnt a big lesson. From now on, we'll be sticking firmly to what we know best.'

Craton Lodge and Knight

For Creenah Lodge, chairman of Craton Lodge and Knight, the new-product development and marketing company, disaster struck when she headed east to enter the Soviet market. Creenah helped to found the company in 1972 and until 1986 they had grown steadily if unspectacularly by sticking close to home.

Swept along with ideas of glasnost, Craton Lodge and Knight knew the Soviets needed to sell their goods to the west and, in turn, they needed to learn western marketing and computing skills. The company had someone who was familiar with the Soviet Union's culture and commerce, so they set up a joint venture with a newly created Moscow publicity agency, Vneshtorgraklama. Despite exploring opportunities with several manufacturing enterprises whose products could easily have been amended and sold to the west, they were finally defeated by Gosplan, the Soviet state planning agency.

The central problem was that the Soviets simply wouldn't or couldn't pay. They played for time, then they would pick holes in the contracts that they had themselves helped to write. By 1990 the Soviet joint venture was haemorrhaging so much that it caused cash flow problems in the whole of the UK operation, to the extent that not only did they have to close down the Russian unit, but they had to sell off three profitable businesses in the UK and return to their core business.

Even the biggest and strongest of firms find diversification hard to handle.

BP

In the mid 1970s, with the Wilson government talking about nationalising the whole oil industry, big companies such as BP began to lose confidence. They started to question their future roles and eventually decided upon a major diversification strategy. During the late 1970s BP moved into coal, minerals, nutrition and information technology (IT).

While the aim was growth, BP found that in coal they didn't have any idea how to differentiate their product from anyone else's. In minerals they lacked knowledge of that type of exploration activity and in IT they were neither users nor providers.

Between 1981 and 1986 BP, under Sir Peter Walters, dramatically rationalised the business, as their 'new' diversifications had been little more than a drain on cash and management resource. They got out of coal, sold their IT business,

Scicon, and their mineral business to RTZ. *In Sir Peter's own words, 'The pity was that if, in the first place, we had put even half of the effort we put into diversification into our core business it would have paid off. But at the time we felt the grass was greener.'*

The theories

Recent research by the Kalchas Group, the strategic management consultants, came down firmly on the side of companies who concentrated on their core business rather than diversifying. In their study they examined 353 quoted UK companies to review the value of business focus from two angles: their market rating, as measured by price-earnings ratios; and the shareholder value created by company performance, measured by growth in earnings per share. Their analysis yields some instructive results, which must certainly be equally valid for smaller and unquoted companies. The market rating of companies declines as the spread of business areas in which they operate increases. The average price-earnings ratios varied from 14 in tightly focused companies (operating in only one or two areas) down to only 10 for the most diversified. This relationship still holds true when examining the companies within individual sectors (as varied as foods, stores and industrial).

The premium accorded to focus is clearly significant for bosses who want to maximise shareholder value and to enlarge their room to manoeuvre for growth. Clearly, the investment community values focused businesses more highly than diversified ones.

The next obvious question asked by Kalchas was whether the higher rating is justified by performance. Growth of earnings per share shows a similar relationship; the tighter the business focus, the higher the earnings growth. Tightly focused companies generated 189 per cent annual growth in earnings since 1984, compared with only 10 per cent for the most diversified. The debate on focus versus diversification has continued over many years. From time to time, focus becomes the latest in City fashion; at other times spreading risk seems more attractive. But this empirical evidence runs strongly in favour of focus. The qualitative reasons advanced by the researchers for supporting this approach are equally compelling.

From an operating point of view, applying the skills of the management team to a business they know intimately is obviously the most sensible course. As the spread of a business widens, the direct contact of managers is dissipated. Extracting value from different businesses requires different skills. Heavy engineering and light manufacturing cannot be managed in a similar fashion; nor can contract assembly as opposed, say, to marketing services. The wider the spread, too, the greater the mix of management talent needed, and the less opportunity there is for one pair of eyes to review, analyse and direct.

There are some obvious caveats to add to the case for focus. The principal one arises where a company operates exclusively in one industry in decline (such as textiles, shipbuilding or tobacco). There the intelligent answer is to diversify into markets where advantage can be taken of in-house skills.

Perhaps we should leave the last word to Sir Ian MacLavin, who joined Tesco as its first management trainee in 1959, became managing director in 1973 and chairman in 1985. Sir Ian has pursued a single-minded policy to expand Tesco's food business in the UK: 'My business experience tells me that you have got to get hold of a market and do not move until you have squeezed every last drop from it', and he should know!

ASSIGNMENT 15

Checking your options out

1. Check your strategies out against the criteria described in this chapter and any others you have, and then list them in your order of preference.

2. Make sure your preferred strategies make up a reasonably balanced portfolio.

3. Make sure the likely sales and profit levels, if achieved, will meet your growth targets. (We'll look at this in more detail when we make the forecasts and projections in the Business Plan in Part 3.)

10.

Financing Growth

Whatever strategic direction you propose to pursue it is almost certain to require money. By now you will have discovered that a healthy business has an equally healthy appetite for cash. For the first years of a business's life its strategic choices are invariably limited by the availability of funds. Once it gathers momentum and begins to plan its strategic direction, the corset elastic is usually the limited availability of good opportunities and the management to exploit them successfully.

The constant search for funds is not in itself a cause for concern. Businesses, after all, exist in part at least to turn money into goods and services, which can be sold on for a profit. It usually takes a while for the business cycle to move from strategic ideas to profit and so, as long as you are growing, more money will be needed.

What should concern you, however, is where that money comes from. There are two main sources of money: internal and external, with a number of sub-divisions of each sector. Getting the right balance of funds from these different sources is the key to profitable growth – and perhaps even to survival itself.

Internal sources of funds

Surprisingly enough, many businesses have much of the money they need to finance growth already tied up in the firm. It may require a little imagination and some analysis to uncover it, but the financial position audit should have given some pointers to how this might be done. Look at the accounts for the High Note Company on page 76. Here you will see that the company is employing 46 per cent more capital in Year 2 to generate additional sales of only 30 per cent. The problem in this example is that High Note has more than doubled its money tied up in fixed assets and is getting very little in return. You should start by looking very carefully at all your capital assets to see if they really are essential to the business. In addition, when you develop your growth strategies, consider carefully both the amount and timing of any major capital expenditure otherwise you could end up scrambling for business at any price, just to cover costs.

Richard Edward Ltd

Richard Edward Ltd was started in 1979, when John and David Moger paid £220 for an elderly little litho press and installed it in a garage. David could not actually lay his hands on his share of the cash at the time and John claims still to be waiting for the £110. The company grew steadily with turnover moving from £254,000 in 1981–2 to £641,000 in 1984–5. By 1989 the company had turnover of £2m in the original printing business and just under three quarters of a million pounds in a new mailing and print finishing business.

By 1989 the Moger brothers were in an expansive mood. The business they had built up was thriving: to invest in better property and better equipment seemed a sensible thing to do. They spent £855,000 on new premises and almost £1m on two new presses.

By July 1990 the company's interest bill wiped out its profits. John Moger confessed at the time, 'We are not making anything at the moment, we are just hoping to survive'. Desperate to keep the presses going they searched for any work from contracts from HMSO down to a few letterheads or a bundle of business cards.

John Moger now admits that his business had grown so fast that there was little time for contingency planning. 'We were a bit too busy,' he said.

Squeeze working capital

Working capital is a further area rich in possibilities for squeezing to release cash for expansion. Debtors and stocks are perhaps the most fertile areas to start. According to figures prepared by the credit management group, Intrum Justitia, British firms wait on average 78 days for bills to be paid while German, Swedish and Norwegian companies wait just 48 days, Danish firms wait 50 days, Dutch companies, 52 days. Italian and French companies wait 90 and 108 days respectively, but they quote 60-day payment terms rather than our normal 30 days, so they are still better off in relative terms.

Intrum Justitia calculates that the total cost of providing customers with the extra 48 days of credit is equivalent to 5.7 per cent of the average business's turnover, and, assuming a net profit margin of 10 per cent, more than half its net profit. Instead of companies being able to borrow to grow the business, they often need to borrow just to fund their sales ledger.

Holliday Chemical Holdings

Companies are turning increasingly to computers to provide them with the information they need to forecast likely demand and the stocks they must carry to meet it. Holliday Chemical Holdings, a Huddersfield-based chemicals manufacturer with UK turnover of £33m, is spending £160,000 on a computerised materials requirements planning system which will allow it to plan production schedules in its two UK plants (employing 367 people). Michael Peagram, head of the new management team which bought into Holliday in 1985, believes tighter controls on purchasing and the computerised systems will allow him to cut £1 million from current stocks of £8m. Stocks have been allowed to grow over the past five years as turnover quadrupled but there is now a need for tighter controls.

Sophisticated computer systems may be appropriate for a company the size of Holliday but smaller businesses can achieve considerable improvements by relatively simple changes in the way they purchase and monitor their stocks of raw materials. Holliday itself is buying in chemicals on a monthly rather than a quarterly basis where possible, to reduce its own stocks.

Mercado Carpets

Mercado Carpets, a Leeds-based carpet wholesaler, has computerised its stock control procedures but combines this with what John Wharton, joint managing director, calls 'gut feel' to decide on the types and volumes of carpets to be purchased. Wharton estimates he devotes five hours a week to stocks and purchasing.

Mercado normally carries between £4 and £5m worth of inventory in its warehouse compared with an annual sales level of £26m. Acquired by its present management by means of a buy-out in 1989, the company employs 168 people.

Wharton keeps stocks low by buying, where possible, from suppliers with short delivery times, though shipment delays mean he is forced to hold 12 weeks' stocks of carpets from his US suppliers. In the wake of the buy-out Wharton persuaded his major suppliers to extend their payment terms by one month.

For businesses which have failed to monitor stock levels closely, the introduction of tight controls can prove daunting. A 'quick and dirty' way of making improvements can be achieved by grading stock as A, B or C according to the value of individual items or of the total number held. Attention is then focused on items in the A category which can provide the greatest savings. These items can then be subjected to regular stock-takes; patterns of demand can be studied to see how frequently orders are placed, if there are peaks and troughs, or whether demand is seasonal. Managers can then decide the quantities they require and when to place their next order or start their next production run if they are making the item in-house. B and C items can be brought into this programme once it is well established.

Much of the cost of many products is incurred in the final stages of manufacture so big stock savings can be made by holding stocks of semi-finished items. Only put the finishing touches to an item when the customer wants it.

Companies frequently maintain larger stocks than are necessary because a new order is triggered automatically when stocks fall to a certain level. These trigger points should be re-examined for each product to see if lower levels can be set.

Make more profit and plough it back

Another internal source of finance is to make your present business more profitable and plough that profit back to grow your business. Five steps you can take to unlock the extra profit potential in your business are:

1. Recognise the iceberg

Just as the small tip of the iceberg showing above water conceals an enormous mass below, the small(ish) percentage of profits the average business makes (typically under 10 per cent of sales), conceals a great volume of money being used to arrive at that profit.

It requires only a few percentage points reduction in costs to dramatically improve profits, as Table 10.1 illustrates.

Table 10.1 *The effects of cost savings on profits*

Before		After 2% cost saving		Extra profit		But if sales drop ...	
£000	*%*	*£000*	*%*	*£000*	*%*	*£000*	*%*
1,000	100	1,000	100	–	–	714	100
950	95	930	93	–	–	664	93
50	5	70	7	20	40	50	7

In the example given in Table 10.1 the last profit-to-sales figure was 5 per cent. Costs, the 'below the water line' mass, are 95 per cent. By reducing those costs by a mere 2 per cent, bottom line profits have been increased by a massive 40 per cent (this is a simplified example from a real life case).

This extra profitability can then be used to finance extra invest-ments, saved as a reserve for bad times, or be used to compensate for lower sales. In the example above, when costs are reduced by 2 per cent, turnover from sales can drop by over 25 per cent to £714,000 before profits will dip below £50,000. That should take care of even the worst recession seen since the 1920s and 30s.

Now much of this will come as no surprise to you – after all most of this is your money, so naturally you are well informed as to where it goes. But the people who work for you have probably never considered (or been given the chance to consider) the phenomenal impact that relatively small savings in costs can have on the bottom line. So why not tell them? You could start by giving your key employees a copy of the above table and inviting their comments.

2. Use the 80/20 rule

Obviously, you can't leave the whole responsibility of reducing costs exclusively to the people who, after all, created the costs in the first place. Just as with any other business, task objectives have to be agreed and strategies adopted.

Fortunately, here you have the 80/20 rule working in your favour. This rule states that 80 per cent of effort goes into producing 20 per cent of the results. Look at Table 10.2 below, which was prepared for one company on a recent business training programme. This more or less confirms the rule, as 18 per cent of customers account for 78 per cent of sales.

Table 10.2 *The 80/20 rule in action*

Number of customers		Value of sales		Value of potential sales	
	%	£000	%	£000	%
4	3	710	69	1200	71
21	18	800	78	1500	88
47	41	918	90	1600	94
116	100	1,025	100	1700	100

A quick glance at figures in your own business will in all probability confirm that 20 per cent of your customers account for 80 per cent of your sales, and yet your costs are probably spread evenly across all your customers. Sales people tend to make their calls in a cycle that suits their administrative convenience, rather than concentrating on customers with the most potential.

Interestingly enough, when the salesman in the company used in the above example was asked where he thought his sales in two years' time would be coming from, (see column 3, Table 10.2) he felt that his top 18 per cent of customers would account for 88 per cent of sales (up from 78 per cent of actual sales this year). And yet an analysis of his call reports showed that he spent over 60 per cent of his time calling on his bottom 68 accounts, and planned to continue doing so. This 'activity' – rather than results-based – outlook was being used to make out a case for an additional salesperson. What was actually needed was a call grading system to lower the call rate on accounts with the least sales potential. So, for example, accounts with the least potential were called on twice a year and phoned twice, while top grade accounts were visited up to eight times a year.

This grading process saves costs, as phone calls are cheaper than visits; it eliminates the need for an additional salesperson, which at first glance the projected growth would have justified; and it even frees up time so the salesman can prospect for new, high potential accounts.

The 80/20 rule can be used across the business to uncover other areas where costs are being incurred that are unwarranted by the benefits. In some areas you just need to open your eyes to see waste. Did you know that the average executive spends 36 minutes a day looking for things on or around the desk? This can waste up to £6000 a year for a fairly senior person – you for example. The same survey conducted for the British Institute of Management, revealed that a quarter of the 500 executives they questioned spent 11 hours a week in meetings – equivalent to 13 weeks a year. Few were satisfied with their investment.

The chances are, if you are anything like many other UK chief executives, you feel that you and your management team waste too much time on the wrong priorities. It's not that managers aren't working hard enough – on average they work 20 per cent more hours than a decade ago. It's just that organising time and daily priorities in a world in which there has been a 600 per cent increase in business information, and the average manager is interrupted every eight minutes, is difficult to say the least. But the 'cost' of wasting time is very real in two senses. First, you end up buying more management than you need – and that cost has to be spread across your products. Second, people are too busy doing the wrong things to have time to do the right things.

3. Zero-based budgeting

The 80/20 rule is helpful in getting costs back into line – but what if the

179

line was completely wrong in the first place?

When you sit down with your team and discuss budgets, the arguments always revolve around how much more each section will need next year. The starting point is usually this year's costs, which are taken as the only 'facts' upon which to build. So, for example, if you spent £25,000 on advertising last year and achieved sales of £1m, the expense would have been 2.5 per cent of sales. If the sales budget for next year is £1.5m, then it seems logical to spend £37,500 next year. That, however, presupposes last year's sum was wisely and effectively spent in the first place, which it almost certainly wasn't.

Popularised in the 1970s by Robert McNamara, zero-based budgeting turns the cost argument on its head. It assumes that each year every cost centre starts from zero spending and, based on the goals of the business and the resources available, arguments are presented for every penny spent, *not just for the increase proposed*.

4.   Cut out mistakes, through training

According to Tom Frost, former Chief Executive of the National Westminster Bank, basic mistakes by employees account for between 25 and 40 per cent of the total costs of any service business – and not just in banking. It is certainly true that people learn from experience, and the more often they do a job, the faster and better they get at it (up to the stage where indifference sets in of course)! What a pity, however, that so many of Britain's smaller firms let their employees practise on their customers, losing money and goodwill in the process.

Training people, on a regular basis, in all aspects of their jobs, is a sure-fire way to reduce mistakes, and get costs down and customer satisfaction up. This is doubly important with the high staff turnover that is all too common today. Some short-sighted employers say: why train them when they stay for such a short time? Answer: it costs 2 per cent of salary to train them, which is less than 10 per cent of the cost of their mistakes, if Mr Frost is right. And once trained who knows, they may even get enough job satisfaction to want to stay – just think how much you'll save if that happens.

Training can be one of the fastest payback routes to cost reduction. One study carried out recently by a major American corporation, concluded that its productivity was improved by 5–20 per cent simply by explaining to people why their jobs matter. This single action saved it a net $9m, after training costs, over the past three years. You can even get government help, through the Enterprise Initiative, to train your staff (contact the Department of Trade and Industry or your local TEC for details of Training for Business Growth).

5.   Incentivise everyone around profit

Lots of companies have incentive schemes, but most end up rewarding the wrong achievement. Some firms actually reward people by how much they spend! So, for example, buyers with the biggest budget get the highest pay and perks. Production staff are paid for greater output and salespeople for more sales, whether or not either activity is particularly desirable at the time it is achieved. In one company (name withheld to protect the embarrassed) one of the largest creditor items on liquidation was sales people's commission.

There are always hundreds of reasons for giving people intermediate incentive, such as sales commission. But unless you build profit targets into your goals and incentives, nine times out of ten you'll end up with the wrong result. You get nothing if the company doesn't make a satisfactory profit, so rewarding others if they don't make money is only encouraging an illusion of reality.

Building incentives for everyone around the profit you make focuses the whole business around customers and costs, and that has to be good. It will make everyone look for: cheaper ways to do things, ways to eliminate waste; more effective ways to spend their time (and your money); and ways to get more money out of more satisfied customers – in short, all the ways to unlock the profit potential in your business.

Medic Aid

Figure 10.1 shows how one participant on a Cranfield business growth programme managed to increase his profit per unit of output. Mark Kirby of Medic Aid, a company that grew from £2m turnover per annum to over £4.5m within 18 months of attending the Cranfield programme, took a detailed look at everything they did with a view to increasing the profitability of every hour they worked. Each process was examined and made the subject of a brainstorming session. For example, one part of the manufacturing process of their nebuliser products required several hundred plastic parts to be tipped on to a table. Invariably, 50 or so fell off the table and were either damaged or took valuable seconds to recover. By putting a 3" high plastic rim around the table, at a cost of £5, the company saved two hours' production time per week. Several hundred simple ideas like this reduced the total production time for one key product by nearly 40 per cent.

The overall effect was quite staggering. At long last Medic Aid managed to grow both profit and sales. Unit profitability, which in the graph below is the difference between the sales line and the break-even line, got progressively bigger from December 1989 when the profit improvement programme (PIP) was introduced. By December 1990 the company was making six times as much profit as before.

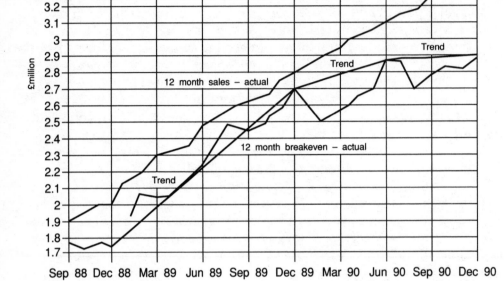

Figure 10.1 *Reducing production time and increasing profits, Medic Aid Ltd*

One final thought on internal sources of finance: do you really need to do everything you do yourself? If you don't you could release all the working capital and fixed capital tied up in that process and use it for better things.

> *For example, Mark Kirby of Medic Aid subcontracted his low value-added production processes to a subcontractor who could actually make them more cheaply. The subcontractor took on the commitment to buy raw material and hold stocks, and Mark used the factory space saved for better things.*

The story below is another example of how this concept can work successfully.

> *No manufacturing. No salesmen. No research and development. Mrs Tina Knight has grown her company from a £4000 launch five years ago to a turnover of £2m a year as much by deciding what not to do as by what she has to sell.*
>
> *She is managing director of Nighthawk Electronics, based at Debden, Essex. The company supplies switches for computer equipment, the kind of gadget that, for example, allows half a dozen personal computers to use one printer between them.*
>
> *She says: 'I didn't want to get into manufacturing myself, but I save myself the headaches. Why should I start manufacturing as long as I've got my bottom line*

right? Turnover is vanity, profit is sanity. I have run companies for other people and I do not have to grow big just for the kudos.' Instead Mrs Knight contracts out to factories in Derby and Bedford. She feels she still has control over quality, since any item that is not up to standard can be sent back. She also has the ultimate threat of taking trade away, which would leave the manufacturers she uses with a large void to fill. *'We would do so if quality was not good enough. Many manufacturers have under-utilised capacity.'*

Mrs Knight uses freelance salesmen on a commission basis. She explains: *'I didn't want a huge salesforce. Most sales managers sit in their cars at the side of the road filling in swindle sheets. Research and development is another area where expenses would be terrific. We have freelance design teams working on specific products. We give them a brief and they quote a price. The cost still works out at twice what you expected, but at least you have a measure of control. I could not afford to employ R & D staff full time and I would not need them full time. Our system minimises the risks and gives us a quality we could not afford as a small company.'*

Indirectly, the tight knit staff of 12 at Debden control and provide work for about 380 elsewhere.

External sources of funds

There are two fundamentally different types of external money which a growing company can tap into: debt and equity. Debt is money borrowed, usually from a bank, and which one day you will have to repay. While you are making use of borrowed money you will also have to pay interest on the loan. Equity is the money put in by shareholders, including the proprietor, and money left in the business by way of retained profit. You don't have to give the shareholders their money back, but they do expect the directors to increase the value of their shares, and if you go public they will probably expect a stream of dividends too. If you don't meet the shareholders' expectations, they won't be there when you need more money – or if they are powerful enough they will take steps to change the board.

Why is borrowing attractive?

High gearing is the name given when a business has a high proportion of outside money to inside money. High gearing has considerable attractions to a business which wants to make high returns on shareholders' capital, as the example in Figure 10.2 shows.

In this example the business is assumed to need £60,000 capital to generate £10,000 operating profits. Four different capital structures are considered. They range from all share capital (no gearing) at one end, to nearly all loan capital at the other. The loan capital has to be 'serviced', that is, interest of 12 per cent has to be paid. The loan itself can be relatively indefinite, simply being replaced by another one at market interest rates when the first loan expires.

		No gearing –	Average gearing 1:1	High gearing 2:1	Very high gearing 3:1
Capital structure		£	£	£	£
Share Capital		60,000	30,000	20,000	15,000
Loan Capital (at 12%)		–	30,000	40,000	45,000
Total Capital		60,000	60,000	60,000	60,000
Profits					
Operating Profit		10,000	10,000	10,000	10,000
Less interest on Loan		None	3,600	4,800	5,400
Net Profit		10,000	6,400	5,200	4,600
Return on Share Capital	=	10,000	6,400	5,200	4,600
		60,000	30,000	20,000	15,000
	=	16.6%	21.3%	26%	30.7%
Times Interest	=	N/A	10,000	10,000	10,000
Earned			3,600	4,800	5,400
	=	N/A	2.3X	2.1X	1.8X

Figure 10.2 *The effect of gearing on ROSC*

Following the tables through you can see that ROSC grows from 16.6 to 30.7 per cent by virtue of the changed gearing. If the interest on the loan were lower, the ROSC would be even more improved by high gearing, and the higher the interest the lower the relative improvement in ROSC. So in times of low interest, businesses tend to go for increased borrowings rather than raising more equity, that is money from shareholders.

At first sight this looks like a perpetual profit growth machine. Naturally owners would rather have someone else lend them the money for their business than put it in themselves, if they could increase the return on their investment. The problem comes if the business does not produce £10,000 operating profits. Very often, in a small business, a drop in sales of 20 per cent means profits are halved or even eliminated. If profits were halved in this example, it could not meet the interest payments on its loan. That would make the business insolvent, and so not in a 'sound financial position', in other words, failing to meet one of the two primary business objectives.

Bankers tend to favour 1:1 gearing as the maximum for a small business, although they have been known to go much higher (a glance at the Laker accounts will show just how far the equation can be taken, with £200m plus of loans to £1m or so equity). Gearing (9) can be more usefully expressed as the percentage of shareholders' funds (share capital plus reserves), to all the long-term capital in the business. So 1:1 is the same as saying 50 per cent gearing.

What balance of debt to equity is right?

A company's gearing will be continuously changing depending on the growth opportunities it sees ahead, the current cost of money and the availability of equity and debt capital. At certain times it is hard to raise more money from shareholders, for example when the general stock market is depressed, or if your profit performance is not up to the mark. Banks or other lenders may be your only hope. Conversely, when the conditions are right, companies frequently raise more share capital to fund growth, well in advance of needing the cash.

Verson International, the West Midlands-based machining manufacturer, raised £10m of extra share capital via a rights issue in the summer of 1990. Mr Tim Kelleher, chairman and chief executive, said the issue, which would halve gearing to close to 53 per cent, would give the group the flexibility to make further acquisitions in the next 12 months.

The board and the two venture capital organisations which have been backing the management and own about 63 per cent of the equity agreed to waive their rights to the issue. Their stake was pre-placed at a premium with institutional investors at a price of 43.5p.

The institutions were underwriting the remainder of the two-for-seven issue, which is being made at 40p, about a 15 per cent discount to the market. According to the annual report released with details of the rights issue, Verson's order book has risen from £80m to £94m since May 1991.

Bankers would generally favour a 1:1 relationship between borrowed funds and share capital. But the nature of the risks involved in your business strategy is a more important factor to consider, rather than pursuing this symmetrical relationship of numbers. A more useful way to look at the debt–equity relationship is to compare money risk to business risk (Figure 10.3).

	Gambling	OK
	OK	Unsatisfactory return

High (top left) / Low (bottom left) — *Business Risk*

Debt — High Risk — Equity — Low Risk

Funding Risk

Figure 10.3 *Funding matrix*

If your business sector is generally viewed as very risky, and perhaps the most reliable measure of that risk is the proportion of firms that go bust, then financing the business almost exclusively with borrowings is tantamount to gambling. Debt has to be serviced whatever your business performance, so it follows that in any risky, volatile market-place, one day you stand a good chance of being caught out. Building firms are a good example of a high risk business sector, who almost always use high risk money. The fallacy is to believe that because houses were thought to be a relatively risk free investment, building them was a safe enterprise too. It's no surprise that building firms top the bankruptcy rolls in both boom years and recessions. A glance at Figure 10.4 will confirm this view.

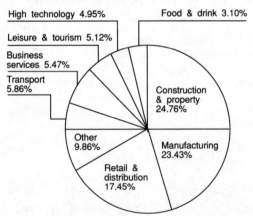

Figure 10.4 *Industry analysis of receivership appointments 1990*
Source: KPMG Peat Marwick McLintock

If your business risks are low, the chances are that your profits are relatively low too. High profits and low risks always attract a flood of competitors, reducing your profits to levels that ultimately reflect the riskiness of your business sector. As venture capitalists and share-holders generally are looking for much better returns than they could get by lending the money, it follows they will be disappointed in their investment on low risk, low return business. So if they are wise they won't get in in the first place, or if they do they won't put any more money in later.

With the funding matrix in mind you can begin to work towards a balance of debt and equity that is appropriate for your business. Very often you will find it attractive to raise both sides of the equation at the same time, as Helene's have done.

Helene, the clothing maker and textile merchant, has announced a £2.62million rights issue to fund its expansion. The company plans to offer 14.4m new shares at 20p each on a 1-for-4 basis. The share price shed 1p recently to close at 24p.

Mr Monty Burkeman, chairman and joint managing director, said the company's sales had grown by 50 per cent last year to £62m – the pre-tax profit was £4.1m. In the first five months of this year turnover was 22 per cent ahead of the comparable period. 'We need to finance it', he said. Mr Burkeman explained that Helene needed to have the capacity to get orders ready for its retail customers, who would have arranged to take delivery at any time over a three-month period. The issue has been fully underwritten by Allied Provincial Securities. Helene has also arranged a £5m unsecured term loan with National Westminster.

What financiers look out for

Successful entrepreneurs with a proven track record can have as many problems raising finance for their ventures as can the relative novice.

Bob Payton, who founded the Chicago Pizza Pie Factory in the late 1970s, related a story at Cranfield making exactly this point.

'I now have a ten-year track record in the hospitality business. My company had a turnover of £10m this year, and made a profit of £1m. But the one constant problem I have had for the past ten years has been raising finance to put my ideas into practice. Getting the £4.5m for my latest venture, Stapleford Park, a country house hotel in Leicestershire will, by the time it opens in May, have taken three years. It has been as difficult and as gut-wrenching as trying to raise £35,000 for my first place, the Chicago Pizza Pie Factory.

Originally EMI had agreed to back my first venture. We'd shaken hands on the deal and I had ordered the ovens and gone off to the States to learn how to make pizza. When I came back I got a 'Dear John' letter. They'd decided, on reflection, not to go ahead. I have that letter still, framed and hanging on the wall in my office. After a lot of trouble I finally raised the money elsewhere and went ahead. EMI were subsequently proved to be wrong.'

Financiers' needs

Anyone lending money to or investing in a venture will expect the entrepreneur to have given some thought to his needs, and to have explained how they can be accommodated in the business plan.

Bankers, and indeed any other sources of debt capital, are looking for asset security to back their loan and the near certainty of getting their money back. They will also charge an interest rate which reflects current market conditions and their view of the risk level of the proposal. Depending on the nature of the business in question and the purpose for which the money is being used, bankers will take a five- to fifteen-year view.

As with a mortgage repayment, bankers will usually expect a business to start repaying both the loan and the interest on a monthly or quarterly basis immediately the loan has been granted. In some cases a capital 'holiday' for up to two years can be negotiated, but in the early stage of any loan the interest charges make up the lion's share of payments.

Bankers hope the business will succeed so that they can lend more money in the future and provide more banking services such as insurance, tax advice etc to a loyal customer. It follows from this appreciation of a lender's needs that they are less interested in rapid growth and the consequent capital gain than they are in a steady stream of earnings almost from the outset.

As most new or fast growing businesses generally do not make immediate profits, money for such enterprises must come from elsewhere. Risk or equity capital, as other types of funds are called, comes from venture capital houses, as well as being put in by founders, their families and friends. Because the inherent risks involved in investing in new and young ventures are greater than for investing in established companies, venture capital fund managers have to offer their investors the chance of larger overall returns. To do that, fund managers must not only keep failures to a minimum; they have to pick some big winners too – ventures with annual compound growth rates above 50 per cent – to offset the inevitable mediocre performers.

Debbie Moore's Pineapple dance studios was one such company. Introduced to the Unlisted Securities Market (USM) in 1982 by its venture capital providers, its shares quickly went to an 85 per cent premium. Profits rose by 50 per cent in 1983, as forecast, and the company raised a further £1.5m via a rights issue. Ms Moore was even given the coveted Businesswoman of the Year award.

But this time the moneymen were not so fortunate. In 1985 aerobics began to lose its popular appeal as health experts cast doubts on its efficacy. By May the company was in a nosedive, showing half-year losses of £197,000. In the latter half of 1985 Peter Bain, a new boardroom recruit, evolved a strategy to turn the company into a marketing services group. After several acquisitions and a total change of direction, Pineapple reported profits of £1.25m in 1986.

But the dance studios clearly couldn't be made to work. 'It soon became obvious', to quote Moore, 'that it was difficult to deliver the kind of money the City wanted out of dance'. Ms Moore resigned from the Pineapple Group in December 1987, taking the loss-making dance studios with her for a nominal sum, leaving the rest of the Group to pursue its new strategy.

Typically, a fund manager would expect from any ten investments: one start, seven also-rans, and two flops. It is important to remember that despite this outcome, venture capital fund managers are only looking for winners, so unless you are projecting high capital growth, the chances of getting venture capital are against you.

Not only are venture capitalists looking for winners, they are also looking for a substantial shareholding in your business. There are no simple rules for what constitutes a fair split, but *Venture Capital Report*, a UK monthly publication of investment opportunities, suggests the following starting point:

For the idea	33 per cent
For the management	33 per cent
For the money	34 per cent

It all comes down to how much you need the money, how risky the venture is, how much money could be made – and your skills as a negotiator. However, it is salutary to remember that 100 per cent of nothing is still nothing. So all parties to the deal have to be satisfied if it is to succeed.

Venture capital firms may also want to put a non-executive director on the board of your company to look after their interests. You will have at your disposal a talented financial brain, so be prepared to make use of him, as his services won't be free – you'll either pay up front in the fee for raising the capital, or you'll pay an annual management charge.

As fast-growing companies typically have no cash available to pay dividends, investors can only profit by selling their holdings. With this in mind the venture capitalist needs to have an exit route such as the Stock Exchange or a potential corporate buyer in view at the outset.

Unlike many entrepreneurs (and some lending bankers) who see their ventures as life-long commitments to success and growth, venture capitalists have a relatively short time horizon. Typically, they are looking to liquidate small company investments within three to seven years, allowing them to pay out individual investors and to have funds available for tomorrow's winners. So, to be successful your business must be targeted at the needs of these two sources of finance (see Figure 10.5).

Lenders (any safe bet)	Investors (winners only)
• Security and low risk • 5–15 year horizon • Ability to pay back loan and interest immediately • Conservative growth • Small sums, with frequent top-ups • No share of future profits but want a loyal long-term customer • No management involvement	• High risk • But high returns • 35% compound growth minimum • Short time horizon, 3–7 years • But no payments until the end of the deal • Exit route evident at outset – Back to founders – Trade buyer – USM etc • Substantial shareholding – For the idea 33% – For management 33% – For money 34% • Hands on involvement • Large sums, with few top-ups

Figure 10.5 *Financiers' needs*

Sources of funds

There are many useful directories and guides to all the sources of funds for a growing business. It would be superfluous to list them again here, or to describe such terms as overdraft, loan, hire purchase, etc. We've concentrated rather on covering the areas that, in our experience, growing firms have often neglected and should certainly address if they are planning significant growth.

Debt capital

The banks are the principal sources of debt capital. As you can see from Table 10.3 the clearing banks are the principal, and sometimes the only, supplier of funds to small and growing businesses. However, the days when you could expect to cultivate a lifetime relationship with either a bank or a bank manager are long gone. Banks are into market segmentation and profit generation, so you need to be prepared to: (a) shop around and (b) manage your relationship with the bank carefully.

As a rough guide, if you are with the same bank for over five years you haven't pushed them hard enough. There are a myriad things to negotiate with your bank, and there is even a new breed of consultants who advise on banking relationships.

Table 10.3 *The principal providers*

Source	Usual financial range		Total per annum
	£000 Min	£ million Max	
Junior Stockmarkets	600	3,200	300
Business Expansion Scheme			
Private Sources	5	155	70
Funds	50	2,000	40
Venture Capital	50	5,000+	300
3i	10	1,000	320
Government loan	1	75	75
Guarantee scheme			
Bank lending	(at present around £20,000 million lent)		
Local Enterprise Boards	85	100	18
Hire purchase	–	–	8,000 total
Leasing	–	–	14,000 total
Factoring	25,000+		4,000 total
Competition	0.4	30	1
Rural Development Commission	1	75	–
Tourist Boards (up to 50%)		300	–
British Overseas Trade Board	–		240
Enterprise Allowance	2		

Matched borrowing

This is a method of getting finance which matches the money against the security of a particular asset. The principal types of matched borrowing are factoring, leasing and hire purchase. The last two most people have explored, but for a variety of reasons many growing companies are highly resistant to using factoring, which is a great pity because it can often be very attractive. The next section is, therefore, devoted to an examination of this under-used financial option.

Factoring comes in a variety of forms

In the full service, as non-recourse factoring is known in the trade, the factoring company takes over once you have delivered your goods (or services) to the customer. All you have to do is send the factor a duplicate invoice, and from then on they assume responsibility for your sales ledger. The factor thus not only has the task of collecting the cash, but also carries the can if the customer doesn't pay up. You can draw on up to 80 per cent of the value of the invoice immediately, and the balance when the customer pays up – or a set number of days after the invoice has been sent out.

For this service you will pay between 0.5 and 3.5 per cent of your turnover, and an interest charge of between 2 and 3.5 per cent over bank base rate on any money advanced. A small setting-up charge of £500–plus will also be made, and normally a minimum level will be set on the service charge – £200 to £300 being a fairly typical base level.

Invoice discounting is the service for companies who want the cash advancing facilities offered by the factor and very little else. The service costs for invoice discounting range between 0.2 and 0.7 per cent of turnover, much lower than for the full service. But in return you have to chase up customers for the money and assume responsibility for any bad debts. Invoice discounting is the fastest growing service in the factoring package, accounting for nearly 45 per cent of all business – up from 20 per cent in 1981.

What's in it for you?

So factoring is on the increase. But exactly what benefits could it bring your business?

- **Helps to avoid over-trading.** Unless you are in a service industry, and you are lucky enough to have your clients pay up front, the faster you get new orders the more cash you consume. You have to pay for raw materials and labour to put products on the market before your customers pay up. If you are not careful the eager pursuit of new business can lead to the cash flow disaster known as 'over-trading'. By factoring your debtors you can get the cash to finance growth as quickly as you can find creditworthy customers and deliver products or services to them.
- **Balancing cash requirements.** The classic source of short-term funds for a small business is an overdraft. Unfortunately, over-drafts seem to be very much a feast-or-famine affair, with facilities being increased when you don't need funds, and the supply restricted sharply when you do. This paradox is not caused exclusively by the bloody-mindedness of short-sighted bank managers – though that surely must play its part. Rather, the problem arises because overdraft limits are usually determined by using historical balance sheet ratios. Hence bankers are always examining the entrails of the past for guidance, while entrepreneurs are extolling the opportunities for the future.

In situations of rapid growth the banker's advice is often 'consolidate', while the factor will say 'go for it'. The factor is able to respond in this way because he is in daily or weekly contact with his client and sees the flow of invoices and payment cheques, in contrast to the banker who often works from out-of-date audited accounts, and only a hazy recollection of what you do and for whom.

- **Improves your operating margins.** By being able to match the cash available to the level of your business activity you can get two important benefits that should have an immediate and positive effect on your operating margins.

First, you can negotiate the finest terms from your suppliers – a luxury usually only available to those who can pay up promptly. Otherwise you have to buy what you need, whenever you can, when you can afford it – not a recipe for great economy.

Secondly, with a predictable cash flow, you can plan production schedules and stockholding in a manufacturing business, to optimise plant efficiencies. This is in sharp contrast to those whose cash shortages force them to move labour and materials around in a haphazard way which inevitably results in more down-time, higher unit labour costs and more material wastage.

- **You can concentrate on what you do best – running the business.** Once you start to view your customers simply as debtors, your marketing focus will become blurred. In any event, the chances are that you are better at making and selling than you are at playing policeman, chasing up late payers. Factoring allows you to concentrate on what you do best, and leaving them to their field – collecting cash.

We know of one company that used to take 90 days to collect money from customers, which is now down to 50 on average a year after introducing factoring. It also leaves your sales people's relationships with customers intact, rather than damaging them through constant pestering for payment. They can also spend more time on selling which should pay handsome dividends. If it doesn't, look carefully at exactly what your salespeople are doing.

- **You can trim overheads.** Not only can factoring allow you to spend more time on managing the business rather than the sales ledger, but you can save the overhead cost currently incurred in running your own credit control department. One company we know gets a factoring service for £12,000 per annum – less than the cost of employing a credit controller and finding a desk for them to sit at!

Factoring will also allow you to optimise the resources needed to collect cash, rather than using the blitz approach that is common to so many small firms. In other words, the effort put into cash collection is always maintained in proportion to the amount of cash to be collected – a feat near impossible to attain when you run your own credit control. The chances are you'll get a more professional service into the bargain, when it comes to such matters as assessing credit risk and insuring against bad debts.

- **Factoring is a source of off-balance-sheet finance.** Under current accounting conventions it is not necessary to reveal how much of the business's funds have been made available from factoring. This means that key balance sheet ratios such as gearing and return on capital employed will be influenced in favour of companies using factoring. Suppose, for example, your present financial structure involved using £100,000 of share capital and reserves, and £100,000 of bank loans: your gearing would be 50 per cent.

If you need a further £100,000 to finance growth and you borrow it from the bank, your gearing would increase to 67 per cent. This would make your business look more risky to any outside observer, such as a potential supplier, customer, or new shareholder. If the extra funds came from factoring your debtors, you could finance the growth – and your gearing ratio would remain unchanged at 50 per cent.

The same argument holds for the return on capital employed (ROCE) ratio. The higher you make the bottom of the equation, the lower the ratio will be for any given level of profit. Once again, the lower your ROCE, the worse your business appears to be performing in the eyes of the financial world.

Of course, loan capital is not the only type of money available to the growing firm. You could raise more share capital – but this route can be expensive and time-consuming and it will dilute your stake in the business. All in all, there will be occasions when factoring is infinitely preferable to taking on board new shareholders.

Can anyone use a factor?

The popular mythology is that only big manufacturing companies can make use of factoring services. Nothing could be further from the truth. Less than half the users of factoring services provided by the Association of British Factors, the main trade organisation for the industry, are in manufacturing. Nearly 70 per cent of users have a turnover below £1m and only 5 per cent have a turnover greater than £5m.

Nevertheless, it is undoubtedly true that providers of relatively uncomplicated goods, services and raw materials are the most attractive type of client from the factor's point of view. This is simply because invoices in this arena are not usually open to dispute in the same way that more complex plant, equipment and major projects are.

When it comes to invoice discounting, the fastest growing sector of this market – where the factor is more exposed to his clients' competence at assessing risk and collecting cash – more stringent criteria apply. Here the factor will be looking for companies with a minimum net worth of around £50,000; turnover in excess of £500,000; goods and services being sold on terms no greater than net 30 days; an efficient sales ledger and credit assessment system in place; and a good spread of debtors with no single customer accounting for more than 30 per cent of debts outstanding.

Before being taken on as a customer for invoice discounting you can expect a visit from the factor's 'heavies'. They will examine your credit control systems in great detail and, on the basis of their findings, agree to provide one of three levels of financial facility: all invoices on all customers; all invoices on selected customers; certain invoices on selected customers, as and when agreed. You can expect your factor to keep in close contact with you thereafter – monthly at least and weekly, perhaps even daily, at the outset.

Who are the factors?

This sector of financial services is dominated by subsidiaries of the clearing banks, but they certainly don't have the market all to themselves. The last few years have seen the entry of a number of new players. S & W Berisford, the food and commodities group, launched Berisford Factors in 1988 with a view to providing companies with the opportunity to diversify their sources of finance, and not simply draw their factoring facility from the bank with which they have loan and overdraft facilities. Also, being relatively small themselves, Berisford Factors expected to appeal to those who would rather deal with a more 'human' organisation.

Another new entrant is Trade Indemnity (TI), the UK credit insurance group, which moved into factoring in January 1989, taking a 50 per cent share in an established firm, H & H Factors.

Of the clearing banks, Lloyds is the most significant force in the market, owning both Alex Laurie Factors and International Factors. National Westminster Bank owns Lombard NatWest Commercial Services, Midland Bank has Griffith Factors, the Royal Bank of Scotland has Royscot Factors, and the TSB has UDT Commercial

Finance. Even Barclays Bank, who pulled out of factoring in 1983, returned in 1987 by buying up 75 per cent of Arbuthnot Factors and renaming them Barclays Commercial Services. The Bank of Scotland entered the market the same year, taking a 95 per cent stake in Kellock.

The industry is loosely clustered under the Association of British Factors and Discounters, 1 Northumberland Avenue, Trafalgar Square, London WC2N 5BW; telephone 0171 930 9112.

Shareholders' funds

There are three principal vehicles for attracting new investors to help finance your growth plans.

Venture capital

In the decade to 1990, the UK Venture Capital Industry grew from a score of firms investing £66m a year, to over 200 who back new and growing firms to the tune of £1.65 billion. The UK venture capital industry is the largest in Europe and second only to the USA in world importance. The largest player in this market is 3i (Investors in Industry) formed in 1945, who account for around half of all this type of funding. They are the only venture capital firm with a comprehensive UK regional office structure. We have already examined what venture capitalists are looking for earlier in this chapter. You can contact these firms via a number of routes.

The British Venture Capital Association, 3 St Catherine's Place, London SW1E 6DX; telephone 0171 233 5212, publish an annual directory of providers, free each year.

Accountants Peat Marwick McLintock, in conjunction with the journal *Venture Economics*, also maintain a comprehensive database of venture capitalists. This allows them to extract, on a selective basis, details of various capital sources as potential investment candidates. For further details contact: *Peat Marwick McLintock*, 1 Puddle Dock, Blackfriars, London EC4V 3PD; telephone 0171 236 8000.

Business angels

For small sums of money, from a few thousand pounds upwards, you could contact a business angel. An angel is a private individual who is willing to put their money and perhaps their efforts into your business. Various industry estimates suggest that upwards of £6.5m of angels' money is looking for investment homes. Not only will angels put in smaller sums of money than conventional venture capital providers, they will be more prepared to back start-ups and riskier projects – if the chemistry is right.

So how do you get in contact with an angel? You will need to use an introductory agency or 'marriage bureau' such as LINC, who circulate to subscribing investors a regular bulletin of abbreviated information on business projects. If you are seeking finance through LINC you should submit a business plan indicating the amount of finance required (sample plans and counselling services are available). Having once been accepted as a bona fide proposal you will be charged a small fee for as many bulletin entries (around 50 words) as are felt necessary. Also, a longer, two-page summary business plan will be prepared to help any enquirers requesting further details. There are now 20 local enterprise agencies in the LINC Network, covering much of the country. You can obtain more details from: LINC, 4 Snow Hill, London EC1A 2BS (telephone 0171 236 3000).

Enterprise Investment Scheme (EIS)

The whole angels sector was given a boost in the 1993 Budget with the introduction of the *Enterprise Investment Scheme* (EIS). The key features of the scheme, which is intended to raise £60 million a year for small firms, are:

- Up-front tax relief at 20 per cent in investments of qualifying unquoted equity
- No tax on capital gains
- Income and capital gains tax relief on losses
- A maximum annual investment of £100,000
- Companies may raise up to £1m a year
- Investors may become paid directors.

Venture Capital Report (VCR)

VCR is a monthly publication of investment opportunities circulated to about 900 subscribers. Each issue contains details of ten or so business projects. VCR charges a flat fee for preparing articles and, in addition, a percentage fee on any risk capital raised. VCR have their own small seed-corn fund, and back a number of ventures themselves. You can obtain more details from: *VCR*, Boston Road, Henley on Thames, Berkshire RG9 1DY; telephone 01491 579999.

A useful annual guide to the whole venture capital industry is VCR's *Guide to the Venture Capital Industry in the UK*. This gives pointers to each company's particular performance, and their method of operation. As you can see from Table 10.4, it's not only high tech ventures that appeal to venture capitalists.

Table 10.4 *Venture capitalists' preferred industries*

	Jan 1991	June 1990
Engineering	1	1
Communications	2	2
Health care	3	3
Chemical	4	5
Leisure	5	6
Electronics	6	4
Publishing & education	7	8
Other services	8	7
Computer services	9	9
Computer software	10	10
High-technology	11	11
Bio-technology	12	14
Financial services	13	13
Computer hardware	14	12
Advertising & marketing	15	15
Entertainment	16	19
Hotels & restaurants	17	17
Property & construction	18	16
Film industry	19	18

The *BBC Small Business Guide,* published bi-annually, gives a directory of all sources of capital for the growing business.

Going public

There are two possible stock markets on which to gain a public listing. A full Stock Exchange listing calls for profits of at least £1m. In practice, unless there are exceptional circumstances, most advisers will insist on profits of between £2m and £3m. A full listing also calls for at least 25 per cent of the company's shares being put up for sale at the outset. In addition, you would be expected to have 100 shareholders now and be able to demonstrate that 100 more will come on board as a result of the listing. This is rarely an appealing idea to entrepreneurs, who expect to see their share price rise in later years, and are loath to sell off so much of the business at what they believe to be a bargain basement price. There is also the threat of a takeover with so many of the shares in so many people's hands.

The Alternative Investment Market (AIM) is a much more attractive proposition for entrepreneurs seeking equity capital. Formed in 1995 specifically to provide risk capital for new rather than established ventures, it has an altogether more relaxed atmosphere. After the failure of the Third Market and the imminent demise of the Unlisted Securities Market, some may ask why the Stock Exchange is bothering to start another secondary share exchange.

AIM was conceived after pressure, mainly from venture capitalists who want a way of investing in companies and realising their profits more quickly.

The authorities accept that small companies suffer generally from a scarcity of investment capital in relatively small amounts. This is an attempt to bridge the gap. The Stock Exchange decided it was easier to start again rather than amend existing rules.

AIM will replace two existing secondary markets. The Unlisted Securities Market, which enjoyed success in the 1980s but will close at the end of 1996, has ceased to be distinct from the official list – the main part of the stock market – partly because European securities laws enforce similar entry requirements.

Costs of joining the USM have risen, making it hardly any cheaper to join. The Rule 4.2 market, which tries to match buyers and sellers of blocks of shares, is not really a market, but an occasional trading facility. Frequently there is no match, leaving the would-be seller with highly illiquid shares. The Stock Exchange hopes AIM will mean lower costs, greater liquidity, and a higher profile for small companies.

AIM will be a separate, less regulated market, run by an independent management team with its own marketing arm, although it will still be part of the Stock Exchange. The shares are not alternatives to mainstream shares.

Small, young and growing companies are likely to be attracted. They may be management buy-outs or buy-ins, family-owned companies, former Business Expansion Scheme companies or even start-up businesses.

Around 75 are expected to join the market in its first year. A young company which may be typical is The Old English Pub Company, which recently raised £2m to refurbish run-down pubs and hopes to be one of the first to trade on AIM. 'Whatever we do, we have always been very aggressive', said managing director Barry Warwick.

Pan Andean Resources, an exploration company, will also join AIM but is not alone in voicing disquiet about the cost. Some companies have been asked to pay up to £100,000 to advisers, but Pan Andean is paying only £25,000.

A public flotation is a major project and proprietors would be well advised to plan some three years ahead to ensure that the company is in the best possible shape when it comes to the Market. The objective must be to present a sound profit record and balance sheet, along with prospects of further growth, which will make the company attractive to investors.

As you draw up your flotation plan and timetable, according to accountants Touche Ross, you should have the following matters in mind:

- **Advisers.** You will need to be supported by a team which will include a sponsor, stockbroker, reporting accountant and solicitor. These should be respected firms, active in flotation work and familiar with the company's type of business. You and your company may be judged by the company you keep, so choose advisers of good repute and make sure that the personalities work effectively together. It is very unlikely that a small local firm of accountants, however satisfactory, will be up to this task.

- **Sponsor.** You will need to appoint a financial institution, usually a merchant banker, to fill this important role. If you do not already have a merchant bank in mind your accountant will offer guidance. The job of the sponsor is to co-ordinate and drive the project forward.

- **Timetable.** It is essential to have a timetable for the final months during the run-up to a float – and to adhere to it. The company's directors and senior staff will be fully occupied in providing information and attending meetings. They will have to delegate and there must be sufficient back-up support to ensure that the business does not suffer.

- **Management team.** A potential investor will want to be satisfied that your company is well managed; at board level and below. It is important to ensure succession, perhaps by offering key directors and managers service agreements and share options. It is wise to draw on the experience of well-qualified non-executive directors.

- **Accounts.** The objective is to have a profit record which is rising but, in achieving this, you will need to take into account directors' remuneration, pension contributions and the elimination of any expenditure which might be acceptable in a privately owned company but would not be acceptable in a public company, namely excessive perks such as yachts, luxury cars, lavish expense accounts and holiday homes.

  Accounts must be consolidated and audited to appropriate accounting standards and the audit reports must not contain any major qualifications. The auditors will need to be satisfied that there are proper stock records and a consistent basis of valuing stock during the years prior to flotation. Accounts for the last three years (two years in respect of the USM) will need to be disclosed and the date of the last accounts must be within six months (nine months for the USM) of the issue.

The rewards

Over the eleven years of the USM's existence more than 500 entrepreneurs have been made millionaires. The top USM millionaires are John Aspinall, the Kent zoo-keeper, and Sir James Goldsmith. They shared £48m in equal halves when the Aspinall Casino Group was floated. In fact, going public is about the only way you can become seriously rich in business and stay in control of your company. With venture capital you are always susceptible to the pressures of the capital providers. They want an exit route so they can plough their clients' funds into new and 'even more exciting ventures', so if the opportunity for a trade sale comes along the chances are they'll sell you to the highest bidder. This may make you rich, but it's unlikely to make you seriously rich and it will certainly leave you in the passenger seat rather than the driver's.

Banks, as we have already discussed, are largely fair weather friends, and you certainly won't get rich borrowing more from them.

Going public also puts a stamp of respectability on you and your company. It will enhance the status and credibility of your business, and it will enable you to borrow more against the 'security' provided by your new shareholders, should you so wish. Your shares will also provide an attractive way to retain and motivate key staff. By giving, or rather allowing them to earn, share options at discounted prices, they too can participate in the capital gains you are making. With a public share listing you can now join in the takeover and asset stripping game. When your share price is high and things are going well you can look out for weaker firms to gobble up – all you have to do is to offer them more of your shares in return for theirs. You don't even have to find real money. But of course this is a two-sided game and you may also now become the target of a hostile bid.

The penalties

So much for the rewards. The penalties are equally awesome, and they can happen before you even get a listing, as described in the story below.

Kevin McNeany, founder and managing director of Nord Anglia Education, spent four months and £300,000 preparing his company for a flotation on the Unlisted Securities Market (USM). In December 1990, on the day before the price of the issue was due to be announced, McNeany decided that his company, which runs 16 private schools and five language schools, was being valued too cheaply and cancelled the flotation.

'I wasn't willing to accept the price because it was 20 per cent less than what had been suggested before', says McNeany, a former teacher who, over the past 18 years, has built up a company with turnover of £8.2m and pre-tax profits of £610,000.

'My financial advisers said: "You can't do this", I said: "I am'", recalls McNeany. Disappointed, despondent and £300,000 poorer, McNeany took the train back to Manchester from London to renegotiate credit lines with his bankers which he had thought the flotation would render unnecessary.

The next penalty is that public companies come under the greater scrutiny of a larger and more perceptive investment community. For example, Spice, the motor parts distributor which went into receivership in 1990, was scuppered in its first attempt to join the USM when the Stock Exchange found out that the financial controller had been convicted of fraud. Another company that came unstuck after its flotation was Sharp and Law, a shopfitter, which joined the Unlisted Securities Market in 1987. Two years later, it discovered errors in its 1987 figures when payments for some large contracts had been double-counted. Arthur Young, the accountants, who were called in to investigate, produced a report calling for improvements to the company's senior financial management, the appointment of a managing director, and organisational systems and computer department review. The company never recovered, however, and went into receivership in 1990.

You may also find that being in the public eye not only cramps your style but it fills up your engagement diary too. Most entrepreneurs find that they have to spend up to a quarter of their time 'in the City' explaining their strategies, in the months preceding and the first years following their going public. It's not unusual for so much management time to have been devoted to answering accountants' and stockbrokers' questions that there is not enough time to run the day-to-day business, and profits drop as a direct consequence.

The City also creates its own pressure both to seduce companies on to the market and then expect them to perform beyond any reasonable expectation.

For example, Michael Aukett, chief executive of Aukett the architectural practice, is less sure that he would not reconsider his options if he had his time again. Aukett went public in February 1988 and maintained its steady promise in June 1990 by turning in highly respectable interims. Profits shot up 24 per cent to

£947,000. Yet Mr Aukett said: 'The City is responsible for creating the hype that any size of business should go on the market, but architectural firms are basically too small. We don't begin to command any position under a market capitalisation of £50m.'

With the benefit of hindsight, Mr Aukett believes now that he would have waited another three years to grow bigger before tangling with the institutions: 'They seduce you to go in and when the market goes on its knees, they don't support you. How do our shareholding staff feel when they see the market dip?'

One final penalty worth mentioning is the apparent lack of a direct relationship between the business's profit performance and its share price. Confidence, rumour and the sentiment for certain business sectors which fall in and out of favour, all play a part in moving share prices up and down – and at the end of the day that's all public shareholders and city institutions care about. Polly Peck is a fairly vivid example of this problem. The auditor's report dated 17 April 1990 showed the company had made £161m profit and the share price stood at 417p, making the company worth £2bn, on paper. By 20 September the company's shares were suspended at 108p on the back of rumours about alleged share dealing irregularities. A month later the company went into administrative receivership and the shares were declared 'worthless'.

Whatever the downside risk on going public it's as well to remember that several thousand private companies go bust for every public company that goes under. In the long run, the only realistic way to get big, very rich and survive is to go public.

Other ways to fund growth

Industry backers

Safetynet is a company that specialises in providing back-up computer services for companies whose computer systems are put out of action in the short term by fire, flood or even human error.

Set up in 1986 by two former IBM salesmen, the company now has 230 subscribers, of whom only 19 have ever experienced a 'disaster'. The company's turnover is £3m and pre-tax profits are around £1m. Their 17 competitors are not doing quite so well, as none makes any money, according to Safetynet's founders.

Compatibility being all important in the computer business, Safetynet has had to specialise. It is only interested in disasters affecting the medium range IBM machines. The decision to concentrate on this area appears to have been influenced by the knowledge that IBM's AS 400 was going to prove a highly popular machine. There are at least 500 of them in the City now. Convinced that they had

*hit upon a sound proposition, they then had to convince others. Venture
capitalists were not enthusiastic but another approach proved more rewarding.*

*Reasoning that their prime requirement would be equipment, they approached
companies in the industry for support. Eventually, United Computers provided
hardware in exchange for a 14 per cent stake. Bluebird Software, now IBM's
largest agency in the mid-range but then a relatively new company which had
bought its first computer from Paul Hearson, agreed to cover all the business's
variable costs, and took a 26 per cent stake.*

*As Safetynet has grown, the founders have been able to buy out their early backers
for more than £600,000. The two founders are now the sole owners of the
company and seem happy to keep it that way. Talk of a flotation has stopped. 'We
feel very cool about going public', says Paul Hearson.*

Franchising

Have you ever wondered why Steve Bishko's Tie Rack is surviving in
this turbulent economy of ours, and Sophie Mirman's Sock Shop has
gone to the wall? Both are (or in Mirman's case were) niche retailers;
both need small high street locations; both founders came from Marks
and Spencer and knew all about their product; neither product is
essential for survival like food – indeed if anything, socks seem more
essential than ties!

One of the key reasons lies in the different ways in which their
respective businesses were funded and managed. All the Sock Shop
outlets were funded by the company itself and in the last year of its life
this was largely provided by the banks. In Tie Rack's case the situation
is rather different. One hundred and seven of their 135 outlets are
effectively owned by the people who managed them. These franchisees, as Tie Rack's 'managers' are called, have stumped up at least
£60,000 each for the privilege of following the Tie Rack formula for
business success. That's a fairly staggering £7m of new money which is
completely risk and cost free to Tie Rack. For Mirman, a similar sum
would have cost her £1.25m a year in interest charges alone – and it
probably did, as £2 in every £3 in the Sock Shop was put up by the
banks.

*Miles O'Donavan's franchise, Material World (named after the Madonna hit
record, 'Living in a Material World'), is a good example of how to turn a
successful conventional business into a franchise. He is an up-market version of a
market trader, buying up manufacturers' ends-of-lines and seconds, and selling
them to an apparently appreciative public. 'It is a very simple business', he says.
And he never doubted that it would succeed because, the way he looks at it, it is*

providing a service at both ends of the equation. Not only is he helping out those people who would love to make their home 'very Sanderson' but currently find themselves strapped for cash; he is also helping out the manufacturers who have to rid themselves of their surplus stock somehow.

This mutually beneficial system is already well established in the clothing business, where disposing of chain store cast-offs is the basis of several retail chains. O'Donavan, however, operates with goods from rather further up-market. Much of what he stocks would normally sell at £15 to £20 a metre but he has a blanket price of £7.95 a yard. The fact that he sticks to yards is not just a hankering for days gone by, it gives him a 10 per cent price advantage.

O'Donavan woke up one morning about 18 months ago and decided that with nine of his own shops he was about as exposed as he would like to be. Watching Coloroll and Lowndes Queensway sink without trace, he decided the time had come to share the risk with others. After a brief flirtation with the idea of venture capital, he plumped for franchising and has never looked back. His new franchisees have helped to lift turnover from £1.8m to £3m in 1991, and his business is now expanding fast both in the UK and Europe. Best of all, he can sleep easy at night with the comfort of knowing his franchisees are as exposed as he is to the consequences of failure, something no Queensway store manager ever was.

Get a grant

One final possible source of money is neither debt nor equity, and in theory is free. The magic money source is called a 'grant'. The EC, the government and many local authorities give grants for one purpose or another. Various estimates put the total figure of grant aid available at between £1/2 billion and £2 billion a year. *Government Funding for UK Business* and *European Community Funding for Business Development* are two guides to this subject, both published by Kogan Page.

Before you rush off and search for this 'free money', do remember that anyone giving a grant wants you to do something that very often doesn't make much commercial sense. There may be millions available to encourage you to set up your satellite production facility in an area that is currently mainly populated by sheep. The grant may or may not compensate you for being miles from markets and potential employees.

The golden rule is: decide what you want to do and that it makes sound business sense – then see if anyone will pay you to do it.

ASSIGNMENT 16

1. Look hard at your working capital and see what opportunities there are to reduce the amount of cash tied up.

2. Review your fixed assets and see if there is any scope for savings.

3. Can you eliminate costs or increase efficiency in any part of your business?

4. Is there anything you do now or that your growth plans include, that it would be better to buy in?

5. Is there any form of funding, for example, factoring, BES, venture capital, that you are not currently using? If so, review these options and locate possible supplies of these funds that could be interested in backing your growth plans.

11.

Acquisitions, Mergers, Joint Ventures and Divestments

Before we look at the pros and cons of each of these strategic options in a little more detail it would be as well to be clear on what each term means.

An *acquisition* occurs when one company buys another – more often than not in a 'friendly' deal, but sometimes events are not so harmonious. The Guinness acquisition of Distillers is one example of a hostile or contested takeover bid. It is the company's shares that are bought so you end up owning the business, warts and all, not just the buildings, machinery and brand names. There may well be unknown and unqualified liabilities lurking below the surface of the deal. Only rarely, as when Sir Owen Green's industrial conglomerate BTR bought Dunlop in 1985, can you uncover a nugget of gold. They found the number plate A1 on a company car which turned out to be worth £250,000 – more than 30 times the book value of the asset they acquired. After the acquisition only the parent company usually exists in any real legal sense and the top management of the 'victim' usually depart quickly.

Mergers are friendly bids where companies join forces and the separate identities of the businesses of the companies concerned continue after the deal is consummated. British Home Stores and Habitat are one such example.

Joint ventures occur when two or more companies decide to set up a separate third business to exploit something together. There is no attempt to harmonise the whole of the two parent businesses, and the joint venture may be disbanded easily when the reasons they joined forces in the first place disappear. No shares in either parent company are changing hands, so you don't have too many hidden problems.

Joint ventures are popular among small and growing firms. Cranfield's 1992 study revealed that over 15 per cent of small firms had plans to set up a joint venture with a European partner.

One example is Brighton-based Epic International Media, a company engaged in interactive computer-based training. They have a UK turnover of £700,000 and a work-force of 14. They have formed a European Economic Interest Grouping (EEIG) with Lang Learning Systems of Brussels and Mentor Consultants of Dublin. An EEIG is a legal formula which allows companies from more than one community country to establish a joint business venture. The grouping is intended to be a simpler and more flexible way of setting up joint ventures and to avoid the need for the partners to choose a particular set of national laws – likely to be unfamiliar to at least one of them – to govern relations between them. The partners are not obliged to contribute capital to the company and there is no requirement either for formal meetings of members or the filing of annual reports or accounts. The EEIG itself pays no taxes; profits are shared among the partners and taxed in their hands. A drawback is the absence of limited liability.

An example of a different type of joint venture is VSW Scientific Instruments, a Manchester-based company with sales of £5m and 100 employees. They are negotiating a cooperation agreement with Sofie Instruments, a company in Esomme, south of Paris, which makes a complementary range of equipment. VSW, which makes instruments for analysing surfaces, wants to start by distributing Sofie's products in Britain and Scandinavia, where it has a sales subsidiary; but is also interested in collaborating on the development of new products. The proposed union between these two companies was prompted by an initiative organised by the Esomme Department Economic Development Board.

The European Commission's Business Cooperation Network is the largest player in the joint venture field. In the two years to June 1990 more than 22,000 small and medium sized firms approached them for help (see Figure 11.1). The network consists of 460 advisers – private consultants, chambers of commerce, development authorities – throughout the community who log their client's business profile with a central computer for matching with potential partners. Computer matching can be notoriously hit and miss and the commission has not yet started to monitor success rates, but it estimates that several hundred businesses have found partners.

Divestments occur when you sell bits of your business to other companies. Any rapidly growing firm ends up with bits of its business that either no longer make sense, or prevent the company from exploiting opportunities that better fit its new strategic direction. This pruning should be done regularly and promptly.

One £3m company in the publishing industry launched an exhibitions business in the late 1980s in a period of rather gung-ho expansion. They were offered £200,000 for the exhibitions business in 1990 by a competitor, who as good as told them it was the wrong business for them to be in. They decided to stick with it and only discovered in 1991 that it really was the wrong business for them – they struggled hard to get £40,000 for the same assets.

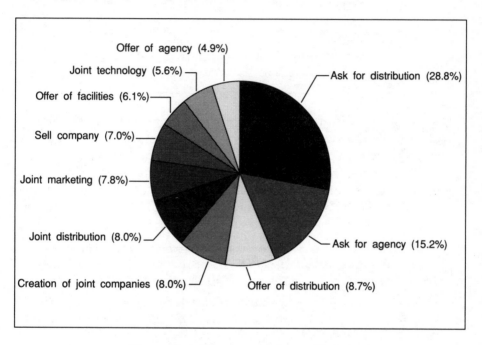

Figure 11.1 *Most popular forms of links*
Source: European Commission

Going on the acquisition trail

Last year 2055 private companies changed hands for a total of £19 billion and many times this number of unincorporated businesses also changed hands. The average size, in turnover terms, of the companies bought and sold was under £5m per annum, with many having sales below £¹/₂m. Forty-five per cent of the acquisitions were viewed as wholly amicable. There was a willing buyer and a willing seller, and no other parties were involved. Another 45 per cent were classified as partly contested, either because there were several interested buyers, or because there was resistance within the vendor to being taken over. Only 10 per cent of the acquisitions were hostile, with a bid being made over the heads of the vendors' board. These contested bids are the deals that make the headlines but, as you can see, the reality is that an awful lot of quite small companies are changing hands in a fairly friendly way, for modest sums of money.

Table 11.1 *Buyers' and sellers' assessment of the results of the acquisition*

	%
Very successful	20
Successful	35
So-so	20
Unsuccessful	17
Very unsuccessful	8

When economic growth is virtually static, or if you want to achieve really dramatic growth, then buying someone else's business can be a very attractive option. But be warned. While 90 per cent of acquisitions took place under friendly or fairly friendly conditions, only 55 per cent were eventually rated as successful or very successful by both buyers and sellers. So buying a company is certainly not always a sure-fire winning strategy.

> *Tom Farmer, who set up Kwik-Fit Exhausts and built it into a £200m turnover business in two decades confessed in the* Independent on Sunday *in 1990 that acquisition as an expansion strategy was his biggest commercial mistake.*

> *'Expanding too rapidly through acquisition was probably the biggest business mistake I ever made. I had started Kwik-Fit in 1971 and we built the company up to 49 depots, all north of Manchester, by 1990. We had a clear corporate identity with our blue and white logo and blue overalls, an excellent reputation with customers, and a good financial control system. By the late-1970s we were thinking of expansion. Towards the end of 1979 we approached a competitor, Euro Exhausts, which had 51 depots south of Birmingham. We acquired the business in January 1980 for £10m, immediately doubling our size.*

> *Now we felt we were really king of the castle, with a national business. We were also excited because our suppliers kept telling us about Euro's computer system and we thought we could just slide our way of controlling the business into their system. The biggest shock came when we discovered that their computer system just produced reams of paper and required even more administrative staff than we had.*

> *We also wanted to change the company's name to Kwik-Fit Euro and create a single company identity. But they had a yellow and brown logo and brown overalls and this turned out to be a very contentious issue. Whose colours would*

win? And we wanted the managers of Euro to do things our way. They didn't want to, so they left the company.

Three months later we were still struggling to put the thing together, desperately short of management, when another deal came along. I made enquiries and found that the Firestone Tyre company had 180 retail depots but was thinking of selling them to concentrate on manufacturing. A month later I met the managing director in London and we did the deal that day. I had to – at £3.25m it was a snip.

Flying back to Edinburgh I knew it would be a bit of a problem breaking the news. So I told the other managers we were a national company and had to keep on expanding. I'm a wee bit of an orator, and as I kept talking they were getting more and more excited. Then I dropped the bombshell and there was a stony silence. Then the boys starting flipping their lids. In the end we did a deal with Dunlop Rubber, which paid £3.25m for 82 of the depots. So in effect we got 98 depots free.

On reflection it was foolhardy to have attempted the Firestone deal. It was a good deal in the end but we were very lucky because I went in without proper planning. Our acquisition turned out to have no financial controls and terrible staff morale. Even worse, the Firestone mechanics wore red overalls and their signs were all red and white!

Prior to that deal we had produced profits of £4m. Now our turnover had gone up fourfold but our profits fell to £1m. I had to stand up and tell the shareholders that this was due to our investment in the future and all the other things you say at such times.

The whole thing caused us a lot of pain and grief at the time. It took two years of dedication and commitment to integrate the administration and financial controls, bring in a proper computer system and train staff. What I learned is that you should never do anything just because it's a good idea. You must spend time on making sure it's a really good idea. Of course you can add instinct based on experience. But don't go on gut feeling – that's just a recipe for indigestion.'

Here is a seven point plan to make sure that you can end up with a very successful acquisition, merger or joint venture.

1. Why do you want to buy?

Big companies end up on the take-over trail for matters of management ego as much as corporate strategy. Over 40 per cent of big companies listed 'sending signals to the City' as their principal reason for buying. A further 35 per cent put it down to the 'chairman's insistence'.

For smaller companies the reasons to buy need to be rather more practical and down to earth. Sound reasons for acquisitions include:

- To increase market share and eliminate a troublesome competitor;
- To broaden your product range or give you access to new markets;
- To diversify into new markets, acquiring the necessary management, marketing or technical skills to enable you to capture a reasonable slice of the market, relatively quickly;
- To get into another country or region;
- To protect an important source of supply which could be under threat from a competitor;
- To acquire additional staff, factory space, warehousing, distribution channels, or to get access to additional major customers more quickly than by starting up yourself.

You should produce a written statement explaining the rationale behind your reason to buy – before you start looking for companies to buy – otherwise you could end up pursuing a 'bargain', just because it seems cheap, that has absolutely nothing to do with your previously defined commercial goals. It's also worth remembering that companies available at knockdown prices are likely to need drastic surgery. So unless you fancy your chances as a company doctor, stay well away.

Martin Blaney, managing director of Winprime, a West London wholesaler of personal computers and printers, says he has a list of gaps in his company's range which he would like to fill and a profile of the sort of business he would like to acquire.

'But a company of our size (170 employees and £40m worth of sales) doesn't have a wonderful research document and reams of paper', he adds. Blaney and his managers keep a close eye on what is happening in their industry and take up suggestions put to them by the City institutions which helped to set up Winprime in 1983.

'It is difficult to have some wonderful acquisition plan', comments Blaney. 'We are always talking to people and making contacts. We may hear of somebody in trouble.' Winprime recently made its second acquisition within 18 months, buying Document Technology (DTL), a supplier of non-impact printers, when DTL's own plans to develop a portable printer failed.

Hugh Charlton, managing director of Pointing, a Northumberland-based manufacturer of food colours and flavours, says his company has a set of written criteria. These cover the product areas Pointing wants to add, the size and profitability of the target company, and the markets and technology in which it is involved.

Pointing, a family company employing 95 people and with sales of £12m, 'would be unlikely to spend more than £3m on an acquisition', notes Charlton.

But even if you have a plan you must remain opportunistic, he adds. Pointing's most recent acquisition, a Manchester-based company making food ingredients, was found by David Garrick. 'We have a hit list but this was a company we were not aware of', says Charlton. 'It is in a peripheral area not specified in our brief.'

2. What do you want to buy?

It can take over one man-year of work, on average, to find and buy a private limited company. The more accurately you describe your ideal purchase the simpler, quicker and cheaper your search will be.

Just imagine trying to buy a house without any idea of where you wanted to live, how much you wanted to spend, how many bedrooms were needed, whether you wanted a new house or a listed building, or if you wanted a garden. The search would be near-impossible to organise, it could take for ever, and the resultant purchase would almost certainly please no one. The same problem is present when buying a company. The definition of what you want to buy should explain:

- The business area/products/service the company is in;
- The location;
- The price range and the cash you have available;
- The management depth and the management style you are looking for;
- The minimum profitability and return on capital employed you could accept. It's worth remembering that if the company you plan to buy only makes 1 per cent profit while you make 5 per cent, and you are of equal size, the resultant profit will be 3 per cent $[(5 + 1) \div 2]$;
- The image compatibility between your company and any target;
- Scope for integration and cost savings;
- The tax status;
- Other key factors for success. Outside the factors listed above you may have vital reasons that, if not achieved, would make the acquisition a poor bet. For example if you want to iron out major cash flow or plant capacity cycles, there is little point in going for a business similar to your own. That will only make the peaks and troughs more pronounced.

John James, chairman of Star Cargo, a privately owned transport and freighting company, started takeover talks with 17 companies in 1989. For a mixture of reasons none came to anything. There were owners who decided not to sell; businesses which appeared less attractive when more was learned about them; and businesses which were clearly not worth the value put upon them by their owners.

The first few weeks of 1990 proved more fruitful and Star Cargo, based in Harpenden, Hertfordshire, sewed up two deals. It bought Viking Shipping Services, a profitable company, from the receivers handling the affairs of its failed parent and later concluded six weeks of negotiations to acquire another small shipping firm.

Despite the unpredictable outcome of takeover negotiations, Star Cargo, which has turnover of £16.6m and 155 employees, is committed to making acquisitions as well as seeking organic growth. 'Negotiations can be enormously time-consuming and costly and can fail after you have gone a long way down the road', says James. 'But you have to put the effort in if you want to achieve results.' Over the past three years Star Cargo's efforts have led to four acquisitions.

3. Start looking

Once you have a profile of the sort of company you would like to buy, you can begin to assemble your shopping list. Two sources are of particular use. ICC (Inter Company Comparisons, telephone 0171 253 3906) produce over 200 business sector reports analysing the performance of over 20,000 UK companies, the vast majority of whom are private. For each sector (for example window manufacturers, retail chemists, the toy industry, employment agencies or software houses), key performance ratios, growth rates and relative performance are analysed over a three-year period. From trade associations you can get membership lists; then either using Extel's cards for unlisted companies, or by getting the accounts direct from Companies House, you can sift through looking for companies conforming to your profile.

You could also read the financial press such as *The Times* on Saturdays, *The Sunday Times* business to business section, or *The Financial Times* on Tuesdays. There are several hundred companies for sale each week in these papers. Alternatively, you could advertise for companies yourself, or approach an organisation that handles the sale of other people's companies. Major accountancy practices or merger brokers are very active in this field. You could start by talking with your professional advisers, then contact:

- *The Business Exchange*, 21 John Adam Street, London EC2N 6JG; telephone 0171 930 8965. Set up by Deloitte Haskins & Sells and Grant Thornton, this is a market for buying and selling companies. Data is fed in by chartered accountants, solicitors and actuaries throughout the country.
- *Christie & Co*, 50 Victoria Street, London SW1H 0NP; telephone 0171 799 2121. Through its 20 regional offices, Christie's claims to

be the country's leading agent for buying and selling pubs, hotels, nursing homes and newsagents.

- *Red Alert* provides you with a weekly newsletter listing companies against which winding up petitions have been presented, companies whose members have passed a voluntary winding up resolution and companies where an administrative receiver has been appointed. Red Alert also provide a telephone enquiry handling service. Contact: MCB University Press, 62 Toller Lane, Bradford BD8 9BY; telephone 01274 777700.

- *Singer & Friedlander Ltd*, 21 New Street, Bishopgate, London EC2M 4HR; telephone 0171 623 3000, operates a company register for those who want to buy a company, sell one or merge with suitable partners. The register is confidential. Its fees, on a graduated scale, are payable only on completion of a satisfactory transaction.

If this all seems like too much hard work you could brief a merger broker or merchant bank to search out prospective companies for you. This will not be cheap – anything around the 5 per cent mark is not unusual for smaller deals and professional advisers could add another couple of percentage points to that figure too.

Table 11.2 *Mergers and acquisitions legislation in Europe*

	Belgium	France	Germany	Netherlands	Spain	UK
Approval generally required for public takeovers	Yes	No	No(9)	No	Yes	No(6)
Approval generally required for takeovers by foreigners	Yes(1)	Yes(1)	No(9)	No	No(8)	No(6)
Limits on voting rights	Yes	Yes(2)	Yes(2)	No(5)	Yes(2)	No(7)
Board able to issue extra shares to its allies	Yes(2)	Yes(2)	Yes(2)	Yes(2)	No	No
National antitrust legislation (& 6)	No	Yes	Yes	Yes(4)	Yes	Yes(4)
Employee rights created by takeover legislation	No(3)	No(3)	Yes	Yes	No	No

Source: KPMG International M & A Network

Notes: This table is intended only as a general guide to illustrate the variety of regulations within Europe. More detailed advice should be sought in specific cases. (1) For non-EC nationals; (2) If authorised by Articles of Association or by shareholders; (3) Workers' council must be informed; (4) But limited application; (5) But often found in Articles of Association; (6) Government has power to block on the grounds of competition or public interest; (7) Except in a very few cases where authorised by Articles of Association; (8) Notification and approval required in special cases; (9) Except for the largest transactions.

If you are going to look overseas for a target company make sure you understand the possible additional obstacles in your way.

KPMG Peat Marwick McLintock surveyed the European mergers and acquisition market in 1991 and concluded that many deals fell through because of the problems of complying with local regulations – see Table 11.2. The motivation of the vendors was also a major problem. Many continentals are much more interested in issues of tax, spreading wealth around the families and ensuring pension rights or annuities.

4. Investigate and approach

Once you have your shopping list of prospective purchases you need to arm yourself with everything you can find out about them. Get their literature, get samples, copies of their advertising, press comment and, of course, their accounts. Then get out and see their premises and as much of their operation as it's possible to see. If you can't get in, get one of your salespeople in to look the business over for you. This investigation will help you to both shorten your shopping list, and put it into order of priority. Now you are ready for the approach.

Although you are technically 'buying', psychologically you would be well advised to think of acquiring a company as a selling job. As such you cannot afford to have any approach rejected either too early or without a determined effort. You have three options as to how to make the initial approach and each has its merits. You can telephone, giving only the broadest reason for your approach – saying perhaps you wish to discuss areas of common interest. You could write and be a little more specific about your purpose, following that up with a phone call to arrange a meeting, perhaps over lunch. Finally, you could use a third party such as an accountant, merchant bank or consultant. Reasons of secrecy could make this method desirable; if executive time is at a premium there may be no other practicable way.

The first meeting is crucial and you need to achieve two objectives. First, you must establish mutual respect, trust and rapport. Nothing worthwhile will follow without these. Then you need to establish in principle that both parties are seriously interested. Time scale, price, methods of integration etc, can all be side-stepped until later, except in the most general sense.

5. Valuing the business

Once you have found a business that you want to buy, and that is probably for sale, you will need your accountants to investigate the business in depth to see exactly what is on offer. This can take several weeks, and it's a little like having a house surveyed. You need to remember that accounts are normally prepared on the 'going concern basis', which implies the company is going to continue trading much as before. This means that the historical cost of fixed assets such as buildings, land, machinery etc, can appear in the balance sheet, rather than the market worth. After all, until you came along they hadn't planned to sell their fixed assets, but now the figures will have to be recast using different principles.

Ultimately, what you are buying is either extra profit or perhaps lower costs in your own business. You have to decide how much that is worth. Public companies usually have rules of thumb for each sector. For example, much of the retail sector is valued on a price/earnings ratio of 12, which means retailers are seen as being worth 12 times last year's net profit. A private company in the same sector would only be worth two-thirds that figure, as their shares are less easily bought and sold. The worth of the assets in the business would also be important, and whatever the business it's usually people – their knowledge and skills – you are buying, unless you are simply asset stripping.

Prices paid for private companies are monitored in a new three-monthly index prepared by accountancy firm, Stoy Hayward. The index is published in the magazine *Acquisitions Monthly* (telephone 01892 515454), and will enable owners of private companies to follow trends in unquoted company acquisitions and help them to assess a fair price for their own businesses.

Based on completed acquisitions, it will track the ratio between the purchase price of private companies sold during a three-month period and their historical earnings. The price/earnings ratio of the index stood at 9.8 during the first quarter of 1990, nearly 20 per cent lower than the trading P/E multiple of companies in the FT 500 Index for the same period.

There is no great science involved in valuing business, just a rather messy art – and at the end of the day you can always work out if it would be cheaper to start up from scratch yourself. That will give you an outer figure for your negotiations.

6. Limit the risks

Buying a business will always be risky. If you have done your homework and got the price right with any luck the risks will be less. Here are some other things you can do to lessen the risks:

- Set conditional terms: for example, you could make part of the price conditional upon a certain level of profits being achieved;

- Handcuff key employees: if most of the assets you are buying are on two legs, then get service contracts or consultancy arrangements in place before the deal is signed;
- Non-competitive clauses: make sure that neither the seller nor his key employees can set up in competition, taking all the goodwill you have just bought.
- Tax clearances: obviously you want to make sure any tax losses you are buying or any tax implications in the purchase price are approved by the Inland Revenue, before committing yourself.
- Warranties and indemnities: if, after you have bought, you find there is a compulsory purchase order on the vendor's premises and the patent on his whizzy new product is invalid, you would quite rightly be rather miffed. Warranties and indemnities set out those circumstances in which the seller will make good the buyer's financial loss. So anything crucial that looks worrying, you could try to include under this heading. Not unnaturally, the seller will resist, but you need to be firm on key points.

7. Manage the acquisition

However well negotiated the deal, most acquisitions that go wrong do so because of the human factor, particularly in the first few weeks after the deal is made public. Some important rules to follow are:

- Have an outline plan for how to handle the 'merger' – and be prepared to be flexible. (Interestingly enough, only one buyer in five has a detailed operational plan of how to manage their acquisition – but 67 per cent of those being bought believe the buyer has such a plan, so it is psychologically important.)
- Let business go on as usual for a few weeks, as you learn more about the internal workings of the company. Then you can make informed judgements on who or what should go or remain in post. Ninety per cent of successful acquisitions follow this rule.
- Hold management and staff meetings on day 1, to clear as much misunderstanding as you can. Do as much of this yourself as you possibly can.
- Never announce takeovers on a Friday. Staff will have all weekend to spread rumours. Wednesdays are best – just enough time to clear up misunderstandings, followed by a useful weekend breathing space.
- Make cuts/redundancies a once only affair. It's always best to cut deep, and then get on with running the business. Continuous

sackings sap morale, and all the best people will leave before it's their turn.

- Set limits of authority and reporting relationships and put all banking relationships in the hands of your own accounts department, as quickly as possible.

On the other side of the Channel two French entrepreneurs, Henri Blanchet and Christian Moretti, a Hanson and White in miniature, have spent the past eight years building a mini-conglomerate by acquisition that has confounded the sceptics. In 1989 Dynaction, their holding company, which controls 32 small firms, turned in a new profit of FF173m, (around £0.5m per company), over 50 per cent up on 1988.

Their philosophy is based on three maxims. The first is that boring businesses are best. Rather than buy small companies in sexy sectors like high technology or luxury goods, Dynaction bids for firms in dull ones like mechanical engineering and packaging. It is, however, fussy about what it buys. Companies on Dynaction's shopping list must be market leaders in their product range, preferably with a healthy export business. Second, they must be cheap, which rules out contested bids. Dynaction rarely pays a price that values its prey at an historic price-earning ratio of more than 6. Dynaction's aim is to float a part of any firm that it buys within four years at twice the price/earnings ratio that it paid.

Their third rule is to let managers manage. It has no centralised cost-control or accounting systems; the executives who run its subsidiaries do almost as they please. Dynaction's approval is required only for big decisions like raising capital or making a significant acquisition. That suits Messrs Blanchet and Moretti. Unlike typical tycoons, they admit they hate hard work and sneak off for a game of tennis at their local club as often as possible.

There is a method in this madness. Good managers suffocated by corporate bureaucracy are queuing to join them. Dynaction's bosses reckon they spend about one-third of their time in search of managerial excellence. Once they have found it the challenge is to turn managers into entrepreneurs. So Dynaction gives managers an equity stake of up to 25 per cent in the subsidiaries they manage.

A hands-off strategy also helps to keep costs down. The holding company employs just four people, and operates from two rooms of a house in an unglamorous part of Paris.

What are the snags? If it grows too fast, Dynaction presumably could soon encounter some of the problems that have afflicted more arthritic giants. For a start, the company could lose its valuable esprit de corps when its network of businesses grows. So far, the flair of Dynaction's two founders for choosing the right people has paid off; but, as the company grows bigger, other executives will have to start hiring. If the calibre of managers deteriorates, and problems appear, the holding company would have little choice but to take a stronger hand in its businesses.

A careful look at any of the most successful companies will reveal that buying up other people's companies played a key part in achieving growth. Some companies – Hanson is a prime example – make buying, repackaging and then selling businesses, a business in itself.

This extract from Henry Barrett's 1990 Chairman's statement gives quite an accurate view of the best you can reasonably expect from acquisitions as part of your growth strategy:

Henry Barrett Group, the Bradford-based steel and industrial products company, recently reported a 23 per cent increase in pre-tax profits to £12.5m in the year to 31 August.

Turnover rose by 44 per cent to £139.66m but earnings per share fell 5 per cent to 19.98p, diluted by the issuing of new shares to fund acquisitions. The final dividend of 3.65p makes a total for the year of 5.65p, an increase of 11 per cent.

Of the 44 per cent increase in turnover, 26 per cent was organic growth and the remainder came from acquisitions. The group said that in spite of investing over £20m on acquisitions and fixed assets, of which £9.4m was raised through issues of shares, group gearing was only 31.2 per cent.

Guy Barrett, chairman, said 'The year ahead promises many opportunities for further developments of core activities, despite the downturn affecting UK industry – indeed more potential exists because of it. We intend to maintain our modest level of gearing and so remain in a strong position to capitalise on opportunities as they arise. In what is likely to be a tough year I have every confidence that the group's financial strength and strategic positioning will enable us to progress.'

In its materials handling division, the group said a recent acquisition, Advanced Storage Systems, had proved disappointing and had been merged with Organised Storage Systems. There had been pressure on margins in the general, industrial sector, and lower than expected levels among edge-of-town retailers.

Licensing

One way to inject accelerated growth into the organisation while minimising the risks associated with either acquisition or new product/ service development, is to buy someone else's revenue stream without taking on either their people or premises: the concept is licensing. Here you buy the rights to make and market a proven product or concept that usually has patent, copyright or some other form of intellectual protection already in place.

Shire Pharmaceuticals was formed in the mid-1980s by a team who broke away from a major multinational pharmaceutical company. They had several product ideas themselves and found backing to take them through the R & D stage and into the market. They sold off one of their products which had world appeal, as they felt too small themselves to properly exploit its potential. The several million they got, along with some venture capital from Schroders, the merchant bankers, allowed them to start building up a UK sales and marketing organisation to exploit their remaining products.

By 1990 it became clear that their present product range was too small to support a national sales-force. Their present force of 20 full-time and 10 part-timers was about half the size needed to get reasonable hospital and GP coverage. They had done a great job of getting sales up to £3m but there the business stuck.

In 1991 they recruited an experienced managing director from Wyeth Laboratories, the UK subsidiary of American Home Products, the giant American pharmaceutical company. Trevor Davis, the new MD, had a solution, which was to license a complementary range of products from Glaxo. He bid for a package of 20 products, too small to be of strategic interest to Glaxo, with a current turnover of £6m. While that may have been small beer to a multinational, it would triple Shire's business overnight and allow them to recruit a national sales-force through which they can now drive their core products.

Glaxo was offered a deal which allowed Shire to put £1m on the table and pay the rest as a 'royalty' on the sale of the drugs. That helps Shire's cash flow and gives Glaxo a share in the extra sales of their old products that will be generated by having someone give them maximum attention.

There are many sources of licensed products, but perhaps the best source of two-way licensing deals (you can license out anything redundant to your needs, too) is the British Technology Group.

BTG works closely with universities, polytechnics, research councils and government research establishments to commercialise the results of their research work. BTG protects the inventions concerned by patenting and other means, identifies potential licensees and negotiates licence agreements with manufacturers. Development funds are available to enhance the prospects of successful licensing.

BTG also funds UK companies planning to develop new products and processes based on their own technology. Through its industrial project finance scheme. BTG can provide up to 50 per cent of the funds required for the development and launch of a new product, recovering its investment by means of a percentage levy on sales of the resulting product or process. Equity financing is also available from BTG.

Divestments

Don't forget that while you are busy adding products and services and making new acquisitions, it may be appropriate to shed some of the old things you were doing.

In the example above Glaxo recognised that its interest and profits were best served by shedding products it could no longer give adequate attention to. This had the double benefit of giving their sales-force time to sell more profitable products and kept a growing revenue stream coming in from the old ones. One small shoe manufacturer has kept every product it ever designed in its stock list, and will make the shoe in minimum batches of ten. This Herculean task has held the company in a time warp bogged down by its past and unable to move forward. Its sales plateaued years ago. Still, perhaps in the UK shoe business that's no mean achievement.

ASSIGNMENT 17

Targeting takeovers

1. Consider whether or not you believe that an acquisition or merger would be desirable at this stage in your firm's life. The deciding question is: *If we buy a company and it goes disastrously wrong can we still survive?*

2. If the answer to the above question is 'Yes', then draw up the profile of your target companies and prepare a plan of campaign along the lines described in this chapter.

3. When it comes to joint ventures you could rephrase Question 1, ie Why shouldn't we start looking for a suitable joint venture partner? If you could operate in Europe but don't, the logic is quite compelling. If you have a market opportunity that you need help in exploiting, joint venture could be a low(ish) risk way in.

4. What products, services or business units should you consider getting out of? Remember that to move forward you have to let go of something.

12.

Visionary Leadership

The former manager of the New York Yankees once said: 'If you don't know where you're going, you might end up somewhere else.'

Today, more and more attention is being paid to articulating the business 'vision'. In fact, many people believe that creating and communicating the vision is the most important job of the leader. The editor of *Fortune* magazine recently said: 'The new paragon of an executive is a person who can envision a future for his organisation and then inspire his colleagues to join him in building that future.'

Visions are about dreams, the 'promised land', a destination shared by everyone, and an inspiration to all. The most successful companies are those whose leaders can see and articulate to others the exciting possibilities of the future. Here is Sophie Mirman talking about her new enterprise in King's Road selling upmarket children's wear and called 'Trotters': 'We shall keep this company small and keep it private. The service has got to be 100 per cent right. It will be impeccable. We want it to be a small, enjoyable business. We want everyone involved to have fun with it.'

Visionary leaders 'have a dream'. There is nothing Sir Terence Conran hates more than 'unfinished dreams'. The same might be said of Mrs Thatcher who, whatever one thinks of her politics, was by general consent a visionary leader. *The Times*, writing about Sheila Pickles, the woman who transformed Penhaligon's, an ailing perfumery business, into an international empire, compares her to Laura Ashley, 'another company built on the nostalgic vision of one woman'.

It is the power and passion of your vision which will translate paper strategies into a way of life. It is vision which puts the mission statement to work by making it something that is shared by everyone, inspirational and clear enough to help people know what kind of decisions not to make in your business. An effective vision centres on people. It also centres on the future and becomes the 'pull-through' for change.

The greatest threat to growing the business comes from the danger that the entrepreneur's thinking and action may be trapped by today's problems, so that the focus is on a 'quick fix' rather than on moving the organisation forward.

In 1980 Ralph Stayer was the head of a successful business – Johnsonville Sausage – that was in great shape but required radical change. Ralph was not a happy man:

'Our profits were above the average . . . we were growing at about 20 per cent annually . . . we were respected in the community, I was making a lot of money, and I had a knot in my stomach that wouldn't go away. For one thing, I was worried about competition . . . What worried me more than the competition, however, was the gap between performance and potential; our people didn't seem to care. In 1980 I began looking for a recipe for change . . . What did I really want Johnsonville to be? I didn't know. This realisation led me to (the) insight that nothing matters more than the goal. The most important question any manager can ask is, "In the best of all possible worlds what would I really want to happen."'

This end state became Ralph Stayer's Point B.

'The detail overwhelmed us and we got nowhere. In short, the early 1980s were a disaster. After two years of stewing, it began to dawn on me that my first reactions to most situations were usually dead wrong. After all, my organisational instincts had brought us to Point A to begin with. Pursuing those instincts would only bring us back to Point A. I needed to start thinking before I acted and the thought I needed to think was, "Will this action help us to achieve our new Point B?"'

(Harvard Business Review *Nov/Dec 1990*)

This chapter aims to help you think afresh about the vision you have for your business, formulate it in such a way that you can get your team on board for the journey and constantly live the values yourself as the ultimate role model.

Developing a vision

When you sit down and write a formal statement of company philosophy you will probably find that 'motherhood' statements are easy, but that it is more difficult to produce a real and relevant vision.

It's rather like the chairman of a large company who is reputed to have written the 'shared' values for his 20,000 staff! A statement of vision or values on its own is meaningless unless it is truly shared by everyone in the organisation. Indeed, in any company with a strong culture any employee at any time can tell you what the company stands for. Developing your business vision isn't therefore a job you can do sitting in splendid isolation, it's an opportunity to involve your people in its design. There are several techniques to help you envision your future with your team:

- Organisation pictures
- Culture statements
- Thoughts about effective organisation
- Core mission
- Vision and value statements.

Organisation pictures

In diagnosing the current state of your organisation (Assignment 10) you drew a picture of how you see your business now. What would your picture of the future look like? Here is Ralph Stayer again describing his business to the *Harvard Business Review*:

> 'The image that best captured the organisational end state I had in mind for Johnsonville was a flock of geese on the wing. I didn't want an organisational chart with traditional lines and boxes, but a "V" of individuals who knew the common goal, took turns leading and adjusted their structure to the task at hand. Geese fly in a wedge, for instance, but land in waves.'

Other visions of the future we have seen recently include:

- A circus ring: 'Ladeez and Gentlemen, the combined skills, synchronised talents, all under one big top'
- An orchestra
- A phoenix rising from the ashes
- A bus with everyone happily on board, knowing the destination
- A formation of Red Arrows (with ears) flying with safety and precision, a quality organisation – achieved through the involvement of the whole work-force of 350 in teamwork
- A TQM hospital, compassionate and caring, prevention not cure, open communications, no 'us' and 'them' type élitism.

Finally, you and your team will find it useful to put some words around your picture. In the 'best of all possible worlds' what will the future look like, and how will you know when you've got there? When BMW dealers were asked to define their business vision, they considered the following questions in order to define the characteristics of their desired 'end state', their Point B:

- What is fundamentally different about our business?
- How will staff behave towards customers?
- What will be the customer image of us?
- What attitude will staff have to their jobs?
- What sort of people will we be recruiting?
- What will be our management style?
- How will staff relate to their managers?
- What training, support and personal development will we offer?
- How will we reward our people?
- How will people work together in team structures?

Culture statements ('The way we do things around here')

In diagnosing your organisation (Assignment 10), we encouraged you to describe your current culture, both historically, as it is now and as you would like to see it in the future. Brainstorming a list of words and phrases with your team can give you a very powerful insight into the kind of company you 'wannabee' (apologies to Prudential's advertising campaign!). Figure 12.1 is an example prepared by the Innovex management team during 1990.

Historical	Current	Future
• Slightly chaotic but very happy family • Self-centred rather than customer-centred • Happy amateurs • Top line driven • Small team playing bar billiards • Passionate attempt to avoid politics • Exciting, a buzz	• We're in transition, losing some of our specialness • Pretty good job with customers, not excellent • More performance orientated • We tolerate failure (which is good) • Reorganisation and management changes • Still a bit disjointed	• International • Customer focused • Experienced elder statesmen • Professional and polished • Attract and keep terrific people • Pride and self worth • Spin off separate units

Figure 12.1 *Example of company culture, historical, current and future*

Doing some navel gazing in this fashion has helped Innovex to decide which aspects of its past it wants to retain (for example, being an open, non-political organisation) and which it needs to change (for example, becoming more strongly customer focused). The words which Innovex uses to describe its future start to provide the management team with a 'vision' of the sort of business they want to build and be part of.

This approach may seem 'soft'; after all it's about values and attitudes rather than facts and figures. However, if you hadn't once had a 'feeling', 'a dream', would the business exist at all? Get back in touch with your own fundamental beliefs about how you want to run your business. In a recent article in *Harvard Business Review* entitled 'Values make the Company', the Chief Executive of Levi-Strauss, Robert Haas, states that it is values which drive the business: 'It is the ideas of a business which are controlling, not some manager with authority.' This is nicely put by the managing director of Glaxo Pharmaceuticals UK Ltd, when he says: 'Attitude is like baking powder, it's what makes the cake rise.'

Values help to bring about the kind of business behaviour you need to stay competitive. Levi-Strauss talk about the impact of an uncertain economic climate on their market share in the 1980s and the need to develop 'a whole new set of attitudes and values'. They describe these as broadly consisting of moving people's behaviour as shown in Figure 12.2.

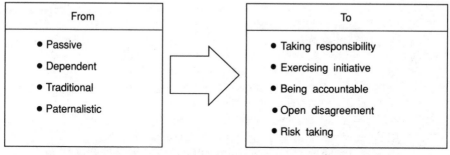

From	To
• Passive	• Taking responsibility
• Dependent	• Exercising initiative
• Traditional	• Being accountable
• Paternalistic	• Open disagreement
	• Risk taking

Figure 12.2 *Moving people's behaviour to develop a new set of attitudes and values*

Thoughts about effective organisation

In Chapter 5, How to Diagnose your Organisation, you benchmarked your business against seven characteristics of effective organisations. Does this give you some clues for how you envisage the future?

Core mission

You may want to revisit your core mission, your *raison d'être*. Here is the newly created mission statement of Innovex:

'We provide marketing, communication, medical and human resource services to the international health-care industry. These services are distinguished by constant innovation and a dedication to excellence, our focus is on client success and constant investment in visionary product development.'

The mission statement should, of course, tell you what's distinctive about your business and the market you operate in. Most important of all, it should give you focus. McKinsey (probably the most prestigious consultancy group in the world) articulate their mission with admirable brevity as:

'To help our clients make positive, lasting and substantial improvements in their performance and to build a great firm that is able to attract, develop, excite and retain exceptional people.'

Vision and value statements

Successful businesses tend to spend a lot of time articulating, communicating and constantly reinforcing their values, business philosophy or credo.

The key job of the chief executive and his top team lies in creating and communicating the vision and values. It's very interesting to put a comment from Deal and Kennedy (*Corporate Cultures*) alongside one by ICL:

'The ultimate success of a chief executive depends to a large degree on an accurate reading of the corporate culture and the ability to hone it and shape it to fit the shifting needs of the market place' (Deal and Kennedy).

'ICL is successful because the top people, probably as much by luck as judgement read the signals right and because there is an emphasis on continuous high profile communication.'

The ICL experience is interesting because it illustrates that having a clear management vision and absolute determination is not enough unless you get others on board as well. ICL barely survived the recession of 1980–81. After a large rescue deal put together by the government and the City, it had to demonstrate very different 'ways of doing things around here'. At the start of their culture change process in 1981, there was intense communication, and Robb Wilmot as chief executive officer was heavily involved. He issued mission statements, he put together a video, he stood on the top of the ICL organisation with his loudspeaker, he preached the new message on every opportunity and . . . 'people nodded but ICL realised nothing much was changing'.

Wilmot knew that things had to change and he found it immensely frustrating that he couldn't get the organisation to move fast enough. To get change in *behaviour, the vision and values must be stated, restated, reinforced and communicated ad nauseam. Wilmot had somehow to get his people as familiar with the reasons for change as he was. He put 2000 of his managers through a core programme, variously known as 'mind expansion' and 'the sheep dip'. It started top down and ran for three years. The programme lasted 5^1/$_2$ to 6 days. The objective was to get people to realise that things had to change. The event is now viewed as a watershed. People realised that there was a real external threat. The world did not owe them a living. People came away saying, 'I understand the problem' and the programme created a common language for ICL.*

Part of this 'common language' was summed up in a glossy brochure distributed by Wilmot in 1983, called 'The ICL Way'. It sums up the ICL philosophy in seven commitments:

'Commitment to Change'

'Commitment to Customers'

'Commitment to Excellence'

'Commitment to Team-work'

'Commitment to Achievement'

'Commitment to People Development'

'Commitment to Creating a Productivity Show-case'.

The initial reaction was disbelief and cynicism, but now the 'ICL Way' is so accepted that it goes out with the offer document to every new recruit.

McKinsey provide a marvellous example of a set of values which have been strongly and clearly articulated since 1926, in such a way that any member of the professional staff who is or ever has been employed with McKinsey, anywhere in the world, can instantly, seriously and passionately tell you what the company stands for. This is done through a set of 'guiding principles'. These are quoted in full in Figure 12.3.

Ericsson, the mighty Swedish telecommunications group, is as lively and enthusiastic as any small entrepreneurial business in stating its values, in the form of three musketeers: 'Perseverance, Professionalism and Respect'. Finally, one of the most famous examples of creating and transmitting the vision of the business is Johnson and Johnson. Their credo is reproduced as Figure 12.4.

Guilding principles

Serving clients
Adhere to professional standards
Follow the top management approach
Assist the client in implementation and capability building
Perform consulting in a cost-effective manner

Building the firm
Operate as one firm
Maintain a meritocracy
Show a genuine concern for our people
Foster an open and non-hierarchical working atmosphere
Manage the firm's resources responsibly

Being a member of the professional staff
Demonstrate commitment to client service
Strive continuously for superior quality
Advance the state of the art of management
Contribute to a spirit of partnership through teamwork and collaboration
Profit from the freedom and assume the responsibility associated with self-governance
Uphold the obligation to dissent

Figure 12.3 *McKinsey's guiding principles*

Building commitment to a shared vision

One managing director outlined his core values as follows:

- Customer orientated
- Quality and value for money
- Caring and helpful
- Appreciative
- Honest, reliable and professional
- Continuously improving

He went on to explain that 'this is what we call our company philosophy. We've had it for some years but we haven't told anyone about it'. Quite! – not all that unusual either and what a missed opportunity.

Visionary leadership means somehow taking your vision for growth and making it live in the hearts and minds of all your people. As a recent *Fortune* article says: 'Yes, a CEO must promulgate a

Our Credo

We believe our first responsibility is to the doctors, nurses and patients, to mothers and fathers and all others who use our products and services.
In meeting their needs everything we do must be of high quality.
We must constantly strive to reduce our costs in order to maintain reasonable prices.
Customers' orders must be serviced promptly and accurately.
Our suppliers and distributors must have an opportuinity to make a fair profit.

We are responsible to our employees, the men and women who work with us throughout the world.
Everyone must be considered as an individual. We must respect their dignity and recognise their merit.
They must have a sense of security in their jobs.
Compensation must be fair and adequate, and working conditions clean, orderly and safe.
We must be mindful of ways to help our employees fulfil their family responsibilities.
Employees must feel free to make suggestions and complaints.
There must be equal opportunity for employment, development and advancement for those qualified.
We must provide competent management, and their actions must be just and ethical.

We are responsible to the communities in which we live and work and to the world community as well.
We must be good citizens – support good works and charities and bear our fair share of taxes.
We must encourage civic improvements and better health and education.
We must maintain in good order the property we are privileged to use, protecting the environment and natural resources.

Our final responsibility is to our stockholders.
Business must make a sound profit.
We must experiment with new ideas.
Research must be carried on, innovative programmes developed and mistakes paid for.
New equipment must be purchased, new facilities provided and new products launched.
Reserves must be created to provide for adverse times.
When we operate according to these principles, the stockholders should realise a fair return.

Johnson & Johnson

Figure 12.4 *Johnson & Johnson's credo*

vision, but the most brilliant vision this side of Paraguay won't budge the culture unless it's backed up by action . . . CEOs encase their mission statements in plexi-glass, hand them out and people laugh. You have to change the way the person who assembles the machine or designs the product acts.'

Envisioning the future of your business is one essential of entrepreneurial leadership but it won't get you very far unless you can also inspire your colleagues to join in building that future. A vision statement on its own won't be the magic bullet. Involvement is the rocket fuel that will launch your vision: compulsively communicating your vision, consulting people at all levels in diagnosing your business problems, promoting your vision and values with a large trumpet.

Here are some examples of how other businesses have built commitment to a shared vision:

Jaguar

When Sir John Egan took over at Jaguar cars as chairman and chief executive, he took time to communicate to the workforce the true financial position of the company. The message was, 'It's not going to be easy but we are getting there.' Jaguar ran quality circles as an ongoing way of getting commitment to the need to do things better and differently, and then organised a sporting and social 'Hearts and Minds' programme for Jaguar employees and their families.

ICL

During 1984–85 ICL put an entire division of 600 people through workshops aimed at creating a greater willingness for change and sharing the vision promulgated by Robb Wilmot in his 'ICL Way'. Each workshop involved a cross-functional cross-level group from the most senior director to the youngest, newest secretary. Each workshop identified major business problems and set up 'projects' to try to address the problems. By turning the organisation on its head in this way, Asa Lanum, the American boss of the division, created a power-house. Instead of denying the need for change, the new level of business awareness and involvement actually generated internal pressure to grow the business for a different future.

Steve Jobs

Steve Jobs has proved to be an extraordinarily visionary leader in the computer world. After leaving Apple he started a new business called Next Computers. He took the entire management team away for a retreat. During this retreat he argued, shared and fine-tuned so that his vision demonstrably became the team's vision. The only technology they had was a flip-chart board. After Jobs' short presentation on his dream, its importance to him and why he thought it exciting, the flip-chart board was rapidly taken over by the members of the team to demonstrate how they intended to make the vision a reality.

Living the vision

Because your people will study your every move for a clue about what really matters to you, your example and your strong leadership are crucial to the business of turning vision into action. There are great risks in the old adage 'Don't do what I do, do what I say'. Most of us place much more weight on actions than words. Your team are bound to look to you personally to demonstrate the values which you are professing. In their dramatic 'culture change' programme the mighty BP (under the strong leadership of Sir Robert Horton) are putting tremendous emphasis on what they call 'walking the talk'; that is on senior management demonstrating the new OPEN* behaviours in everything they do.

You are the 'X factor', it is your personal leadership style which will make all the difference to whether the vision in your head truly becomes the tune to which people's feet are marching. Fortunately, there is a lot to help you develop your visionary leadership. There is also a lot around to get in the way, starting with Machiavelli's definition of leadership in *The Prince* as 'achieving one's ends through guile, deceit and flattery'. There has been much unhelpful mythology around the cult of the personality – the leader as 'hero', a great man with powerful charisma and an ego to match. The *Financial Times* recently stated, of a famous business leader, 'He is not held back by lack of self-esteem'. However, the concept of leader as hero and great man has had its day. These days even Sandhurst relies on methods other than the development of 'officer-like qualities'. Are leaders born or made? Well some Sandhurst comments (ancient folk-lore) are salutary:

'Smith is not a born leader yet.'

'Men will follow this officer anywhere – out of sheer curiosity.'

The mythology has been exploded, it is not leadership qualities' – whatever they are – that make visionary leaders. In the *Leadership secrets of Attila the Hun*, Attila advises us that: 'Seldom are self-centred,

---

*The acronym stands for Open thinking, Personal impact, Empowerment and Networking.

conceited and self-admiring chieftains great leaders but they are great admirers of themselves.' The leader as hero shouts 'over the top' but when he turns round he may find that no one is following him. The trouble with the hero is that he creates dependency in the organisation. He is playing a losing game. Entrepreneurs quite like to accept responsibility and to see themselves as hero or heroine. There is a certain satisfaction in pulling the rabbit out of the hat yet again , to the cries of amazement from the audience! However, in proving his own worth by solving crises, the leader is playing a losing game. By now there's no one around who has any capabilities. Every time he pulls the rabbit out of the hat, he creates more dependency. That's the trap in becoming a hero.

The essence of leadership is the activity of orchestrating the resources of others towards solving problems – not in being the hero oneself. Unfortunately, many entrepreneurial chief executives learn this lesson the hard way. They like to keep on being the hero. That's one reason why successful CEOs often have to leave at a certain point. They have to leave because there is a dependency on them which they can't shift, and they can't let go. Most entrepreneurs will have to learn the transition from 'meddler' to 'strategist' if they are to avoid being a constraint on the growth of their own organisation. The essence of visionary leadership lies in two aspects, first articulating the vision or direction of the business, second in mobilising the energies of all people towards the vision:

> The managers of Innovex have a clear expectation of their chairman, whom they regard as a visionary leader: 'His role should be to lead ten paces ahead, like a magnet, dragging us after him and challenging our way of doing things.'

Leadership can best be described not as a quality, or as a combination of technical skills demanded by particular situations, but as an activity. This is why John Adair's 'action-centred leadership' model has proved so successful both in training the officers of Sandhurst and in many walks of business life. The leader must satisfy three distinct but inter-related sets of needs as shown in Figure 12.5.

Lao-Tzu said quite a few years ago: 'When the best leader's work is done the people say – we did it ourselves.' The idea of leader as hero has been replaced by the concept of leader as conductor of his orchestra of players.

A very useful guide to assessing your visionary leadership capability is the 'Visionary Leader', Leader Behaviour Questionnaire by Dr Marshall Sashkin available in the UK and Europe from MLR Ltd, PO

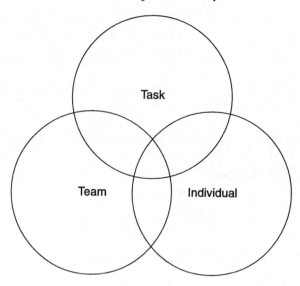

Figure 12.5 *The action-centred leadership model (From John Adair's* Training for Leadership)

Box 28, Carmarthen SA31 1OT; telephone 01267 281661. This question-naire helps you to plot where you are on the 'mountain' of leadership from being 'at the Piedmont' through 'on the final ascent' to 'at the summit'. As well as appealing to mountaineering entrepreneurs it also enables you to assess (if you work with feedback from others) just how visionary a leader you are against ten characteristics which research has shown to be associated with effective leadership. These are:

1. Focused leadership — Effective leaders focus on a few key issues
2. Inter-personal skills — Communication skills in getting messages across to others
3. Trustworthiness — The leader takes clear positions and avoids 'flip, flop' shifts
4. Respect for self and others — The leader has genuine concern for others, what Carl Rogers calls 'unconditional positive regard'
5. Risk taking — The leader is willing to take risks and doesn't spend time in 'cover-your-ass' type activities
6. Bottom line leadership — Effective leaders have a sense of self-assurance and a belief that they can make a difference

7.	Empowered leadership	Effective leaders don't want power for its own sake, they share power to give everyone influence. They 'empower' others
8.	Long-term vision	Effective leaders are able to think over relatively long time spans of at least a few years
9.	Organisation leadership	Effective leaders help the organisation to change
10.	Cultural leadership	Effective leaders create, articulate and communicate shared visions and values

ASSIGNMENT 18

Checking out your leadership ability

1. Develop a statement of your company vision and values, through the involvement of key members of your team and using any combination of the methods described in this chapter, for example:

- Drawing an organisation picture
- Culture statement of what you are moving from/to
- Thoughts about effective organisation (your benchmark exercise)
- Revisiting your core mission.

2. Assess your personal leadership capability using the visionary leadership questionnaire.
3. What practical action can you take to involve everyone in the company in enthusiastically understanding and promoting your vision?

PART 3:

How Will We Get There?

Completion of your basic marketing SWOT and Critical Success Factor analyses, together with reviews of strategic options, people and financial audits, will have placed you in a strong position to redefine your company's future growth strategy. In the light of the analyses you have undertaken so far, you must begin the third and final phase by:

- Revisiting and possibly revising your company's mission statement, first outlined in Chapter 1. Rowing harder does not help if the boat is headed in the wrong direction!

- Setting specific objectives to focus your marketing, financial and operation efforts.

Revise company mission statement

Mission statements do change and should be revisited regularly.

> Martin Sorrell at WPP set out in 1985 with the mission to 'establish a large multinational marketing services company and to be one of the best', rather than simply being the best boutique agency in London. By 1989 the mission statement had altered marginally to be 'the largest multinational marketing services company and the best, by acquisition and adding value to customers products/services'.

Overgearing and debt crisis conditions in the early 1990s are undoubtedly causing a rewriting of mission *statements at WPP, probably nearer to their original statement. In the light of your current trading conditions now, and forecast for the next 18 months, re-examine your mission statement, remembering that it should contain three basic elements:*

1. *A statement of the business you are in and your purpose: e.g. Connectair stated: 'We are in the commuter/feeder airline business and we want to establish a profitable air-link between Cranfield and Heathrow as a forerunner for other links.'*
2. *What you aim to achieve over the next one to three years; the Metropolitan Police state: 'We aim to maintain a peaceful society, free of fear of crime and disorder' (pessimists may argue this may take a little longer than one to three years, but it is certainly a desirable aim!).*
3. *How this aim is to be achieved (values and standards): Sainsbury's aim 'to be leaders in our trade by acting with complete integrity, working to the highest standards and by contributing to the quality of life in the community'; British Airways expressed it 'by putting people first'; IBM 'by dedication to customer service'.*

Mission statements are important as, unlike specific financial or marketing objectives which may be kept board-level confidential, they are meant to be communicated to all company employees, investors and even customers. But above all, as the management writer Peter Drucker has said:

> *'A mission statement has to focus on what the company/institution really tries to do so that everybody within the organisation can say, "This is my contribution to the goal". No hospital worker can tell you what action or behaviour follows from saying "Our mission is healthcare"; but "it's our mission to give assurance to the afflicted" is simple, clear direction for a hospital emergency room. Every mission statement has to reflect the market opportunity or need, your company competence and gain the commitment of your people. Without all three it will not mobilise the human resources of the organisation to get the right things done.'*

How Will We Get There?

The mission must not simply be a statement of good intentions; it must be simple and clear and meet the tasks described above. As new tasks are added, old ones can be removed. Sub-units in a company will have their own unique mission statements, provided they contribute to the overall group mission. This is probably why the group missions most admired by Drucker are the simplest and yet the most motivating; they include the mission of the Salvation Army, 'to make citizens out of the rejected' and of Dr Arnold of Rugby School, 'to make gentlemen out of savages' (like the Metropolitan Police mission statement cited above, this again may be somewhat optimistic!).

> *Solglas Ltd set itself the mission of becoming the largest and most profitable company in the UK glass merchanting and glazing market sector, within five years, by acquisition and commitment to customer service. Its subsidiary company, Autoglass, could contribute to this overall group mission by aiming to become Number 1 in the windscreen and automotive glass replacement business, by similar policies of acquisition and customer service.*

Having revised or renewed your group and unit mission statements, you are now able to proceed to set specific targets and goals, to focus your specific marketing, financial and organisational plans.

Set specific objectives and goals

Objectives, goals and tasks flow naturally from the mission statement and contribute to its achievement. Thus, continuing with the Autoglass example, in order to achieve 'the most profitable, number one position, in the windscreen and automotive glass sector', Autoglass needed to set the following realisable objectives:

1. Marketing. *Achieve a minimum 25 per cent UK market share; partly by internal growth and own depot expansion, partly by acquisition of competitors;*

2. Financial. *Achieve a minimum 20 per cent return on assets, by ensuring new depots and*

acquisitions matched, within time deadlines, the 25 per cent return on assets achieved in the existing depot network;

3. Operations. *Achieve a basic 30 windscreens fitted per month per employee target, by improved training and recruitment policies.*

4. Social goals. *To invest half of 1 per cent of profits in social reconstruction projects, eg Project Fullemploy.*

Goals such as these should be specific, measurable and achievable; reflecting quantity, quality and cost-effectiveness. These are as important in non-profit as profit related businesses, witness the extraordinary (to businessmen) debate in UK education and health today, in introducing simple objectives and measurement systems. It needs to be done, as Peter Drucker again has noted:

> *'Non-profit organisations find it very hard to answer the question of what "results" are. Results can be quantified – at least some of them. The Salvation Army is fundamentally a religious organisation. But it knows the percentage of alcoholics it restores to mental and physical health and the percentage of criminals it rehabilitates. It is highly quantitative ... because it realises that work is only done by people with a deadline. By people who are monitored and evaluated. By people who hold themselves responsible for results.'*

Many have argued that if something cannot be measured, the venture should not be undertaken! By setting clear and concise objectives, in accordance with the company's mission, detailed tasks can be assigned to responsible individuals, and the basis of properly managing results and resources can be set in motion. To achieve the Autoglass 25 per cent market share objective, tasks would include:

1. *Opening three new depots in Midlands region, in next six months;*

2. *Initiating discussions with two south-western competitors, to complete national coverage;*

How Will We Get There?

3. *Recruiting and training staff for new depot openings;*

4. *Developing new promotion material to help launch new, and build additional sales at existing depots.*

All of these tasks and actions need to be set down and incorporated, with attendant costs and results, in the company's or unit's detailed business plan.

13.

The Marketing Plan

The final step in the marketing process, is the Marketing Plan (see page 32). Your detailed one-year marketing plan (sometimes up to three years for major groups) for each operating unit, should encapsulate much of the analysis and description included so far in this book. In outline it should contain:

- Your company's mission statement plus supporting unit mission statements where relevant. (Chapter 1).
- Description of market sector (Chapter 2), including size and sector growth rates over the last three to five years (eg windscreen replacement market is currently £30m pa, with average growth rate of 3 per cent pa compound, without inflation), your market share performance to date and your competitive analysis, to provide evidence for the opportunity and forecast you are making.
- Your company's differentiation and marketing mix strengths and weaknesses (Chapter 3), marketing options and strategy (Chapters 8 and 9), to explain the course you have chosen.
- Your marketing objectives, following from your unit mission and SWOT analyses (Chapter 7).
- The detailed marketing strategy, marketing plan and sales forecast (Chapter 13).

Throughout this book, we have been emphasising that your unit marketing plan should seek to focus on specific customer segments and demonstrate as far as possible the differentiation of your product or service from competitive offerings.

Harvard Professor Michael Porter has described the three basic marketing growth strategies as being overall cost leadership, differentiation and focus.

Overall cost leadership

Where markets are large, requiring large-scale capital investment (eg airlines, basic industries such as iron and steel) producing economies of scale from long runs, the winning marketing strategy is frequently to be the most efficient, lowest-cost producer. Tight control, with low margins creates effective barriers to new entrants and prevents creation of substitutes. Amstrad, for example, is a typical low-cost producer (sourcing computer products from third world countries) and has built a significant market and market share by low pricing.

This is a dangerous marketing strategy, however, for new, small entrants to pursue, for example the airline industry is littered with low price carriers, where unexpected market falls can create havoc for low margin businesses. It is a characteristic of mature industries where one or two major corporations hold dominant market share (eg Pilkington and St Gobain in glass). This may be seen, therefore, as a marketing strategy, primarily for world class competitors and matching resources!

Differentiation

By imaginative design, good image, developed networks and high margins, companies able to demonstrably differentiate their goods or services, are able to build brand loyalty by their demonstrated uniqueness. A recent City University Business School study noted that:

> *'In the strongly advertised mineral water market, the manufacturers' brands enjoyed a 22 per cent premium over the own-labels. Evian, the brand leader, had a 19 per cent share against the combined 26 per cent of the own labels. In the less advertised fruit-juice market, some own-labels were dearer than manufacturers' brands!'*

Those companies which complain in their commodity-like industry it is impossible to create differentiation and get good prices, should stop and reflect on the achievements of Perrier with water (surely the most basic commodity business of all!) and Everest with double-glazing.

Focus

By focusing on one target market at a time, building product differentiation and good margins, focused companies are able to build barriers to entry, frequently in narrow markets unattractive to major competitors (for example Autoglass in the small UK windscreen replacement business), by creating high switching costs for customers or by erecting distribution barriers. Several examples of well focused companies emerged in the UK in the 1980s:

> *Rohan clothing, a UK equivalent to Patagonia in the USA, was developed by founder Paul Howcroft as a provider of light-weight clothing for climbing clubs in*

the Yorkshire Dales. Growing by mail order to similar clubs throughout the UK, the light-weight trousers in particular were quickly seen as a boon to travellers, the next target market. With long lasting zips and ample pockets and attractive design, the clothing subsequently began to appeal to the fashion-conscious, leisure market, leading to the opening of retail stores in Covent Garden and Kensington. As a successful, specialist retailer, the company was subsequently acquired by the Clark Shoe and Fashion Group, allowing Mr Howcroft to devote more time to his passion for car rallying!

While Michael Porter has noted 'there is no formula for achieving competitive advantage, only approaches that are tailored to individual companies', you can see from the above why the growing business should concentrate on trying to achieve differentiation and customer focus – world class domination by overall cost leadership is for later. In the marketing plan, under each heading of the five Ps (Product, Price, Promotion, Place and People) you should endeavour to follow best practice to maximise your competitive advantage.

1. Product

We have seen earlier that all products have service elements and vice versa, and in consequence achieving differentiation entails an endless battle or trade-off against cost, quality and service level. In this battle you have to seek improvements along two or even all three dimensions, simultaneously! In the 1960s, British manufacturers, particularly in the automobile industry, appeared to have neglected the quality dimension, in largely the mistaken belief that 'dynamic obsolescence' (the marketing flavour of that moment) was almost good for that industry. The Japanese car manufacturers, in changing their image within 20 years from 'cheap and cheerful' in the sixties to reliability and performance in the eighties (which proves quality can be brought back!) showed that quality need not be neglected while fighting costs and the rising service levels expected by customers.

Product quality is clearly vital for the growing company:

James Koch, in developing the Boston Beer Company, noted that the biggest problem for the new and growing company was in creating in customers' minds an image of product quality. 'You can't sell a product you don't believe in and in cold calling the only thing standing between you and the customer's scorn is the integrity of your product'.

Those people making pasta who believe it is the freshest and best around, are likely to be the long-run winners. Product differentiation is important for profits, as the matrix in Figure 13.1 shows.

	Low	High
Low	OK eg Pilkington Glass	Superb eg Colman's Readymix Mustard
High	Awful eg High Street Computer Dealers	OK eg Everest Double Glazing

COSTS (row label between Low and High)

Figure 13.1 *Differentiation*

High costs with low differentiation is clearly the box to avoid, confirming again the importance of working with and controlling suppliers' costs, seeking good design and image (that people buy with their eyes is as true for industrial products as for High Street goods), ensuring features and benefits match customers needs. But, above all, you must ensure that quality is not lost while you integrate these functions. Quality is not, of course, just what you do, but also *how* you do it, as Jan Carlson of Scandinavian Airlines noted in listing these 'moments of truth' in customer contacts:

Customer contact point	*Customer expectation*	
Sales	Reliability	
Invoices	Responsiveness	
Telephone	Competence	What does customer
Reception	Courtesy	think of you at each
Packaging	Credibility	contact point?
Delivery	Security	(each 'Moment of
	Tangibles	Truth')

So, quality is hearts and minds, attitudes and standards, and your product marketing plan must include some quality targets and indications as to how you will audit your performance. Achieving British Standard 5750 might be expensive for the growing company, in terms of extra personnel and procedures, but it is now firmly on the agenda of many growth companies, particularly given the quality discipline and assurance it gives to customers, at home and abroad.

2. Price

Price and quality are closely linked in the minds of most customers. Concentration on good quality should provide greater flexibility in your pricing plan. Differentiation can be achieved by careful focus on the needs of different target groups of customers. Above all, attention has to be paid to the gross margins (ie the gap between sales and variable costs) on each of your product groups. As Brian Warnes has explained in his Genghis Khan guide:

> *Ignoring cash and service companies like banks and supermarkets, most manufacturing companies achieving less than about 25 per cent gross margin are likely to fail sooner or later. Companies begin to achieve real strength, cash flow and financial durability once margins get over about 40 per cent. The real high fliers, like properly structured electronics companies, begin to get into their stride at over 60 per cent.*

Many companies survive on smaller margins, but survive is perhaps all they do. Without a good margin there is no overhead room for building further differentiation by extensive promotion, research and development, or distribution experimentation with low margins. Goods have to be sold on, with the barest minimum of service, in order to survive. Yet thriving retailers, even in depressed times, concentrate on margins and different target groups of customers by using price and quality across the range:

> *Marks and Spencer used a 'tiered catalogue' with three main price ranges for St Michael brands: Easy, Mid and Upper, to suit different customer groups. Ratners offered customers jewellery at prices they could afford, rather than quality they could not: in many stores you can find a one carat diamond ring at £1,600, a silver plated tray and decanter at £14.99 and 9 carat earrings at £2. As a result Ratner's doubled Samuels' turnover per square foot from £32 to £62 a year.*

The pricing decision has to be revisited regularly, particularly in inflationary times; margins, like quality, must be maintained by constant attention to cost, quality and competition. Price increases should be combined with improvements in quality or service:

> *Rabone Tools commissioned a new corporate design for its wide range of hand-held tools. Featuring a single logo, distinctive colour schemes for product groupings, and highlighting new product features, permitted the company to relaunch its existing product range with a 5 per cent price increase, leading to a 60 per cent increase in profits.*

3. Promotion

Advertising (and PR) is a major way for companies to differentiate and focus their activities. In many ways this must be true, if one compares one mineral water with another, or if you try to choose among comparable double glazing systems; you may choose Perrier and Everest through the sheer weight and differentiation achieved by their distinctive advertising, which their good gross margins permit!

Your promotion plan is in many ways a mini-marketing plan. Advertising is simply an expensive way for one person to talk to another and, as such, must be rigorously controlled. Thus, procedures to follow include those recommended by Tim Bell, formerly of Saatchi and Saatchi:

- set specific campaign objectives (building sales, market share)
- decide strategy (budget, media choice, geographical profile)
- target audience (market segment, demographic profile)
- decide advertising content (specific product/service benefits to highlight)
- execution and style (humour, hard sell?). Ask yourself, if your product/service was a car or a newspaper, which kind of car (Rolls or a Mini), which kind of newspaper (*Sun* or *The Times*) do you want to be seen as.

Leaflets and brochures for exhibitions have to be written with the specific exhibition visitor in mind; press releases are written for professional editors, as Hyde and Partners, advertising agency, explain:

> 'It is the Editor who decides to print, not you, as when you supply and pay for advertisements. You must, therefore, attract the Editor's attention, with a snappy headline and a stimulating first paragraph. British Rail did it when their PR release entitled their new rail-airport link as 'Gatquick'. Your release must be short, it must be factual. It is not a 'sales message'. Print always in double space, to allow the Editor to make changes.'

Issue targeted press releases regularly, including photographs, personality and performance quotations, and write in a sunny story style! Good newspaper or trade journal coverage can provide good copy to help improve the normally low, $2\frac{1}{2}$ per cent, response rates on direct mail, if you include them in your mailing.

Above all, monitor carefully the cost/effectiveness of each campaign undertaken; either by comparing tear-off coupon replies against the cost of the advertisement, or ensuring customers are questioned, at the till or on the invoice, as to how they came into contact with your company. Popular mythology has it that only half of your advertising works, but you must know which half.

4. Place

The distribution plan must match the other elements of the marketing mix, noted above, to maintain the differentiation and focus sought by the company. If your product is of the highest quality, with price and promotion to match, it must be available in the major quality stores. Different channels must be used to reach different customer segments as Table 13.1 denotes:

Table 13.1 *Means of reaching target groups*

	Channel	Target group
Farm goods producers	Pick your own	DIY
	Farm shop	Commuters/Trippers
	Mail order	Specialist interest
	Specialist shop	Groups (eg health, vegetarian etc)
	Wholesale/Retailer	Diverse socio-economic groups
	Restaurants	Variety of income groups
	Health farms	Health/high income group

The choice of distribution channel, therefore, can make an important contribution to both your company differentiation and to reaching your target group of customers. The chosen channel must be consistent with the differentiation/focus chosen for the company. Remember also, that if you are investing in 'safe' property, to protect your distribution channel, that until very recently the world's biggest bankrupt in the *Guinness Book of Records* was the 'owner' of 20,000 Freshwater flats in Central London! Property aspects of distribution are often best left to the real property specialists!

5. People

The final ingredient in the marketing plan jigsaw must be quality salespeople to consistently maintain your key marketing differentiation. It is not entirely impossible! People generally prefer to work for quality companies; there are frequent reports among companies committed to quality, like Sainsbury's, of better staff morale, job satisfaction and even admiration of leadership (compared with surveys showing most managers are regarded by staff as being 'misleading'). Attention to maintaining good margins can ensure staff are properly rewarded; as the Relocation Services Institute has observed:

'There is probably, for example, a direct connection between the generally low estate agents' sales fees in the UK (1¹/₂ to 2¹/₂ per cent compared with 7 to 8 per

*cent in France and the United States) and the low staff performance in the UK,
compared with the energetic sales support provided in the US and Continental
housing market.'*

A well-remunerated and motivated staff will act as enthusiastic sales
promoters of the quality company as well as being more willing to
travel long distances to work and to act as the eyes and ears of the
company in the competitive market-place. None of this will come
about simply by accident, as Chapter 14 will explore; but just as
customers see quality companies as caring companies, meeting and
responding to customer requirements, so also, all other things being
equal, do employees.

With all the above five Ps consistently in place in the marketing plan,
the basis is set to construct an operations (people) and financial plan to
match the marketing strategy proposed. The natural link with these
important activities is the sales forecast.

Sales forecast and control

The sales forecast should be the natural outcome and quantification of
the marketing planning. It should reflect:

- known industry or market segment growth rates (eg if your
  growth is to be faster than the industry average growth rate, say 5
  per cent versus 3 per cent for the industry sector as a whole, it
  should reflect explanations why – such as investment or extra
  promotional support).
- estimated own and competitive market shares (with explanations
  as to why your market share is to increase at the expense of
  competitors).
- your own targeted and costed plans to increase market share (for
  example, new depot openings will add 2 per cent market share).

Comparisons should then be made between the above and the short-
term forecasts of your sales team, based on known customer contacts.

Inevitably the smaller, growing business cannot always achieve
total levels of precision in all of the above areas; particular attention
must be given to making best estimates, nonetheless, and learning
from experience.

*In making growth plans, the Directors of Autoglass were hampered by lack of
market information. Through discussions with leading windscreen suppliers it
was possible to guess the total size of the UK windscreen replacement market.
This was compared with the known average windscreen breakage rate (3½ per
cent pa) applied to the total car population (17 million) to corroborate market size.*

The average car population was growing at 3 per cent pa, so forecasts of the future replacement market could be made; own unit sales indicated Autoglass market share, and forecasts could be tied to a programme of new depot openings and market growth'.

Attention must also be given to:

- Known industry production and distribution capacity, with the effect of planned additions or deletions;
- Allowing for both the impact of seasonality and the effect of economic trends on your business;
- Relating the timing of your promotional expenditures to planned sales increases and monitoring their impact closely.

Some companies produce both optimistic and pessimistic forecasts and steer a middle course; conservatism is always recommended, particularly where new products are involved, especially because, as a rule, less than 20 per cent of your first customers will become repeat clients. Sometimes the recent past can be a poor guide to even the immediate future:

Coldshield Windows, as one of the first national double glazing companies, grew at annual interest rates of between 25 and 30 per cent throughout the early 1970s, benefiting from customer concern with the first oil price rise and the rapid spread of central heating. Attempts were made to correlate the percentage of homes with central heating (60 per cent by 1979) and the low percentage of homes with double glazing (under 10 per cent in 1979), to show that growth could continue at these rates throughout the early 1980s. Depot expansion plans were developed and promotional expenditure committed on this basis. The sharp economic downturn of 1980–82 halted market growth completely, and only the more conservatively planned double glazing companies remained in the black!

So, do not let the natural optimism of the sales team outweigh the careful reasoning and logic of the marketing plan. This can best be done by ensuring that your control system regularly monitors the effectiveness of your marketing efforts, regularly recording, for example, the cost of promotional sales leads, or sales per sales person, to give some early indication of market maturity or turn-down. Continuing the Coldshield example:

Recording promotional expenditure per sales lead was only introduced in 1980 and showed an average cost of £40 per direct newspaper lead; this compared with under £10 cost per sales lead for Wallguard's new company in France. The disparity emphasised the growth of UK competition in double glazing as well as the maturity of the market, soon to be shown in static sales figures.

Armed with a sensible marketing plan and a conservative sales forecast, you are now able to develop your matching operations (people) and financial plan.

ASSIGNMENT 19

Prepare your marketing plan

1. Summarise your unit mission statement:

2. What has been your average percentage industry/market growth rate in the last three to five years, and what is your current market share percentage compared with main competitors?

3. What SWOT conclusions have most relevance for your marketing plan (strengths to build on, weaknesses to repair), what strategic role is your unit performing (invest/disinvest)?

14.

The People Plan

Where people fit into the business plan

If the business plan describes the journey you intend, the people plan explains how you will get your team on board to make it happen. A vital part of your business plan will be the power of the executive summary, in which a description of the management team and the company's culture and history will be essential to the 'feel' of what you're trying to do.

Equally important will be the evidence that you have assessed and are using existing organisation capability as fully as possible before asking for additional resources. At the same time you need to spell out in detail the management and staffing strategies which will be needed for future growth: numbers, skills mix, and how you will recruit, retain and reward.

You may have carried out the most sophisticated environmental scan, financial forecasts and marketing SWOTs but if you haven't put in place the organisation and people to make it happen, then you haven't got a business plan. Organisation is strategy. Yves Doz commented that the reason the Japanese are such superb strategists is that they have both environmental flexibility and organisation resource. This chapter aims to help you plan to get resource in place. None of it comes about by accident, and unfortunately every source of people resource (recruitment, training, re-skilling) tends to take a lot of money, effort and most important – time – to get in place.

Your people objectives

Where you put your people is the direction in which your business will move. In carrying out earlier work of organisation diagnosis, you have assessed your people, structure and systems, the potential fits and misfits with your plans for growth and the key items on your organisational agenda for change. What are the organisational levers which you will need to pull to achieve change? Are they primarily to do with people, or process, or changing your structure? It is likely that your people objectives will fall around some, or all, of the following:

- Recruiting new skills
- Developing the management team
- Building your company culture and identity
- Reviewing 'people systems' such as appraisal, career planning, selection processes
- Rewarding your people
- Putting in a process to communicate and co-ordinate as the organisation grows
- Changing the organisation structure.

Key elements of the people plan

Having decided your primary people objectives, you are in an excellent position to outline the initiatives you intend to take to turn a paper business plan into an organisation reality. The following elements will be key:

- Vision and values
- Recruitment and selection
- Retaining and motivating staff
- Appraisal
- Recognition and rewards
- Roles and responsibilities
- Communication and team building
- Training and development plan.

Vision and values

Your business plan needs to excite both your management team, who will make your money for you, and the potential backers who will give you more. No one wants to put their life or their money into a business that's as boring as Scunthorpe on a rainy day. A mission statement is vital evidence of a clear focus, but it is a passionate and inspirational vision of what's special about you and your company philosophy that will bring in the punters. The product branding which you sell to customers is nothing without the 'internal' branding. The executive summary of the business plan is the perfect opportunity for flaunting your company vision.

Recruitment and selection

Recruitment is perhaps the biggest worry for growing businesses. It can be a major constraint on development plans. A Cranfield survey in February 1990 identified the problems of small businesses (see Table 14.1).

Table 14.1 *The key problems of small businesses*

Key priorities	Percentage of respondents
Recruiting key staff	83
Finding customers	59
Raising new finance	31
High interest rates	27
Red tape	21

Getting the right people is a difficult, time-consuming and costly business. Getting it wrong is even more expensive and can be extremely painful. Few growing businesses can claim not to have fallen into this trap. However, you can increase the odds on success by putting in place some basic process and discipline which is likely to include:

- deciding on the numbers and skills mix you are going to need over the next one to three years;
- preparing job descriptions as a guide to recruitment covering job title and purpose, to whom responsible, for whom, limits of accountability and main tasks;
- preparing a person specification, outlining the sort of person you think is likely to be effective in the job (the seven point plan covers physical make-up, attainments, general intelligence, special aptitudes, interests, disposition, circumstances);
- sourcing your requirements creatively, through networks of contacts, employment and search agencies, newspaper advertisements, hotel wine evenings etc;
- weeding out from application forms or CVs those who don't fit the job description and person specification;
- using psychometric tests to supplement your interview process. A huge range of tests covering aptitude or ability are available, tests of general intelligence, tests of attainment, personality inventories. You can locate the appropriate test for your business through

the British Psychological Society (0533 549568) or the IPM (071-946 9100).

Retaining and motivating staff

Having got the right people to implement your strategy, the problem is to keep them. If morale and levels of job satisfaction are low, then performance will suffer, the team will be affected and often people (usually those you want to keep!) will leave. 'Holcot Press is a service business,' Richard Meredith says, and 'Keeping people and good morale is crucial to our business.'

One of the biggest mistakes you can make is to assume that money alone is the way to motivate staff. See Figure 14.2 which gives a graphic example of how minor is the motivating effect of a salary increase by itself.

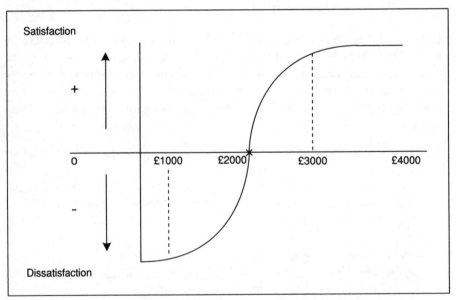

Figure 14.2 *The effect of a salary increase on job satisfaction*

In fact, it's not so much the amount of money awarded that is important – expectation is all. The 'S' shaped curve shows that the effect of a salary increase on job satisfaction and, therefore, performance, depends on what you expected. Thus, if you expected a salary increase of £2000 and this is what you got, then the effect is zero. If you expected an increase of £2000 and were given £3000, then your job satisfaction will increase. You will have a warm glow but the feeling

Question	Rating* 0...5...10	Comment
1. How would you assess your morale right now? Please explain why.		
2. What action would help to move your score up and increase your job satisfaction?		*Comment only*
3. How well does the management team manage?		
4. How effective are our internal communications up down and across? What improvements would you suggest?		
5. How clear are you about what is expected of you (targets etc)?		
6. How adequately are you rewarded & recognised for good performance?		
7. How well does the appraisal process work? Any recommendations?		
8. How fully are we using all your talents? How could we do better?		
9. What do you most like about working for this business? (What's special about us?)		*Comment only*
10. To what extent do you feel part of the total team? How could we involve you more?		

*Rating: 0 = very poor; 5 = average; 10 = excellent

Figure 14.3 *Some ideas on a simple attitude survey (to use as an annual benchmark)*

soon tails off! Similarly, if you expect £2000 and are given £1000, you will actively be de-motivated!

Maslow's famous hierarchy of needs shows just how many other factors are involved in job satisfaction, from physiological, through security and social needs to the needs for self-esteem and self-actualisation. In fact, the problem isn't so much that of motivating people, but of avoiding de-motivating them! If managers can keep off the backs of employees, it is quite possible that they will motivate themselves. After all, as Herzberg established years ago in his interviews at Pittsburg Iron and Steel, most of us want the same things: a sense of achievement or challenge, recognition of our efforts, an interesting and varied job, opportunities for responsibility, advancement and job growth.

You can gain a lot of mileage by arranging the context of work so that people can find more motivators in the jobs they do. You will also keep them longer and they will be more likely to empower the business change you are seeking.

There are some key measures which you can use to benchmark the morale of your people. They are:

- Monitor labour turnover regularly;
- Carry out exit interviews;
- Survey levels of job satisfaction.

When ICL was trying to stay alive in 1983–84 the annual labour turnover of the Reading Division was 25 per cent. This was against a Thames Valley norm of around 12 per cent. A clear signal of low morale! When anyone leaves, it is a good idea to get a reliable and trusted member of staff to carry out an exit interview. In this way you can discover the real reasons why people are leaving and identify sources of internal dissatisfaction. If, every year or every two years, you carry out a simple internal survey of staff attitudes you will be able to pin-point problem areas in the parts of your business which you can't reach (see Figure 14.3 for a sample survey questionnaire). Even a simple 0–10 scale will give valuable information. For example, Holcot

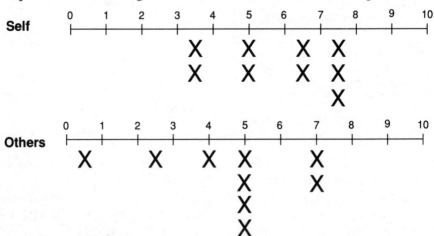

Figure 14.4 *The morale of Holcot Press management team and their subordinates in 1990*

Press management team defined their morale and the morale of those under them on a simple scale, reproduced in Figure 14.4. The difference in rating indicates the work they had to do in 1990 to bring the motivation of all employees up to the level of the management team.

Appraisal

Appraisal lies at the heart of assessing, improving and developing people's performance for the future of the business. However, to be an effective tool, appraisal needs to be approached seriously and professionally by all involved.

Take Innovex, providing marketing services to the pharmaceutical industry. Two years ago Innovex had a fairly half-hearted appraisal system. Not all managers carried out appraisals, some interviews took only half an hour or so, assessment of areas for improvement was distinctly lacking, there were no clear objectives, people were assessed against personality characteristics (such as common sense) rather than results. Yet the great issue for Innovex is the lack of depth of management resource. This could easily become a limitation on its phenomenal growth rate. There are no obvious successors, and managers are already 100 per cent stretched in their current jobs. The requirement is 'to grow people to run businesses in the UK and Europe'. There are some significant gaps between the management 'animal' of today and the one Innovex will need for the future. As Barrie Haigh says, 'The key is to look hard at our people, look hard and develop.' The mechanism for doing this is appraisal.

Innovex has put all its managers and secretaries through appraisal interview training (video), taken a good look at its appraisal system and revamped it along the following lines:

- *Appraisal as a 'talk between people who work together'.*

- *Open two-way discussion, both appraiser and appraisee prepare for the interview in advance.*

- *Results orientated rather than personality orientated. The appraisal interview starts with a review against objectives and finishes by setting objectives for the year to come.*

- *The appraisal discussion is kept separate from salary review.*

- *The appraisal starts with performance and only later moves on to reviewing potential.*

- *The appraisal format is a narrative rather than a tick boxes and ratings process. It covers a discussion of achievements, areas for improvement, overall performance, training and development, and career expectations.*

- *Plenty of time is allowed for each appraisal interview (one and a half hours on average).*

- *Appraisals are carried out once a year, with more regular quarterly reviews.*

- *Training needs are identified and acted upon by those concerned.*

Recognition and rewards

As businesses grow it is common to find that rewards are encouraging the performance you needed in the past rather than the performance you need now. Different stages of growth demand different reward packages, from the hands-on, commission-based, sales-linked rewards of a Phase 1 business, through the cost and budget management of Phase 2, into the challenges of giving the whole management team a share of the future which comes in Phase 3.

As the business grows up the Greiner curve it is likely that the recognition and reward package will need to be slanted to:

(a) Encourage genuine 'ownership' of and commitment to the business (share options?);
(b) Provide some element of reward for team performance as well as individual success;
(c) Demonstrate a direct relationship to performance.

Roles and responsibilities

Although managers, and certainly consultants, are often over-enthusiastic in pulling the lever for change which is marked 'structure', you will need to consider whether the current structure of your business is a constraint on growth. For example, if you have a traditional, functional, hierarchical structure with lots of layers of management, it is very likely that it will preclude you from rapidly diversifying into new businesses. Unfortunately, restructuring means more than just rewriting the organisation chart of today. It means getting people to behave in new ways.

If you want to get people to behave differently, rather than telling them to do so, it's usually much more effective to give them different things to do. This is why realigning individual roles and responsibilities can be a powerful force for change.

Glaxo UK, the UK's leading pharmaceutical company and single largest supplier of medicines to the NHS, talks about its behavioural guide-lines, written in

September 1989 as an outline for the working practices needed to achieve the strategic plans of the 1990s. Of the five guide-lines, two refer specifically to roles:

Role clarity
Clear definition of job parameters so that each individual's contribution to outputs and objectives is understood and overlapping responsibilities are minimised.

Accountability
Clear definition of responsibilities so that individuals understand both their contribution to achieving business goals and the scope of their decision making.

Communication and team-building

The young, entrepreneurial business needs to give little attention to its internal communication. Its people tend to be a highly motivated small team who spend a lot of time together at work and socially. As the business grows in numbers, sheer size will start to crack the foundations of its camaraderie, the introduction of new people without the original motivation will change the flavour of relationships. It is at this point that you will find yourself consciously having to introduce ways and means of getting the team together and keeping them facing the right way. Involving your team in the preparation and presentation of the business plan can, in itself, be a good way of providing co-ordination to a growing business.

In addition, you will probably have to start putting in processes to address what happened quite naturally in Phase 1 growth. It's amazing how many businessmen expect a team to work as a team without any practice. After all it (presumably!) doesn't work this way for football teams. The way to build a team is to find many formal and informal ways of bringing them together: cascade briefings, state of the nation addresses, lunches, social events, special project teams, happy hours. Fun is actually quite compatible with profit. The importance of informal contact between people, as a way of building productive networks, cannot be over-emphasised but again it won't happen without the mechanisms to make it happen.

It's absolutely clear that the more you are trying to grow and change the business, the more you will have to communicate. Briefing groups are an excellent discipline for downward communication but there's a lot more to it than that. You need processes to ensure upward communication and especially to co-ordinate across the barriers which your organisation will establish as it grows. There are plenty of examples to help here and plenty of ways of building your team: for example, outward bound programmes, internal team building events – giving everyone the same language. The Belbin team profiles, for example, are particularly useful as a way of identifying individuals' preferred team roles, accepting that difference is essential to effective team-working and learning to live with each other. Belbin suggests that successful teams need a mix of eight roles.

Chairman/team leader
  Stable, dominant, extrovert
  Concentrates on objectives
  Does not originate ideas
  Focuses people on what they do
    best

Plant
  Dominant, high IQ, introvert
  A 'scatterer of seeds', originates
    ideas
  Misses out on detail
  Thrustful but easily offended

Resource investigator
  Stable, dominant, extrovert
  Sociable
  Contacts with outside world
  Salesperson/diplomat/liaison
    officer
  Not original thinker

Shaper
  Anxious, dominant, extrovert
  Emotional, impulsive
  Quick to challenge and respond
    to challenge
  Unites ideas, objectives and
    possibilities
  Competitive
  Intolerant of woolliness and
    vagueness

Company worker
  Stable, controlled
  Practical organiser
  Can be inflexible but likely to
    adapt to established systems
  Not an innovator

Monitor evaluator
  High IQ, stable, introvert
  Measured analysis not
    innovation
  Unambitious and lacking
    enthusiasm
  Solid, dependable

Team worker
  Stable, extrovert, low
    dominance
  Concerned with individuals'
    needs
  Builds on others' ideas
  Cools things down

Finisher
  Anxious, introvert
  Worries over what will go
    wrong
  Permanent sense of urgency
  Preoccupied with order
  Concerned with 'following
    through'

Figure 14.5 *Belbin's team profiles*

Training and development plan

It is inevitable as the business grows that through no fault of their own, people's knowledge and skills, which were once adequate, become inappropriate for the next phase of growth. One option is to get rid of people with obsolete skills and bring new ones in. But this is both extremely expensive and time-consuming, and very disruptive to your team identity and culture. Clearly a preferable option is to keep training and developing your existing people resource (see Figure 14.6).

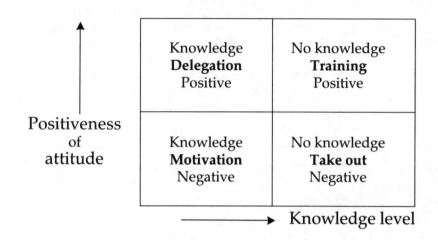

Figure 14.6 *The role of training*

Even those who have been recruited with the skills they need, require training to do things your way, which may not be the way they have been taught in the past. Figure 14.7 is a typical training 'menu' resulting from a training needs analysis within a small publishing business:

Unfortunately, when asked what training they need, most people find it difficult to answer. It is therefore essential to spend time identifying training needs for your team, for each key individual and also for yourself. Training needs are the gap between performance now and the performance you would like in the future. For example, Innovex has historically employed managers with a sales and marketing background; what it needs for the future is strong all-round businessmen who can run bits of the growing business. The appraisal interview provides one good opportunity for identifying training needs, another approach is to carry out a training needs

Technical/Job related	• For example accounting or sales skills • Negotiation skills • Computer skills
Management skills (existing and potential managers)	• Leadership and motivation • Team building • Appraising, counselling and disciplinary interviews • Managing change • Recruitment and selection • Training and developing staff
Business	• Basic finance • Principles of marketing • Putting together the business plan • Understanding strategy

Figure 14.7 *An example of a training menu*

analysis. This analysis depends on interviewing members of staff to determine key issues such as their background, role, skills needed in the job, strengths and weaknesses, career aspirations. A good survey will also include a discussion of changing business requirements, and the gap between these demands and present capability.

The former government Training Agency, now called TECs (Training and Enterprise Councils) operate on a local basis to provide up to 50 per cent of the costs of management training as part of Business Growth Training (BGT Option 3). Under BGT Option 3 the local TEC will form an agreement with your business, and approve an appropriate training consultant who, typically over a 12-month period, will:

Phase 1 Carry out a training needs analysis.
Phase 2 Prepare a plan for change to include a training and development programme.
Phase 3 Provide the agreed management training.
Phase 4 Complete quarterly progress reports, document all the programmes and prepare a final report.

Checklist: Minimum requirements for people systems

Recruitment and Selection

- Job descriptions for all jobs
- A person specification
- An application form
- An advertising/sourcing procedure

Retaining and Motivating (including staff appraisal)

- Monitoring annual labour turnover
- Carrying out exit interviews
- Annual or biennial survey of staff attitudes (you can do it yourself)
- At least an annual appraisal interview – an opportunity for two-way discussion available to all staff
- An appraisal format covering objectives, performance, training needs and review of potential

Reward

- A pay system which distinguishes good performers from poor performers (and rewards the behaviour you want!)
- A pay system comparable with the going rate in the market place
- Recognition of team performance (at a local and/or corporate level)
- 'Little, immediate and often' reward and recognition

Training and development plan

- A training plan which specifies the needs of the total team
- Training needs analysis of key individuals' strengths, weaknesses and requirements (appraisal will help)
- A self-development plan for you

Communications

- A monthly management meeting
- Twice yearly state of the nation talks when you bring everyone together to put across the realities of the business and its performance

- A cascade system for briefing downwards (the Industrial Society will advise)
- Informal/social/cross-functional meetings, ie weekly happy hour, peanut party or lunches.

ASSIGNMENT 20

Putting the people plan in place

Prepare a people plan for your business

1. Your Vision (see Assignment 18)
2. Key People Objectives (develop from agenda for change, Assignment 12).
   The structure, people or systems levers you need to pull
3. The People Plan

Topic	Action	Who will do by when
Recruitment and Selection (Getting the right people)		
Retaining and Motivating (keeping them)		
Appraisal (Assessing them)		

The People Plan

Topic	Action	Who will do by when
Recognition and Rewards (Rewarding them)		
Communication and Team-building (Team involvement)		
Roles and Responsibilities (Structure change)		

15.

Managing Change

Managing change effectively is intrinsic to the business plan. Only if your business plan uses existing resources to the full and only if it gains the commitment of those who have to implement it, will it become a reality. When examining the present state capability in Assignment 12 you will have already identified candidates for your organisational agenda for change. The question which this chapter addresses is how best to manage people through the transition state in order to achieve the future state of your business plan.

Change is no longer a matter of gradual and cosy adaptation. Major organisational change follows a predictable and rather uncomfortable pattern characterised by:

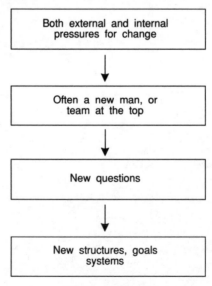

Change hurts

We have only to observe people in a meeting or the staff canteen or relaxing in the pub to know that the human being is a creature of habit, who likes familiar patterns: the same bar stool, the same group of friends to talk to over lunch. Most of us don't like change, we like things to stay the same. By definition change means the unknown; it's risky, uncertain and worrying, and that applies to organisational change just as much as to personal changes such as divorce.

In 1983 ICL was rescued from the brink of disaster by a combined City and government deal. Sir Michael Edwardes was put in as the new man at the top. Of his earlier experience in BL he had written:

> *'It is easier to lead a defence of the status quo than to lead people into something new with all the attendant uncertainties and the innate fear of the unknown which change implies.'*

Thus, even while Robb Wilmot, then MD, was announcing that: 'every part of our business has changed, is changing and will continue to change', people within ICL perceived change as a temporary and unnecessary disruption of the status quo. They believed that once management got it 'right', change would go away and their lives could get back to normal. They didn't really want to see how inevitable change was for ICL's survival – the costs were too great.

Of course, change has productivity costs, but change also costs emotionally – it hurts. Here are some comments from ICL from the 1983–84 period:

- **Fear:** 'Don't think the company realise how frightened people are.'
- **Loss:** 'Teams broken, relationships broken, lack of commitment to keeping our unit.'
- **Discomfort:** 'We feel very battered.'
- **Stress** (causing personal overloads): 'In the past we worked hard and played hard, and people laughed – they don't any more.'

Individual resistance to change shouldn't be a surprise, it's the normal reaction. Resistance stems from:

- Fear of the unknown
- Lack of information
- Threats to status
- Threats to established skills and competencies
- Fear of failure
- Reluctance to let go
- Lack of perceived benefits
- Threats to power base
- Low trust organisational climate
- History and previous custom

- Fear of looking stupid
- Feeling vulnerable and exposed
- Threat to self-esteem
- Loss of control of one's own destiny
- Loss of team relationships
- High anxiety
- Stress

The predictable process of change

Almost any major change will make things worse before it makes them better. The concept of the productivity curve means that the immediate impact of change is a decrease in productivity as people struggle with new ways of doing things, cope with their own learning curve and desperately try to 'keep the shop open'. It may be months or even years before productivity recovers let alone exceeds original levels (see Figure 15.1).

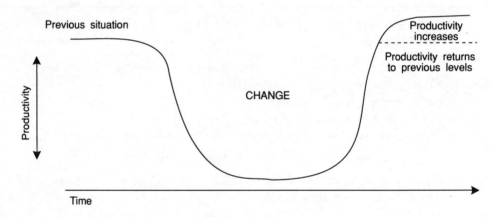

Figure 15.1 *The productivity curve*

Unfortunately, the inevitable fall-off in production increases the likelihood that managers who have an unrealistic expectation of how long change will take to achieve, will panic and pull the plug on the change just when they are about to start to see the pay-off! This phenomenon is well described by John Philipp and Sandy Dunlop, adapting an idea from Darryl Connor and depicting it as 'the long dark night of the innovator' (see Figure 15.2).

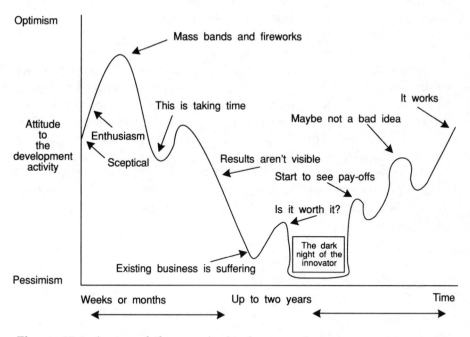

Figure 15.2 *A map of the organisational energy during any major transition programme*

Everything looks like a failure halfway through. It takes courage to stay with the vision during this period to persevere, to maintain enthusiasm and commitment. Here's one company who didn't make it:

> ABC Retail is part of an American consumer chain. It has been established in the UK for about 70 years. It employs over 2000 staff in the UK with almost 150 branches. In 1988 a new French chief executive was appointed. His job was to implement a vast programme of change, moving the organisation from formal traditional values towards greater delegation of authority levels and greater personal responsibility. He said it would take time. One and a half years later in 1990, the shareholders, concerned about low profits, forced the new CEO out. An American CEO was brought over from the States to undo the changes made by his predecessor and to 'bring the UK operation back into the family'.

Change always takes longer than you think. For example, it is said that a major programme of attitude change in a large organisation will take five years. One or two of the big and extremely prestigious Swedish banks maintain that it has taken them the best part of 20 years to turn unwieldy organisations around to be decentralised and customer responsive. Even in a small responsive business, the temptation is to assume that change can be made to happen overnight. For example, one chief executive we know asked his consultant to devise a totally new 'culture' and to have it in place by the next board meeting.

The risk of not allowing sufficient time for the change to 'bed down' is that the embryo change plant will be pulled up and thrown on the rubbish heap, to be succeeded by yet another change and another after that – all equally likely to meet the same fate. The change process predictably takes time, costs money and effort, and causes an immediate fall-off in productivity. Perhaps by expecting this scenario, the businessman can help to maintain his cool and ride the rapids.

In responding to a significant change, people also go through a predictable pattern of personal response. This has been described as a transition curve, showing an individual's response to change over time (see Figure 15.3).

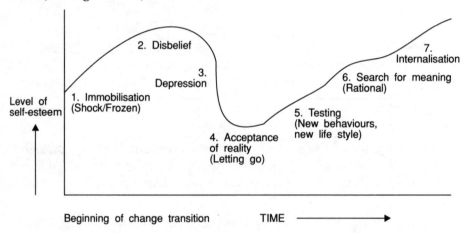

Figure 15.3 *Self-esteem changes during transitions; based on Adams, Hayes & Hopson (1976) 'Towards an understanding of transition, understanding and managing personal change'*

Similarly, Fink, Beak & Taddeo describe a four-stage process through which people typically pass in learning to adjust to a personal change such as bereavement or an organisational change such as a relocation, redundancy or restructuring (see Figure 15.4).

The most important lesson for anyone who is trying to grow a business is that change doesn't happen automatically, and that the way in which the CEO handles innovation and change will have a critical effect in helping people to go through the change process as rapidly and painlessly as possible. Managerial support is crucial, just as support for a grieving spouse is crucial. It's an interesting but sad fact that most people who are trying to cope with bereavement get the support from friends and family when they least need it, in the early stages of shock. When they most need encouragement, months later, most of the relatives have gone home!

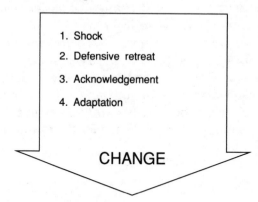

1. Shock

2. Defensive retreat

3. Acknowledgement

4. Adaptation

CHANGE

Figure 15.4 *Typical response to significant change (organisational or individual)*

Identifying and managing resistance

Like sales objections, resistance to change should be expected and even welcomed. By expressing their resistance people can convert themselves into believers and create their own momentum for change. Any organisational change will have pros and cons, it is the balance

$$C = (A\ B\ D) > X$$

C	=	Change
A	=	Dissatisfaction with status quo
B	=	Desirability of proposed change
D	=	Practicability of change (minimum risk/disruption)
X	=	Cost of changing

Figure 15.5 *Managing resistance*

between the driving forces and the resisting forces which will determine whether change happens. This balance can even be expressed as an equation, which states that unless the cost of changing is exceeded by the weight of dissatisfaction with what you've got, plus the desirability of the proposed change, plus its practicability, the change won't happen (see Figure 15.5).

For example, you may see a house which you and your spouse find very desirable. But unless you are pretty dissatisfied with the one you've already got (too few bedrooms) and unless the move is practicable (doesn't disrupt school arrangements) then the 'cost' of changing will outweigh the benefits and you won't do it. The same applies to organisational change. Consider the examples opposite.

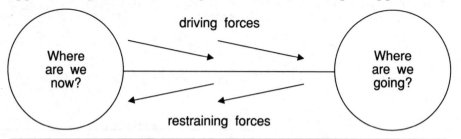

The process of force field analysis

1. What is the problem?
   (Write it down and define it in specific terms, who is involved, what is the magnitude?)

2. Where are we now?

3. Where do we want to get to?
   (Define the desired end result and try to make it measurable)

4. What are the things going **for** us? – Driving forces
   (List all the forces; organisational, individual, motivational, which are helping the change along)

5. What are the things going **against** us? – Restraining forces
   (List all the sources of resistance to the change)

6. What **action** can we take to maximise the driving forces and minimise the restraining forces?

Figure 15.6 *Kurt Lewin's force field analysis*

Managing Change

An oil company in the United States decided to reorganise into independent oil and gas companies. The change involved relocation, causing geographic and personal dislocation for hundreds of people. Senior managers were surprised by 'significant resistance' from employees. Given the following comments from their consultants should they have been surprised by strong resistance?

'The rationale for change was obscure since the existing organisation was very profitable and displayed no obvious evidence of the need for transformation.'

Kurt Lewin's force field analysis is a useful technique for assessing the forces for and against the change in such a way that you may be able to change the balance between them (see Figure 15.6). After all, if the driving forces and the resisting forces are opposite and equal, then even a non-scientist can see that no movement will take place.

In this second example the technique is applied by John Elliot owner/founder of EBAC Ltd to a stock control problem.

1. *What is the problem?* Poor stock control.

2. *Where are we now?* Production stoppages due to shortages but high stock levels.

3. *Where do we want to get to?* Low stock and no stoppages.

4. *What are the driving forces?*   5. *What are the resisting forces?*

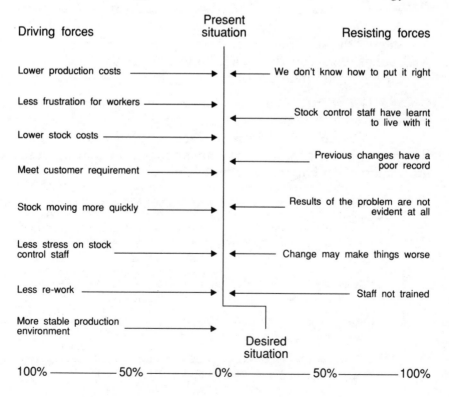

6. *Action*
   We need to devise a solution, devise a detailed plan and describe as clearly as possible the system as it should be.

Interestingly, the evidence is that in handling resistance, there may be greater benefit in eliminating the negative rather than accentuating the positive. Thus, rather than putting on his boxing gloves in an effort to outweigh resistance by hammering the positive benefits of change, the manager may do better to adopt a more laid back, judo approach, allowing people to express their resistance – the Zen rather than the macho approach. It pays to resist rushing into aggressive mode and to spend some time listening and understanding. As in the ethos of the Samaritans, merely expressing a problem may help in coming to terms with it.

There are already some clues for the manager who is concerned with handling the inevitable resistance and increasing the odds for successful change. These include:

- Involve people as early as possible in the change.
- Anticipate the impact on people, those who will perceive themselves as winners and those who will see themselves as losers.
- Do not underestimate resistance.
- Identify the key influencers.
- Use coalitions and alliances to build critical mass for change.
- Expect organisational inertia.

On the last point of organisation inertia it is worth reminding ourselves that resistance to change isn't just an individual phenomenon. Organisations resist change too. For example, here are Rosabeth Moss Kanter's ten commandments for making sure that innovation never happens in your business!

1. *Regard any new idea from below with suspicion because it's new, and it's from below.*

2. *Insist that people who need your approval to act first go through several other levels of management to get their signatures.*

3. *Ask departments or individuals to challenge and criticise each other's proposals. (That saves you the job of deciding; you just pick the survivor.)*

4. *Express your criticisms freely, and withhold your praise (that keeps people on their toes). Let them know they can be fired at any time.*

5. *Treat identification of problems as signs of failure, to discourage people from letting you know when something in their area isn't working.*

6.   Control everything carefully. Make sure people count anything that can be counted, frequently.

7.   Make decisions to reorganise or change policies in secret, and spring them on people unexpectedly. (This also keeps people on their toes.)

8.   Make sure that requests for information are fully justified, and make sure that it is not given out to managers freely. (You don't want data to fall into the wrong hands.)

9.   Assign to lower-level managers, in the name of delegation and participation, responsibility for figuring out how to cut back, lay off, move people around, or otherwise implement threatening decisions you have made, and get them to do it quickly.

10. Above all, never forget that you, the higher-ups, already know everything important about the business.

Diagnosing readiness for change

Greiner puts particular emphasis on organisational readiness for change existing when there is both considerable external pressure for change (ie from new market or technology trends) combined with internal pressures (ie from low morale or pressure for profits). Terry Cooke-Davies, a consultant we know, has really decided that this time he will lose weight! Despite years of external pressure from his wife, his doctor and his friends, he's stayed the same. It was only when the external pressure for change was equalled by the internal pressure to maintain his image on the ski-slopes that he really changed! Similarly, the greatest organisational readiness for change exists when, for example, the external pressure from disgruntled shareholders is echoed by internal pressure, for example, from an attitude survey indicating dissatisfaction. Readiness for change is greatest where there are neither very high security levels, nor very low security levels. If people are too insecure then they tend to dig-in, re-trench and resist change; when they are too secure, for example some of our famous insurance companies, then it is difficult for the organisation to see the warning signal that times may be changing.

The likely commitment, or readiness for change of key individuals can also be plotted using the technique of 'commitment charting' (Beckhard and Harris *Organization Transitions*). Clearly, there is a critical mass of individuals or groups whose active commitment is necessary to provide the energy for the change to occur. Before this time, the change leaders may find they have few friends, afterwards everyone climbs aboard. The steps in developing a commitment plan are:

1. Identify target individuals or groups whose commitment is needed
2. Define the critical mass needed to make change happen
3. Develop a plan for gaining commitment of the critical mass
4. Monitor progress.

Commitment charting will help you to form a diagnosis and an action strategy for the key players you need for critical mass. The technique works on the assumption that for each key player it is necessary to gain some degree of personal commitment or the change won't happen. To make a commitment chart, list all the members or groups who are part of the critical mass on the vertical axis of the chart. Then consider the degree of commitment you must have from each (see Figure 15.7). The range of possibilities is:

- no commitment
- let it happen
- help it happen
- make it happen.

The 0 indicates the minimum commitment you need, the X indicates where you think that person's commitment is at the moment. When the 0 and the X are in the same box, breathe a deep sigh of relief; where they are not draw an arrow connecting the two, this will give you a map of the work to be done.

Key players	No commitment	Let it happen	Help it happen	Make it happen
1.		X ——————————→		0
2.		X ——→ 0		
3.		X ——————————→		0
4.		0 ←—— X		
5.			(X0)	
6.	X ——→ 0			
7.		X ——————————→		0
8.		(X0)		
9.	X ——————————→		0	
10.			0 ←—— X	

Figure 15.7 *A sample commitment chart*

Bruce Elliot of Elliot Brothers has used commitment charting as a way of looking at whether he has the momentum within his team to move the company culture nearer towards 'growth through delegation'. His force field analysis is shown in Figure 15.8 and his commitment chart in Figure 15.9.

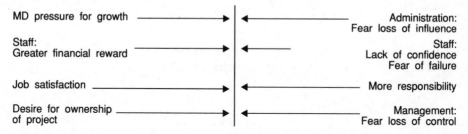

MD pressure for growth ——————►	◄—————— Administration: Fear loss of influence
Staff: Greater financial reward ——————►	◄——— Staff: Lack of confidence Fear of failure
Job satisfaction ——————►	◄—————— More responsibility
Desire for ownership ——————► of project	◄—————— Management: Fear loss of control

Figure 15.8 *Growth through delegation retaining existing strengths*

Key players	No commitment	Let it happen	Help it happen	Have it happen
BRUCE			0 ◄——— X	
GUY	X ——► 0			
STEWART	X ——————————► 0			
ANDREW	X ——————————► 0			
JULIE		X ——► 0		
CHRIS		0 ◄——————— X		
STEVEN		0 ◄——— X		
STUART		(X0)		
DAVID	X ——————————► 0			

Figure 15.9 *Elliot Brothers' commitment chart*

These pose some interesting issues for Bruce. Should he back off from trying to drive the change through? How to increase the 'buy in' of two key members of the team, how to persuade Chris not to be too enthusiastic!

Unfortunately, managing people through organisational change isn't a straightforward step-by-step process. It's messy and it involves doing lots of things at the same time. The change star model (Figure 15.10) has proved a useful framework to help get people through the change process as quickly and painlessly as possible.

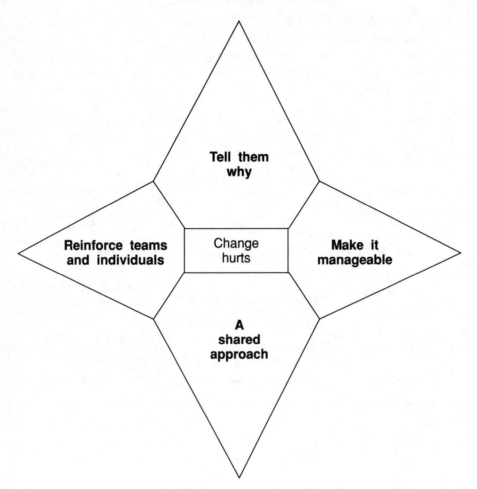

Figure 15.10 *The change star*

It starts from the belief that if a businessman has to make an assumption about how people react to change, it is wisest to assume that change hurts. This model is based on ICL's experience in 1983 when managers felt they needed some pointers to start to get change to happen in an organisation which just wasn't moving fast enough to ensure its own survival. Using the change star model increased ICL's chances of changing the perception 'change hurts' into the perception that 'our business is change'.

There is no right place to start on the star, it is an iterative model (see Figure 15.11). 'Tell them why' may seem the obvious start point but unless you have 'made it manageable' it may be that the resistance you will meet will make the change too hot to handle. Similarly, you can't afford to wait until the later stages of the change to adopt a 'shared approach'; this must come right at the beginning. The fourth pointer of the star talks about the need to 'reinforce teams and individuals' in order that people feel safe enough to take the risks of change. This climate of positive thinking and 'people matter' cannot be built overnight. If you have a punitive culture where people 'keep their heads below the parapets' and come out of every meeting with their boss feeling uncomfortable, then it will be a long time before your employees will feel they can risk making mistakes without being cut off at the knees.

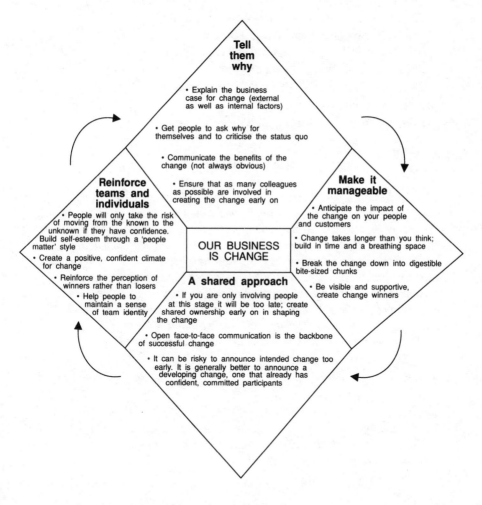

Figure 15.11 *Using the change star*

Checklist of questions to help anticipate the size/potential impact of a change on your people

- How far do people see the need for change?
- How many people will be affected by the change?
- Will existing teams be broken up?
- Is a change of boss involved?
- Will retraining be needed?
- How many people will perceive themselves as losers?
- What levels of resistance do you anticipate?
- How will career opportunities be affected?
- How long will the change take to achieve?
- Will relocation be necessary?
- What are the effects on travel time to work, social and domestic arrangements?
- How much will customers be affected?

A cautionary tale

John Squires ran a successful software house of 150 people based near Reading. He was committed to growth in a market place which presented many opportunities. He had set the business up six years previously and lived, ate and breathed it. The business consisted of three separate teams, one based in Bracknell doing 'leading edge' work, one near Reading covering routine operations and a new business start-up outside Henley. Over the last year or so he had begun to see a strong argument for co-locating the teams on one office site which had become available in the centre of Reading. It made good business sense to him and he had tossed the idea around in his mind for many months. He didn't want to get the grapevine working overtime so he kept things to himself and refined his plans.

At last arrangements were finalised. On the Friday afternoon he called in his three direct reports to tell them the news. They were not pleased. Fred Jackson who ran the Bracknell operation, asked him to work through the implications for staff and reconsider. But Bracknell was only 23 miles from Reading and John Squires couldn't see the problem. He left in his new Jaguar for an urgent meeting in London, after instructing his secretary to place an announcement on the noticeboard elaborating his dictation:

'As from 10 December, Project Teams A, B and C will relocate in the newly acquired office in Queens Road, Reading. The revised organisation chart is attached. There will be no available car parking spaces so you are asked to make alternative arrangements.'

Over the weekend, lines between the Squires' employees buzzed angrily. On the

Monday morning, Fred Jackson gave in his resignation and that of two of his key systems analysts. One was a divorced woman, living alone in a Bracknell flat with a handicapped child. She said she would now find it impossible to get home at lunchtime and to shop conveniently, and would rather find another job than make the move. The other, who had recruited many of the bright young team at Bracknell, said that he wasn't prepared to see his people absorbed by the Reading group – who did most of the 'bread and butter work', were not of the same calibre and would only degrade the prestige of his group. By Monday lunchtime John Squires was ruefully considering what had gone wrong with a change which, to his mind, made so much sense.

ASSIGNMENT 21

Planning for change

1. Complete a force field analysis (overleaf) related to a major problem/change issue associated with implementing your business plan.

Force field analysis

1. What is the problem/change issue?	
2. Where are you now?	
3. Where do you want to get to?	
4. What are the things going for us?	Driving forces Present status quo Resisting forces
5. What are the resisting forces?	
6. What action can minimise resisting forces and maximise driving forces?	

2. Complete a commitment chart of the key people within your business team, outlining what movement of attitude will be needed to achieve your business plan.

Commitment chart for achieving your business plan

Key players	No commitment	Let it happen	Help it happen	Make it happen
1.				
2.				
3.				
4.				
5.				
6.				

X = The level of commitment of that key player right now
0 = The minimum commitment you will need to make the change happen

3. Produce a plan for change, identifying key change issues and outlining actions within the change star framework.

Managing Change

Plan for change

How can you ensure that your business plan can be implemented by the people you have – under fire?

What are the likely change issues for people?
(ie resistance levels, winners and losers)

1.

2.

3.

4.

5.

Outline a change plan for achieving 'buy in'

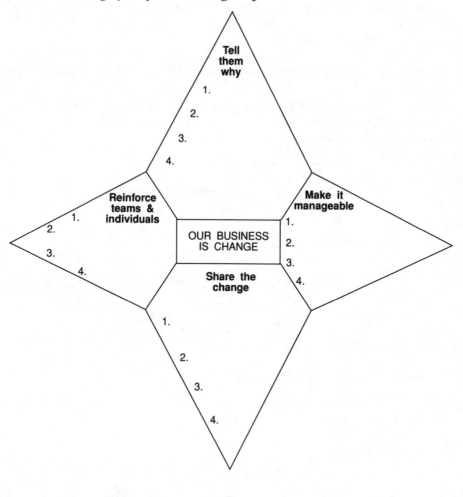

16.

The Financial Plan

Financial objectives are both the starting and finishing point of a good business plan. At the outset you need specific objectives covering such areas as return on capital employed, profit growth, gross margin, gearing and liquidity (see Chapter 4), which to achieve you must develop new marketing strategies and improve performance in your existing areas of business.

The financial plan seeks to reflect the financial implications of your marketing, people and operational plans in the form of profit and loss accounts, cash flows and balance sheets. In this respect it will be an iterative process as different strategies or variations of existing ones are tested to validate their effect on the company's financial performance (see Figure 16.1).

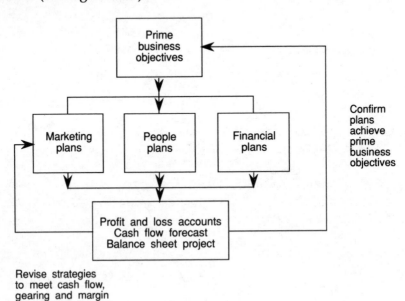

Figure 16.1 *The Financial Plan: an iterative model*

So, for example, a particular marketing strategy might have a satisfactory effect on profit growth and meet marketing objectives such as market share, but strain cash flow critically or cause the gearing ratio to become unacceptably high.

Financial plans also have a strategic dimension of their own which is reflected in the amount of extra funds the company is prepared to commit to achieve growth and the balance of where those funds will come from – for example, debt vs equity (see Chapter 10).

Before looking in detail at the financial plan, it will be useful to see why financial data is such an important element of the business plan, and what sort of information on financial performance is needed.

The sales forecasts are the essential input from which financial projections contained in a business plan are made. These projections are not the business plan, rather they should be viewed as the financial consequences of pursuing a particular course of action. Every business plan should contain them. If additionally you can demonstrate a sound grasp of financial matters, you will be talking the same language as financiers, which has to be an advantage in any negotiation for funds. But more importantly, the financial reports used for planning the business are also used for monitoring results and controlling events once the venture is under way.

Liquidators, who ought to know why businesses fail if anyone does, have at the top of their reasons for failure: 'lack of reliable financial information'. Many failed entrepreneurs believe accounting to be a bureaucratic nuisance carried out for the benefit of the Inland Revenue alone. These same people, who would never drive a car without a fuel gauge, speedometer or oil pressure indicator, frequently set off at breakneck speed running their business with only a 'gut feel', or perhaps the annual accounts to guide them. For them the end of the first year is often the end of the business. Financiers recognise this syndrome only too well, which is one reason why they take the 'financials' so seriously. The other reason is that it's their money that is at stake.

Taking the analogy further, the motorist must also plan ahead to arrive successfully at his goal – to reach his destination safely and on time. The success of any journey, particularly a long one, depends very much on the care taken at this planning stage. The preparation must centre around three distinct areas:

- *The car*. Making sure it is serviced, filled with fuel, and generally in a fit state to make the journey.
- *The route*. Choosing one which takes account of the traffic, possible roadworks, and en route facilities such as petrol, refreshments etc.

The Business Growth Handbook

You should also choose the route which is both the shortest practical route, and one with which you are familiar.

- *The travellers.* Ensuring that everyone is prepared for the journey. This may mean seeing that the children have been to the loo, and some games and toys have been packed to keep them occupied on the journey. It will also mean ensuring that the luggage is packed and loaded into the car, and the house is left secured.

If this stage is accomplished with reasonable care and attention, the travellers and their vehicle have a very good chance of success in the next phase, which is the journey itself.

The soundest approach to any journey is to calculate how far the distance to be travelled is, determine an average travelling speed that is maintainable and safe, and from these two calculate the time needed to travel this distance. Working back from when you want to arrive at your destination and allowing a margin of safety for petrol stops, refreshments etc, you can calculate when you should set off.

The rest of the journey, given that phase 1 has been carried out properly, should be plain sailing provided you follow your plan, follow the map correctly, and take account of the warning signs along the route. In all probability you will arrive at your destination safely and on time.

There are many parallels between the planning, information needs, and decisions made by the safe motorist and the successful entrepreneur's business plan as the financial reports described below will illustrate.

Planning assumptions

The believability of any business plan will depend greatly on the assumptions that underpin it. These assumptions should cover the key areas of the business and its operating environment. You also need to assess the downside risk and show how far things can go before new action has to be taken. Your assumptions can be recorded and monitored using a table such as Table 16.1.

These assumptions may be slightly different for each major objective/strategy. An example of these assumptions is given in the extract from a business plan below.

Celtic Carveries will set up and operate a small chain of carvery restaurants in Scotland. These will provide traditional food in a relaxed atmosphere offering value-for-money food in the middle price market.

288

The Financial Plan

Table 16.1 *Assumptions underpinning your objectives and strategies*

Key assumptions	Basis of assumption	Confidence in assumption	What would happen if assumption proves incorrect	When contingency action can be taken, and when should it be taken
1.				
2.				
3.				
4.				
5.				

These assumptions may be slightly different for each major objective/strategy

The carvery is already a proven concept in parts of England, serving roast meals on a quick throughput basis but without the fast food image. Labour costs are low and, with a limited menu, waste is avoided and in turn makes value for money possible. One carvery has been in operation for six months in Stirling, so the following assumptions have been drawn partly from experience and partly from market research.

Profit and loss assumptions
(a)   Sales
*   ● Carveries in operation will be:*
        Year 1   2
        Year 2   4
        Year 3   7
        Year 5 onwards 10
*   ● Opening six days per week, meals sales will be:*
        Year 1   40 per day
        Year 2   50 per day
        Year 3 onwards 60 per day
*   ● Sales value per meal will be:*
        Food – £6.50
        Drink – £2.50

(b)   Cost of sales per meal:
        Food   £1.75
        Drink   £1.00
        Labour   £2.70
        *   £5.45*
This equals 61 per cent of sales.

(c) *Wages. Each carvery will employ seven staff at a cost of £42,600 per annum (labour costs = 30 per cent of sales which compares favourably with a general restaurant's 40 per cent).*

(d) *Directors. Paid £15,000 in first year, rising to £20,000 from year 3.*

(e) *Administrative staff. Needed mainly from year 2. Costs will rise from £5000 to £40,000 over seven years.*

(f) *Rent and services. £30,000 per carvery per annum.*

(g) *Alterations, equipment and decoration. £40,000 per carvery.*

(h) *Advertising. £2000 per carvery per annum.*

(i) *Inflation. All income and expenditure is stated at current prices.*

Cash flow assumptions:
(a) *No debtors – all meals paid for in cash.*

(b) *Salaries and wages paid monthly.*

(c) *Purchases paid monthly.*

(d) *Rent paid half yearly.*

(e) *Rates paid monthly.*

(f) *Loan interest paid quarterly from month 1.*

(g) *Overdraft interest paid quarterly from month 3.*

(h) *Sales spread evenly over each month of year (sensitivity analysis described later shows how this assumption can be varied).*

Balance sheet assumptions:
(a) *Closing stock. Building up to six weeks' sales.*

(b) *Depreciation of fixed assets. Improvements and office – 20 per cent per annum; fixtures and fittings 25 per cent per annum.*

(c) *Creditors. Equivalent to one month cost of sales.*

The cash flow forecast

The acid test of whether or not your growth strategies are desirable and achievable will show up in the long-term cash flow projections.

In practical terms, the cash flow projections and the profit and loss account projections are parallel tasks which are essentially prepared from the same data. They may be regarded almost as the 'heads' and 'tails' of the same coin – the profit and loss account showing the owner/manager the profit or loss based on the assumption that both sales

	1	2	3	4	5	6	7	8	9	10	11	12	From sales TOTAL
Inflow	18,667	18,667	18,667	18,667	18,667	18,667	18,667	18,667	18,667	18,667	18,667	18,667	224,000
Owners capital introduced	15,000												15,000
Other capital introduced	30,000												30,000
Loan capital	42,258												42,258
	105,925	18,667	18,667	18,667	18,667	18,667	18,667	18,667	18,667	18,667	18,667	18,667	311,258
Outflow													
Capital expenditure	90,000												90,000
Food and wine	5,703	5,703	5,703	5,703	5,703	5,703	5,703	5,703	5,703	5,703	5,703	5,703	68,436
Wages, cooks etc	5,680	5,680	5,680	5,680	5,680	5,680	5,680	5,680	5,680	5,680	5,680	5,680	68,160
Rent	12,000						12,000						24,000
Rates	500	500	500	500	500	500	500	500	500	500	500	500	6,000
Advertising	4,000												4,000
Overheads	2,500	2,500	2,500	2,500	2,500	2,500	2,500	2,500	2,500	2,500	2,500	2,500	30,000
Administration	400	400	400	400	400	400	400	400	400	400	400	400	4,800
Drawings	1,250	1,250	1,250	1,250	1,250	1,250	1,250	1,250	1,250	1,250	1,250	1,250	15,000
Loan interest	938			938			938			938			3,750
Overdraft medium-term loan interest			891			707			881			696	3,175
	122,971	16,033	16,924	16,971	16,033	16,740	28,971	16,033	16,914	16,971	16,033	16,729	317,321
Net inflow (outflow)	(17,046)	2,634	1,743	1,696	2,634	1,927	(10,304)	2,634	1,753	1,696	2,634	1,938	(6,063)
Cumulative in (out) flow	(17,046)	(14,412)	(12,669)	(10,973)	(8,339)	(6,412)	(16,716)	(14,082)	(12,319)	(10,623)	(7,989)	(6,051)	

Figure 16.2 *Celtic Carveries: Cash flow for year 1*

income and the cost of making that sale are 'matched' together in the same month; and the cash flow statement looking at the same transactions from the viewpoint that, in reality, the cost of the sale is incurred first (and paid for) and the income is received last, anywhere between one week and three months later.

Obviously, the implications for a non-cash business of this delay between making the sale and receiving the payment and using a service/buying goods and paying for them are crucial, especially in the early years of the business and when your business is growing quickly.

Celtic Carveries' cash flow projection for one year is shown in Figure 16.2. Cash inflows are at the top and outflows below, with the next monthly and cumulative position to date shown at the bottom of the sheet. From this we can deduce that despite a fairly hefty injection of funds, they expect to end up with an overdraft of £6063 at the year end, and a worst cash position in month 1 of minus £17,046. An overdraft facility of around £20,000 should be included in the business plan proposal. The negative figures at the bottom show how much money you will need to fund your growth plans – and when and for how long you will need the funds.

In practice you will find it desirable to produce your long run cash flow projection on a quarter by quarter basis.

The profit and loss account

So much for cash flow. It is also important that your strategies are delivering the desired profit, growth and the appropriate margins.

You now need to match income and expenditure to the appropriate time periods, ignoring the cash implications. For example, if a customer orders and takes delivery of your goods and service, but does not pay for 100 days, the figure won't appear in the first quarter's cash flow, but it will form part of the income for profit and loss purposes. The same applies to expenses incurred, whether paid for or not.

Returning to Celtic Carveries, their history and projection are shown in Figure 16.3. A couple of years' history on the same chart with the projections can make your growth plans much more clear.

The date at the top of the profit and loss account shows the period over which income and expenditure has been measured, in this case a year. For your business plan the earlier years should be shown in greater detail – either quarterly or preferably monthly for year 1 at any rate, quarterly for year 2, and annually for years 3 to 5 should be acceptable.

£000	2 Yrs Ago	Last Year	Year 1	Year 2	Year 3	Year 4	Year 5
Sales Income	224	504	995	1,432	1,600	1,685	1,685
Cost of goods sold	137	307	583	874	976	1,028	1,028
Gross Profit	87	197	372	558	624	657	657
Expenditure							
Administration	5	28	30	30	40	40	40
Rent	24	48	84	120	120	120	120
Rates	6	12	21	30	30	30	30
Advertising	4	8	14	20	20	20	20
Overheads	30	60	105	150	150	150	150
Depreciation	22	38	61	77	63	50	39
Total	91	194	315	427	423	410	399
PBIT (profit before interest & tax)	−4	3	57	131	201	247	258
Interest	7	8	18	26	11	10	0
Taxation	−1	5	28	55	80	92	95
Directors' emoluments	15	18	20	25	25	25	25
Profit & tax	−24	−28	−9	26	85	120	138

Figure 16.3 *Celtic Carveries – Profit and loss account for the year to 31 October*

The balance sheet

The balance sheet shows what assets we will deploy and how those will ideally be financed for each year of the plan. So in the Celtic Carveries example in Figure 16.4 you can clearly see that additional capital is required to fund the fixed asset improvement programme, essential to the success of the restaurant group.

Sensitivity analysis

While you have been realistic in preparing your forecasts of sales and related costs it is highly probable that actual performance will not be as expected over the planning horizon. This could be for one or more reasons, such as resistance to innovation (if a new product), over-estimate of market size, change in consumer demand, slow take-up of product etc. All these could mean that sales forecasts are significantly wrong. It is advisable to pre-empt any potential investor's question, such as, 'What happens if your sales reduced by 20 per cent?' by asking yourself the question first and quantifying the financial effects in your business plan. You need not go into any great detail – it is sufficient to outline one or two scenarios.

	This year	Year 1	Year 2	Year 3	Year 4
Net assets employed					
Fixed assets					
Improvements	48,000	86,400	141,120	184,896	14,916
Fixtures and office	30,500	43,900	82,995	97,051	85,631
	78,500	130,300	224,115	281,947	233,547
Current assets					
Stock	1,887	38,425	72,819	109,250	109,250
Cash	0	2,366	2,029	10,863	120,641
	1,887	40,791	74,848	120,113	229,891
less					
Current liabilities					
Creditors	11,383	25,617	48,546	72,833	72,833
Overdraft	6,063	27,929	60,974	45,657	0
Tax	0	4,000	25,000	58,000	80,000
	17,446	57,546	134,520	176,490	152,833
= Net current assets	(15,559)	(16,745)	(59,672)	(56,378)	77,058
Total assets less current liabilities	62,941	113,545	164,463	225,569	310,605
Financed by:					
Share capital					
Owners	15,000	15,000	15,000	15,000	15,000
Other directors	10,000	10,000	10,000	10,000	10,000
New Venture Capital	20,000	90,000	120,000	150,000	150,000
Profit/loss for year	(24,317)	(28,455)	(8,557)	25,569	85,036
Retained earnings/ reserves	–	–	–	–	25,569
	20,683	86,545	136,443	200,569	285,605
Loan capital					
Long term	25,000	25,000	25,000	25,000	25,000
Medium term	17,258	2,000	3,000	–	–
	42,258	27,000	28,000	25,000	25,000
TOTAL	62,941	113,545	164,463	225,569	310,605

Figure 16.4 *Celtic Carveries – Balance Sheets at 31 October*

Celtic Carveries' sensitivity analysis

In arriving at sales forecasts, estimates were made by comparison with the accounts of X Ltd who have a similar operation. If, however, these estimates were incorrect and our sales were 20 per cent lower, then turnover would be £180,000 with costs of sales falling to £110,000 and the company would still produce a gross profit at the end of year one of £70,000. Given a fixed cost of £90,000, our first year loss would be extended from £4000 to £20,000. This position could be largely offset by cutting the directors' pay for that year.

Summary of performance ratios

When you have completed your pro forma profit and loss accounts for years 1 to 5, together with your pro forma balance sheets for years 1 to 5, you should prepare a summary of your business's performance in certain key areas. This summary will help both yourself and any potential outside investor to compare your business's performance:

1. One year against the next, for example has gross profit grown or declined between years 1 and 5?
2. Against other similar businesses, for example does your business give as good a return on investment as others?
3. The ratios can be used as an aid in making future financial projections. For example, if you believe it prudent to hold the equivalent of a month's sales in stock, once you have made the sales forecast for future years the projections for stock in the balance sheet follow logically.

Year	1	2	3	4	5
	%	%	%	%	%
Gross profit	39	39	39	39	39
Total expenditure	41	38	33	30	26
Profit before tax	(10)	(5)	2	6	10
ROI	–	–	–	13	30
Gearing	67	24	17	11	8

Figure 16.5 *Summary of Celtic Carveries' performance ratios*

This summary of key ratios should include:

Sales. Actual sales, to be used as the base figure for all other calculations.

Cost of goods sold. Expressed as a percentage of sales to highlight any increase/decrease in this key area over the period.

Total expenditure (expenses). Expressed as a percentage of sales to indicate how well these have been controlled over the period.

Profit before tax. Expressed as a percentage of sales to show how well sales have been converted to bottom line profit. Perhaps the key measure of operational performance (add back tax to profit after tax).

Profit growth. Experience as a percentage year on year.

Net worth. This is actual investment in the business, ie share capital plus reserves, which on its own gives a valuable measure of absolute growth.

Return on net worth. This is also referred to as return on investment (ROI), and is undoubtedly the key measure of profitability used by outsiders to compare your business with others. It is calculated by taking your net profit (after tax and before dividends) and dividing this by the average value of your share capital and reserves.

Debt to equity. Frequently referred to as *gearing*, this is calculated by taking total borrowings (both long and short term) divided by total capital reserves (net worth) and expressing the result as a percentage. This ratio is, however, a two-edged sword in that if your gearing is high (mainly financed by borrowings) potential investors will see high rewards, assuming your business performs well, but if you are asking a bank or similar institution for interest bearing funds then they will normally expect to see low gearing, to show a certain level of your commitment, expressed as share capital, to reduce the risk of their not being able to recover their loans.

Net current assets. This is calculated by subtracting current liabilities from current assets, thereby giving creditors an indication of your liquidity or ability to meet current liabilities when they fall due.

Current ratio. This is calculated by dividing current assets by current liabilities and expressing the result as a ratio, thereby giving an indication of your ability to meet short-term obligations as they become due. It is often refined to include only those current assets 'quickly' convertible to cash (ie excluding stocks) and all current liabilities repayable within 12 months. In this form it is known as a *quick ratio*.

Three other useful working capital ratios which both reveal the strength of financial control in a business plan and can be used in financial forecasting are:

$$\text{Average debtor collection period} = \frac{\text{Debtors}}{\text{Sales}} \times 365$$

This gives a guide to how long you expect to take (or have taken) getting money owed to you back in.

$$\text{Days' Stock held} = \frac{\text{Stock (or inventories)}}{\text{Cost of goods sold}} \times 365$$

This shows the stock level held, in proportion to your sales. This is more useful than comparing figures alone, as you would expect levels to change with increases or decreases in sales.

$$\text{Average credit period taken } = \frac{\text{Creditors}}{\text{Purchases}} \times 365$$

This shows how much credit you are taking from your suppliers. As a rough guide, if you are allowing your customers 30 days to pay then you should be looking for that credit period yourself.

Look back to Chapter 4 for further classification of key ratio calculations. If your accounting is a little rusty read *Financial Management for the Small Business*, second edition, by Colin Barrow.

Financing requirements

Your business plan may look very professional, showing that you have a very high probability of making exceptional returns, but it will fall at the first hurdle if your funding requirements have not been properly thought out and communicated to potential investors. It is *not* sufficient for you to look at your pro forma cash flow statement and, taking the maximum overdraft position, say:

'The management require £150,000 to commence business, which may come either from bank loans or a share capital injection. The cash flow projections show that if the funding was by way of loan it would be repaid within three years. If the funding came from an issue of share capital an excellent return would be available by way of dividends.'

Such a statement leaves many questions unanswered, such as:

- Why do you need the money?
- What type of money do you need?
- When will you need it?
- What deal are you offering your investors?
- What exit routes are open to your investors?

Let's examine each of these questions in turn, as your business will have to include answers to them.

Why do you need the money?

You probably have a very good idea of why you need the funds that you are asking for, but unless the reader of your business plan has plenty of time to spare (which he has not) and can be bothered to work it out for himself (which he can't), you must clearly state what you will use the funds received for.

An example might be: A net investment of £150,000 is required, which will be used as follows:

	£
To purchase:	
Motor vehicle	5,000
Plant and Equipment	100,000
To provide:	
Working capital for first	
6 months	75,000
Total requirement	180,000
Less investment made by (you)	30,000
Net funding requirement	150,000

This statement clearly tells the reader how the funds will be used and gives clear pointers as to appropriate funding routes and the timing of the funding requirements.

When will you need it?

In the example above a net investment of £150,000 is required, which is likely to come from several different funding routes, depending on how it is to be used. However, one thing is apparent: the whole £150,000 is not needed immediately or even at the same time, so don't ask for it all to be provided at the same time.

The £100,000 needed for plant and equipment will be needed several weeks or months before trading can begin, and the £5000 for the motor vehicle can, in all probability, be left until closer to the time you will need it. The working capital requirement of £75,000 is needed in varying amounts over the first six months or so of trading. Your funding request should clearly show this 'Timetable of Anticipated Funding'. An example of this timetable might be as shown in Figure 16.6. The statement should be carried on for as long as external funding is required and shows that:

1. An equity investment of £100,000 is made three months prior to implementing your growth plan and remains in the business for the medium- to long-term future.
2. A bank overdraft facility of £75,000 is required, which is first used during month 3, reaches a peak of £70,000 during month 5, and is cleared by month 9 (ie the sixth month of trading). Note that the full £75,000 facility appears not to be needed, but it is advisable to obtain more than is required to cover the unforeseen.

3. An HP loan of £5000 is required in month 3, and is repaid over three years.

Date	Requirement per cash flow forecast	Anticipated funding			
		Share issue	Your cash introduced	Bank loan	HP loan
	£000	£000	£000	£000	£000
Year 1					
Pre commencement of growth plan					
Month 1	100	100	30	–	–
2	5		–	–	–
3	70		–	45	5
Commencement of growth plan					
Month 4	20		–	60	4.85
5	10		–	70	4.70
6	(5)		–	65	4.55
7	(20)		–	45	4.40
8	(21)		–	24	4.25
9	(25)		–	–	4.10
10	(20)		–	–	3.95
11	(10)		–	–	3.80
12	(10)		–	–	3.65

Figure 16.6 *Example of timetable of anticipated funding*

What type of money do you need?

The amount of money you need and what you require it for will help you to decide what type of money you need to finance growth.

Two points need stressing here; they have already been covered in Chapter 6, but are so crucial as to be worth revisiting.

Gearing. Do not allow your business to have more debt than equity over the whole horizon of your business plan. Highly geared companies, unless the risks are minimal, are simply fruit machines which ultimately won't shell out as much money as you put in (see Chapter 10).

'Giving away' equity. Always a contentious issue with successful entrepreneurs. For many the problems start with the idea of giving away a share of their business because they feel that they are losing

control by so doing. The problem can be alleviated by looking at other successful business people who have already been down this route: Anita Roddick, founder of the Body Shop, Richard Branson of Virgin and Alan Sugar of Amstrad are all minority shareholders in their companies, yet nobody would dispute that they are in control.

The deal on offer

People can and do sell off varying amounts of their business to raise funds. While ideally you should retain 51 per cent of the voting power in your company, it is possible to achieve this by owning less than 51 per cent of the shares. Part of the negotiating process will hinge round voting rights of shares, and it is not uncommon for outside investors to accept restricted voting rights on their shares. Don't forget that you want their money and you have got to give up something in return.

So far the question of how much the business is worth has been avoided, and since this is what will determine how much equity you will need to sell to raise the required funds, it needs to be answered. There is no one way to value a business and once you start to try, you will find it's more of an art than a science, but you can begin to get a feel for value using the present value formula. The formula used to calculate it is quite simple, but the factors used in arriving at the valuation are somewhat subjective. However, a simple valuation of a company by way of an example is shown below.

Cranfield Engineering Ltd

Cranfield Engineering Ltd (CEL) is a new start-up business which needs a £200,000 equity injection to achieve its business plan objectives. A brief summary of its financial projections shows:

	Turnover £	Profit after Tax £
Year 1	200,000	(25,000)
Year 2	500,000	100,000
Year 3	750,000	200,000

Assuming that a P/E ratio (the ratio of a share's price to its earnings) of 10 is used as the accepted multiplier of earnings in their industry, then using the formula:

$$Present\ value\ (PV) = \frac{Future\ valuation\ (PV)}{(1 + i)^n}$$

Where
FV = Maintainable profits X applicable P/E ratio

i = Required rate of return (to investor)

n = Number of years until date of forecast earnings; used to calculate valuation

Assuming that the figures provided by CEL are accepted at face value (which is unlikely) and that maintainable profits are achieved in year 2, and that our investor is seeking a 60 per cent return (because of the high risk involved), then the valuation of the company would be as follows:

$$PV = \frac{£(100,000 \times 10)}{(1 + 0.60)^2} = \frac{£1,000,000}{2.56} = £390,625$$

If the company is valued at £390,625 and CEL requires £200,000, then the percentage of the equity that the investor will acquire will be 200,000/390,625 which is 51.2 per cent. Obviously, while the above is mathematically correct there would be much negotiation about the acceptability of the factors being used and perhaps which year's profits represent 'maintainable profits'. In the above example, if year 3 had been used, the investor's share of the equity would have fallen to 41 per cent.

Exit routes also have to be considered at the point of raising funds. This matter is dealt within Chapter 18.

ASSIGNMENT 22

Pulling together the financials

Prepare a three to five year profit and loss account projection based on your marketing strategy for growth.

Reflect the cash flow and balance sheet implications and calculate key ratios to show how your business performance helps to meet your key business objectives.

You may find a spread sheet or a business plan writer helpful.

Summary of key ratios

	Last Year	This Year	% Change	Year 1	% Change	Year 2	% Change	Year 3	% Change
1. *Percentage Sales Growth*									
2. *Percentage Profit Growth*									
3. *Headcount Growth*									
4. *Sales Number of Employees*									
5. *Profit Number of Employees*									
6. *Value added per employee [Profit + Wages/Salaries ÷ Number of Employees]*									
7. *ROCE Profit Before Interest & Tax Capital Employed*									
8. *ROSC Profit after Tax Share Capital & Reserves*									
9. *Share Capital & Reserves All Long-term Capital Gearing:*									
10. *Operating Profit Loan Interest*									
11. *Gross Profit Sales*									

	Last Year	This Year	% Change	Year 1	% Change	Year 2	% Change	Year 3	% Change
12. Operating Profit / Sales									
13. Net Profit / Sales									
14. Current Assets / Current Liabilities — Current Ratio:									
15. Debtors & Cash / Current Liabilities — Quick Ratio:									
16. Average Collection Period: $\dfrac{\text{Debtors} \times 365}{\text{Sales}}$									
17. $\dfrac{\text{Creditors}}{\text{Purchasers}} \times 365$									
18. $\dfrac{\text{Stock}}{\text{Cost of Sales}} \times 365$									
19. $\dfrac{\text{Sales}}{\text{Working Capital}}$									
20. $\dfrac{\text{Sales}}{\text{Fixed Assets}}$									
Other key ratios									

17.

Writing Up and Presenting Your New Business Plan

Up to now the assignments have focused on gathering and analysing data needed to validate and confirm your strategy for growth, to assess your business team's capability to implement their chosen strategy and to quantify the resources needed in terms of men, machinery, money and management.

Getting this data together along the lines we have suggested can take anything between 200 and 400 man hours depending on the nature of your business and how much data you already routinely gather. Your task will have been made that much easier if you have involved all your staff in gathering and analysing the information, and in writing up the business plan. They will also be that much more committed both to implementing the ensuing strategy and to preparing future business plans.

However onerous the overall task of preparing a new business plan, it is essential if you are to shift the business through from being almost exclusively entrepreneurial and opportunity driven to having a strategic focus that allows the whole management team a share in the future of the firm. (Remember Greiner!)

Some benefits from having a current business plan include:

- Few businesses can grow without additional finance. While it would be an exaggeration to say your business plan is a passport to sources of finance, without it you will not really know how much money you need to finance growth and no one today will lend or invest in a business without a plan.

- A systematic approach to planning enables you to make your mistakes on paper, rather than in the market-place. One potential entrepreneur made the discovery while gathering data for his business plan that the local competitor he thought was a one-man band was in fact the pilot operation for a proposed national chain of franchised outlets. This had a profound effect on his marketing strategy!

Another entrepreneur found out that, at the price he proposed charging for a new product, he would never recover his overheads or break even. Indeed 'overheads' and 'break even' were themselves alien terms before he embarked on preparing a business plan. This naive perspective on costs is by no means unusual.

- Your business plan will make your management team more confident that they can achieve the strategic goals set. They will then be better able to communicate the company's strategy to others in a way that will be easier for them to understand and so appreciate the reasoning behind your plans.

  This will give both the appearance and substance to your having management 'in depth': absolutely essential for organisations moving along the continuum from one-man band to major enterprise.

  Remember the secret of making money is to make others content to make it for you.

Now the information gathered so far in carrying out the assignments has to be assembled, collated and orchestrated into a coherent and complete written business plan aimed at a specific audience.

In this chapter we will examine the six activities that can make this happen:

- Packaging
- Layout and content
- Writing and editing
- Who to send it to
- The oral presentation
- What financiers look out for in a business plan

Packaging

Every product is enhanced by appropriate packaging and a business plan is no exception. The panellists at Cranfield's enterprise programmes prefer a simple spiral binding with a plastic cover on the front and back. This makes it easy for the reader to move from section to section, and it ensures the plan will survive frequent handling. Stapled copies and leatherbound tomes are viewed as undesirable extremes.

A near letter quality (NLQ) printer will produce a satisfactory type finish which, together with wide margins and double spacing, will result in a pleasing and easy-to-read document.

Layout and content

There is no such thing as a 'universal' business plan format. That being said, experience at Cranfield has taught us that certain layouts and contents have gone down better than others. These are our guide-lines to producing an attractive business plan which tries to cover both management requirements and the investor's point of view. Not every sub-heading will be relevant to every type of business, but the general format can be followed, with emphasis laid as appropriate.

First, the cover should show the name of the company, its address and phone number, and the date on which this version of the plan was prepared. It should confirm that this is the company's latest view of its position and financing needs. If your business plan is to be targeted at specific sources of finance, it's highly likely that you will need to assemble slightly different business plans, highlighting areas of concern to lenders as opposed to investors, for example.

Second, the title page, immediately behind the front cover, should repeat the above information and also give the founder's name, address and phone number. A home number can be helpful for investors, who often work irregular hours – rather as you probably do. He or she is likely to be the first point of contact and anyone reading the business plan may want to talk over some aspects of the proposal before arranging a meeting.

The executive summary

Ideally one but certainly no longer than two pages, this should follow immediately behind the title page.

Writing up the executive summary is not easy but it is the most important single part of the business plan; it will probably do more to influence whether or not the plan is reviewed in its entirety than anything else you do. It can also make the reader favourably disposed towards a venture at the outset, which is no bad thing.

These two pages must explain:

1. The current state of the company with respect to product/service readiness for market, trading position and past successes if already running, and key staff on board.
2. The products or services to be sold and to whom they will be sold, including details on competitive advantage.
3. The reasons customers need this product or service, together with some indication of market size and growth.
4. The company's aims and objectives in both the short and longer term, and an indication of the strategies to be employed in getting there.

5. A summary of forecasts, sales, profits and cash flow.
6. How much money is needed, and how and when the investor or lender will benefit from providing the funds.

Obviously, the executive summary can only be written after the business plan itself has been completed. The summary below, for instance, accompanied a 40-page plan.

Pnu Cleen will assemble and market an already prototyped design for a vacuum cleaner. The design work was carried out by myself and my co-director when we were at Loughborough University taking a BSc course in design and manufacture. The prototype was made during my postgraduate course in industrial design engineering at the Royal College of Art in London.

The vacuum cleaner is somewhat special. Its design, powered by compressed air, is aimed at the industrial market and fulfils a need overlooked by cleaning equipment manufacturers.

The vacuum cleaner offers to the customer an 'at-hand' machine that can be used by their employees to keep their workplace or machine clean and tidy during production. This produces a healthier and more productive environment in which to work.

It is cheaper than electrical vacuum cleaners and more versatile. It is also far less prone to blockage which is especially important considering the types of material found in manufacturing industry.

The vacuum cleaner can be produced at low unit cost. This, together with the market price it can command for what it has to offer, will mean that only a small turnover is needed for the company to break even. However, with the prospect of a sizeable market both in this country and abroad, the company has the chance of making substantial profits.

The company will concentrate on this product for the first five years to ensure that it reaches all of its potential market and this will make a sound base from which we can either expand into other products or incorporate the manufacturing side of the product into our own capabilities.

The financial forecasts indicate that breakeven will be achieved in the second year of operations, and in year 3 return on investment should be about 40 per cent. By then sales turnover will be a little over £1m, gross profits about £400,000, and profit before tax but after financing charges around £200,000.

Our P/E ratio from year 3 will be 10 to 1, which should leave an attactive margin for any investor to exit, with comparable stock being quoted at 19 to 1.

We will need an investment of £300,000 to implement our strategy, with roughly half going into tangibles such as premises and stock, and the balance into marketing and development expenses. We are able and willing to put up £100,000. The balance we would like to fund from the sale of a share of the business, the exact proportion to be discussed at a later stage.

The table of contents

After the executive summary follows a table of contents. This is the map that will guide the new reader through your business proposal and on to the inevitable conclusion that they should put up the funds. If a map is obscure, muddled or even missing, then the chances are you will end up with lost or irritated readers unable to find their way around your proposal.

Each of the main sections of the business plan should be listed and the pages within that section indicated. There are two valid schools of thought on page numbering. One favours a straightforward sequential numbering of each page – 1,2,3,4...and so on. This seems to us to be perfectly adequate for short, simple plans, dealing with uncomplicated issues and seeking modest levels of finance.

Most proposals should be numbered by section. In the example that follows, the section headed 'The Business and its Management' is Section 1, and the pages that follow are listed from 1.1 to 1.8 in the table of contents, so identifying each page as belonging within that specific section. This numbering method also allows you to insert new material without upsetting the entire pagination during preparation. Tables and figures should also be similarly numbered.

Individual paragraph numbering, much in favour with government and civil service departments, is considered something of an overkill in a business plan and is to be discouraged, except perhaps if you are looking for a large amount of government grant.

The table of contents below shows both the layout and content which in our experience is most in favour with financial institutions. Unsurprisingly, the terminology is similar to that used throughout the book. For example, Chapter 2 covers the items covered in 3.2 in the sample table of contents below. For competitive strengths and weaknesses you can look back to Chapter 3 for guidance and inspiration. Performance ratios mentioned in 8.1 are explained in Chapter 4. If in doubt use the index which will guide you to relevant areas of the text.

Sample Table of Contents

Objectives, Near Term	1.3
Objectives, Long Term	1.4
The Current Key Management Team	1.5
Legal and Existing Capital Structure	1.6
Professional Advisers	1.7

2. Products or Services

Descriptions and Applications	2.1
Readiness for Market of New Products/Services	2.2
Development Cost Estimates	2.3
Proprietary Position/Barriers to Entry	2.4
Comparison with Competition, Performance and Economics	2.5
Guarantees and Warranties	2.6
Future Potential/Product Development	2.7
Sources of Supply (if not a manufacturing/assembling business)	2.8

3. Market & Competitors

Description of Customer Needs and Benefits	3.1
Market and Segment Size and Growth	3.2
Customer Decision Criteria	3.3
Target Market Segments (showing differentiation from competition)	3.4
Marketing Objectives	3.5
Competitive Strengths and Weaknesses, and the Opportunities and Threats Ahead	3.6
Marketing Strategy	3.7
The Sales Forecast	3.8

4. Selling

Current Selling Method(s)	4.1
Proposed Selling Method(s)	4.2
Sales Team	4.3
In-house Support	4.4

5. Management & Staffing

Specific Management Roles for existing and planned staff and general organisation of the business under each	5.1
Strategies for Retaining and Motivating Key Staff	5.2
Planned Recruitment and Selection	5.3
Reward and Recognition Packages and their relationship to the required business performance	5.4

Appendices should include:
Management team biographies
Names and details of professional advisers
Technical data and drawings
Details of patents, copyright, designs
Audited accounts
Consultants' reports or other published data on products,
  markets etc
Orders on hand and enquiry status
Detailed market research methods and findings
Organisation charts

Writing and editing

You and your colleagues should write the first draft of the business plan yourselves. The niceties of grammar and style can be resolved later. Different people in your team will have been responsible for carrying out the various assignments in the book, and writing up the appropriate section(s) of the business plan. This information should be circulated to ensure that:

1.   Everyone is still heading in the same direction;
2.   Nothing important has been missed out.

A 'prospectus', such as a business plan seeking finance from investors, can have a legal status, turning any claims you may make for sales and profits (for example) into a contract. Your accountant and legal adviser will be able to help you with the appropriate language that can convey your projections without giving them contractual status. This would also be a good time to talk over the proposal with a friendly banker or venture capital provider. They can give an insider's view of the strengths and weaknesses of your proposal.

When your first draft has been revised, then comes the task of editing. Here the grammar, spelling and language must be carefully checked to ensure that your business plan is crisp, correct, clear and complete – and not too long. If writing is not your trade then, once again, this is an area in which to seek help. Your local college or librarian will know of someone who can produce attention-capturing prose, if you yourself don't.

However much help you get with writing up your business plan it is still just that – *your* plan. So the responsibility for the final proof-reading before it goes out must rest with you. Spelling mistakes and typing errors can have a disproportionate influence on the way your business plan is received.

311

The other purpose of editing is to reduce the business plan to between 20 and 40 pages. However complex or sizeable the venture, outsiders won't have time to read it if it is longer – and insiders will only succeed in displaying their muddled thinking to full effect. If your plan includes volumes of data, tables, graphs etc, then refer to them in the text, but confine them to an appendix. The text (not the tables or appendices) of your final business plan should be eminently readable if you want to stay out of the reject pile in lenders' and investors' offices.

The Fog Index can help you to make sure the business plan is readable. Research into the subject has shown that two things make life hard for readers: long sentences and long words. Back in 1952 Robert Gunning, a business language expert, devised a formula to measure just how tough a letter, report or article is to read. Called the Fog Index, it takes four simple steps to arrive at.

1. Find the average number of words per sentence. Use a sample at least 100 words long. Divide total number of words by number of sentences to give you the average sentence length.
2. Count the number of words of three syllables or more per 100 words. Don't count: (a) words that are capitalised; (b) combinations of short, easy words – like 'bookkeeper'; (c) Verbs that are made up of three syllables by adding 'ed' or 'es' – like 'created' or 'trespasses'.
3. Add the two factors above and multiply by 0.4. This will give you the Fog Index. It corresponds roughly with the number of years of schooling a person would require to read a passage with ease and understanding.
4. Check the results against this scale:

   4 and below very easy – perhaps childish
   5 fairly easy: tabloid press, hard sales letters
   7 or 8 standard: *Daily Mail*, most business letters
   9 – 11 fairly difficult: *The Times*, good product literature
   12 – 15 difficult: *The Economist*, technical literature
   17 or above very difficult – *New Scientist* – no business use, except to bamboozle.

Who to send it to

Now you are ready to send out your business plan to a few carefully selected financial institutions who you know are interested in proposals such as yours.

This will involve some research into the particular interests, foibles and idiosyncrasies of the institutions themselves. If you are only interested in raising debt capital, the field is narrowed to the clearing banks for the main part. If you are looking for someone to share the risk with you, then you must review the much wider field of venture capital. Here, some institutions will only look at proposals over a certain capital sum, such as £250,000, or will only invest in certain technologies. It is a good idea to carry out this research before the final editing of your business plan, as you should incorporate something of this knowledge into the way your business plan is presented. You may find that slightly different versions of 9.4, The Deal on Offer (sample table of contents), have to be made for each different source of finance to which you send your business plan.

Don't be disheartened if the first batch of financiers you contact don't sign you up. One Cranfield Enterprise Programme participant had to approach 26 lending institutions, 10 of them different branches of the same organisation, before getting the funds she wanted. One important piece of information she brought back from every interview was the reason for the refusal. This eventually led to a refined proposal that won through. It is well to remember that financial institutions are far from infallible, so you may have to widen your audience to other contacts.

> *Anita Roddick, the Body Shop founder, was turned down flat by the banks in 1976, and had to raise £4000 from a local Sussex garage owner. This, together with £4000 of her own funds, allowed the first shop to open in Brighton. Today there are 87 outlets in the UK and a further 169 abroad. The company has a full listing on the Stock Exchange, Ms Roddick is a millionaire many times over – and at least one Sussex bank manager must be feeling a little silly!*

Finally, how long will it all take? This also depends on whether you are raising debt or equity, the institution you approach and the complexity of the deal on offer. A secured bank loan, for example, can take from a few days to a few weeks to arrange. Investment from a venture capital house, on the other hand, will rarely take less than three months to arrange, and will more usually take six or even up to nine months. Two Cranfield Business Growth participants raised substantial six figure sums during the 1991 recession and both took 13 months from first approach to getting the cheques in the bank! Although the deal itself may be struck early on, the lawyers will pore over the detail for weeks. Every exchange of letters can add a fortnight to the wait. The 'due diligence' process in which every detail of your business plan is checked out will also take time – so this will have to be allowed for in your projections.

The oral presentation

If getting someone interested in your business plan is half the battle in raising funds, the other half is the oral presentation. Any organisation financing a venture will insist on seeing the team involved presenting and defending their plans – in person. They know that they are backing people every bit as much as the idea. You can be sure that any financier you are presenting to will be well prepared. Remember that they see hundreds of proposals every year, and either have or know of investments in many different sectors of the economy. If this is not your first business venture they may even have taken the trouble to find out something of your past financial history.

Keep these points in mind when preparing for the presentation of your business plan:

- Be well prepared, with one person (you) orchestrating individual inputs. Nevertheless, you must also come across as a team.
- Use visual aids and rehearse beforehand.
- Explain and, where appropriate, defend your business concept.
- Listen to the comments and criticisms made and acknowledge them politely. You need to appear receptive without implying you have too many areas of ignorance in your plans.
- Appear businesslike, demonstrating your grasp of the competitive market forces at work in your industry, the realistic profits that can be achieved, and the cash required to implement your strategies.
- Demonstrate the product if at all possible – or offer to take the financiers to see it in operation elsewhere. One participant on a Cranfield enterprise programme arranged to have his new product, a computer-controlled camera system for monitoring product quality in engineering process, on free loan to Fords for the three months he was looking for money. This not only helped financiers to understand the application of a complex product, but the benefit of seeing it at work in a prestigious major company was incalculable.
- What empathy is there between the financiers and the entrepreneurs? You may not be able to change your personality but you could take a few tips on public speaking. Eye contact, tone of speech, enthusiasm and body language all play their part in making the interview go well, so read up on this, and rehearse the presentation before an audience.

What financiers look out for in a business plan

If you need finance then, as well as the operational benefits of preparing a business plan, it is important to examine what financiers expect from you, if you are to succeed in raising those funds.

It is often said that there is no shortage of money for new and growing businesses – the only scarce commodities are good ideas and people with the ability to exploit them. From the potential entrepreneur's position this is often hard to believe. One major venture capital firm alone receives several thousand business plans a year. Only 500 or so are examined in any detail, fewer than 25 are pursued to the negotiating stage, and only six of those are invested in.

To a great extent the decision whether to proceed beyond an initial reading of the plan will depend on the quality of the business plan used in supporting the investment proposal. The business plan is the ticket of admission giving the entrepreneur his first, and often only, chance to impress a prospective source of finance with the quality of his proposal. It follows from this that to have any chance at all of getting financial support, your business plan must be the best that can be written and it must be professionally packaged. These subjects were covered earlier in this chapter. But it may be helpful, when evaluating your business plan before sending it out to sources of finance, to try to get under the skin of those financiers.

In our experience at Cranfield, the plans that succeed meet all of the following requirements.

Evidence of market orientation and focus

David Stapleton, who took his company Pinneys from sales of £100,000 per annum in 1977 to over £30m in 1987, learnt the lesson of concentration the hard way. He started out aiming to sell lamb, beef, venison and grouse, all products close to hand in his Scottish Borders home, to overseas markets. Full of enthusiasm he made a sales trip to the Far East, and went into the Peninsular Hotel in Hong Kong carrying, literally, a side of lamb on his back. But they didn't want to know about anything – except the smoked salmon. He made a loss of £14,000 on that trip, but he did discover what customers wanted. On the strength of that he raised £20,000 and bought out his smoked salmon supplier, and his company now makes £1m per annum profit.

Entrepreneurs must demonstrate that they have recognised the needs of potential customers, rather than simply being infatuated with an innovative idea. Business plans that occupy more space with product descriptions and technical explanations than with explaining how products will be sold and to whom, usually get cold-shouldered by financiers. They rightly suspect that these companies are more of an ego trip than an enterprise.

But market orientation is not enough in itself. Financiers want to sense that the entrepreneur knows the one or two things their business can do best – and that they are prepared to concentrate on exploiting these opportunities.

Blooming Marvellous

Two friends who eventually made it to an enterprise programme – and to founding a successful company – had great difficulty in getting backing at first. They were exceptionally talented designers and makers of clothes. They started out making ball gowns, wedding dresses, children's clothes - anything the market wanted. Only when they focused on designing and marketing clothes for the mother-to-be that allowed her still to feel fashionably dressed was it obvious they had a winning concept. That strategy built on their strength as designers, their experiences as former mothers-to-be, and exploited a clear market opportunity neglected at that time by the main player in the market-place – Mothercare.

From that point their company made a quantum leap forward from turning over £200,000 a year into the several million pound league in a few years.

Evidence of customer acceptance

Financiers like to know that your new product or service will sell and is being used, even if only on a trial or demonstration basis.

The founder of Solicitec, a company selling software to solicitors to enable them to process relatively standard documents such as wills, had little trouble getting support for his package house conveyancing once his product had been tried and approved by a leading building society for their panel of solicitors.

If you are only at the prototype stage then, as well as having to assess your chances of succeeding with technology, financiers have no immediate indication that, once made, your product will appeal to the market. Under these circumstances you have to show that the problem your innovation seeks to solve is a substantial one that a large number of people will pay for.

One inventor from the Royal College of Art came up with a revolutionary toilet system design that, as well as being extremely narrow, used 70 per cent less water per flush and had half the number of moving parts of a conventional product, all for no increase in price. Although he had only drawings to show, it was clear that with domestic metered water for all households a distinct possibility, and a UK market for half a million new units per annum, a sizeable acceptance was reasonably certain.

As well as evidence of customer acceptance, entrepreneurs need to demonstrate that they know how and to whom their new product or service must be sold, and that they have a financially viable means of doing so.

Proprietary position

Exclusive rights to a product through patents, copyright, trademark protection or a licence helps to reduce the apparent riskiness of a venture in the financier's eyes, as these can limit competition – for a while at least.

One participant on a Cranfield enterprise programme held patents on a revolutionary folding bicycle he had designed at college. While no financial institution was prepared to back him in manufacturing the bicycle, funds were readily available to enable him to make production prototypes and then license manufacture to established bicycle makers throughout the world.

However legally well protected a product is, it is marketability and marketing know-how generally that outweigh patentability in the success equation. A salutary observation made by an American Professor of Entrepreneurship revealed that less than 0.5 per cent of the best ideas contained in the US *Patent Gazette* in the last five years have returned a dime to the inventors.

Believable forecasts

Entrepreneurs are naturally ebullient when explaining the future prospects for their businesses. They frequently believe that 'the sky's the limit' when it comes to growth, and money (or rather the lack of it) is the only thing that stands between them and their success.

It is true that if you are looking for venture capital, then the providers are also looking for rapid growth. However, it's as well to remember that financiers are dealing with thousands of investment proposals each year, and already have money tied up in hundreds of business sectors. It follows, therefore, that they already have a perception of what the accepted financial results and marketing approaches currently are, for any sector. Any company's business plan showing projections that are outside the ranges perceived as acceptable within an industry will raise questions in the investor's mind.

Make your growth forecasts believable; support them with hard facts where possible. If they are on the low side, then approach the more cautious lending banker, rather than venture capitalists. The former often see a modest forecast as a virtue, lending credibility to the business proposal as a whole.

ASSIGNMENT 23

Writing up the business plan

Write up your three-year business plan.

18.

Exit Routes

Why sell up?

Every year, tens of thousands of entrepreneurs sell up all or part of their business. The reasons for doing so are legion. Some want to retire, others want out of a business they are bored with and the resources to get into something new. Some feel their business has reached the point where association with a larger business is either desirable or even essential.

Many firms who have taken venture capital on board will find their erstwhile partners become restive after a few years and seek to influence both the choice and the timing of an exit-route for their investee firms.

These examples give a flavour of some of the main reasons for selling up.

Scientific instruments

From its origins in a garage in the early 1970s one small British manufacturer of scientific instruments managed to finance expansion from retained profits. Despite all the efforts of its management, however, the company faced three seemingly insuperable barriers to growth.

It lacked the resources to develop its own computer systems; it was unduly dependent on an overseas supplier; and it was unable to break into the US market because its products were not sufficiently competitive. These problems were compounded by a new product which suffered from technical and design failings.

By 1978, the company, which then employed 20 people, appeared to have reached a limit to its growth. It was helped out of this impasse when it was acquired by a larger company. This allowed the smaller firm to finance a new research and development programme and invest in production capacity.

With the help of its larger parent the smaller company has since grown to turnover of £11m (in 1987) and a work-force of 245. Seventy per cent of its production is exported and it spends 12 per cent of turnover on R & D.

Thomas Goode

In January 1991 Thomas Goode's 60 family shareholders decided that the business, which has been financially weakened in recent years by failed diversifications and the tough retailing market, could best be taken forward as part of a larger organisation. They also wanted to realise some of the capital tied up in the business, which they hoped would fetch about £10m.

Hambros Bank was asked to look for suitable buyers and very quickly received several preliminary offers from potential purchasers in the UK as well as from North America, Japan and continental Europe.

The business started in 1827, when Thomas Goode opened à china store in Hanover Square. The shop moved in 1845 to its present site in South Audley Street and consists of an enticing maze of small showrooms displaying ornate glassware, porcelain and fine china.

Mrs Robinson, a former executive editor of Vogue *magazine who also worked as a main board director at Debenhams, gradually transformed the business after her appointment as managing director in 1988, and also brought in outside professional managers.*

They modernised the shop, speeded up service, introduced computer technology, achieved faster stock turn-round and improved the availability of goods. They also introduced a range of branded goods, ranging from pottery to playing cards, and are looking at further licensing and franchising opportunities. Thomas Goode has retained three royal warrants, which are proudly on display near the entrance. Other precious objects are also on show and two seven foot high Minton china elephants stand guard in the window.

However, by 1991 the company had reached an impasse and was finding it hard to expand without further injections of cash. The company was hit badly by the collapse of a pottery manufacturer it ran in Stoke-on-Trent and an unfortunate – and expensive – attempt to stage an exhibition in the US on the day the Wall Street market crashed in October 1987.

Like many other UK retailers, Thomas Goode suffered from the harsh trading climate in the early 1990s and was further hampered when some large orders from Kuwait and Iraq were cancelled because of the Gulf War. Sales in the 12 months to 31 January 1991 rose from £3.4m to £3.6m but the company still made a small loss at the pre-tax level.

Technophone

Finland's largest private company, Nokia, became the world's second biggest manufacturer of cellular telephones after Motorola of America, after paying £34m for Technophone, a British company set up seven years ago with a share capital of just £3.3m. The agreement made Hans Wagner, Technophone's chairman, and Nils Martensson, managing director, millionaires many times over. Together, they held 60 per cent of the share capital. Mr Martensson remained in charge of Technophone and joined the board of Nokia-Mobira, the cellular telephone arm of Nokia.

The 1991 deal was the fruit of more than 12 months of talks between the companies. It put Nokia in a position to take advantage of the rapid expansion in demand for cellular telephones expected in the wake of agreement on a common European technical standard and fast-rising usage of the equipment world-wide. Mr Martensson claimed at the time that both companies would benefit from economies of scale as production volumes increased, and from shared research and development.

Technophone was set up in Camberley, Surrey, in 1984 and established a reputation for innovative lightweight telephone designs. It has manufacturing plants at Camberley and in Hong Kong, which together employ 500 people, as well as a research and development staff of 150 at Camberley.

A study at Cranfield published in 1989 by Sue Birley and Paul Westhead, with support from Price Waterhouse and Lloyds Bank came up with the following statistics on why entrepreneurs sell up (see Table 18.1). For the 2000 owners who responded to this part of the research study, 17 per cent indicated specific strategic reasons, 23 per cent either wished to retire or were selling due to ill health. By far the largest majority, however, were either in receivership (28.7 per cent) or administration (23.9 per cent).

Where are the exits?

The Cranfield study mentioned earlier revealed for the first time the overall pattern in business sales for a five-year period (see Table 18.2). By far the most common method used by owners to realise their investment in their business is sale through advertisement. The option of a listing on the Stock Exchange, whether it be a full listing, or a partial listing on the Unlisted Securities Market (USM; replaced in June 1995 by the AIM, see page 198), or the then Third Market, was a route used by just over 1000 businesses during the period studied. Moreover, a listing on the Stock Exchange does not automatically imply that the owner(s) or investor(s) have realised the whole of their equity stake in the business, but that they have merely diluted their ownership. Thus, for example, only 22 per cent of businesses admitted to a full listing sold shares through an offer for sale. This caveat also applies to the 446 independent acquisitions listed on the Stock Exchange.

Table 18.1 *Reasons why private company owners sell up*

Reasons for sale	Number	Percentage
(a) Strategic		
1. For development	41	2.1
2. Cash for incorporation of business	4	0.2
3. Lack of funds	5	0.3
4. Exchange shares for PLC shares	11	0.6
5. Wishing to diversify	3	0.2
6. Seeks acquisition	14	0.7
7. Strategy/policy misfit	190	9.5
8. Explore other interests	59	3.0
(b) Personal		
9. Retirement	397	19.9
10. Ill health	53	2.7
(c) Ceased to trade		
11. Receivership	574	28.7
12. Liquidation	82	4.1
13. Insolvency	1	0.1
14. Administration/joint administration	478	23.9
15. Minimise capital gains	1	0.1
16. Tax losses/ ceased trading	87	4.4

Table 18.2 *Exit routes for each year 1983–1987*

Year	Private advertised sales	Public listing	USM listing	Third Market listing	Mergers listed on the Stock Exchange	Independent acquisitions on the Stock Exchange	Management buy-outs	Receiver independent company management buy-outs	Private/ family/ retirement/ company management buy-outs
	No	No	No	No	No	No	No	No	No
1983	868	79	88	0	68	43	189	6	13
1984	1,168	87	101	0	90	69	209	8	19
1985	1,393	80	98	0	104	94	255	0	53
1986	1,338	136	94	0	132	115	312	2	56
1987	1,522	155	75	35	161	125	335	1	49
Total	6,289	537	456	35	555	446	1,300	17	190

Over the five years, the results show a clear growth in exit route activity in all markets except for the USM which has remained fairly stable at around 90 businesses per year. The smaller number in 1987 reflect the October stock market crash of that year. The Third Market was initiated in 1987 as a response to the perceived need for a market in the shares of the smaller, newer business, but in the first year only 35 businesses were traded. These positive trends in exit route activity are also reflected in the growth of management buy-outs, which continue to be an attractive option for entrepreneurs and managers alike.

Who can help?

Leaving aside going public which was dealt with in Chapter 10, where the main problem is how to *value* the business rather than finding someone to sell it to, Table 18.3 covers the principal organisations involved in selling private companies in the UK.

Over the five-year period covered in the Cranfield study, 624 agencies were involved in advertising 3322 private business sales. A significant minority of companies advertised their own firms themselves. Not surprisingly, the majority of agencies represented the leading firms of chartered accountants, most of which have significant geographic coverage, although five leading agencies (Edward Symmons and Partners, Henry Butcher Business Brokerage, Humberts Chartered Surveyors, Christie and Co and Levy Gee & Partners) were dealing with real estate based retail businesses. However, even the 20 most active agencies listed in the table accounted for only 27.4 per cent of the advertised sales. Indeed, 537 firms (86.1 per cent) appeared to have very little experience on which to draw, since they were only involved with one or two sales during the five-year period. On the basis of this evidence, it was decided in the Cranfield study to classify active agencies as being those agencies which had dealt with more than ten private sales each over the five-year period.

The media used by these organisations to sell private companies were studied in a two-month sample out of the whole period. To do anything else would have involved an enormous volume of data and perhaps little greater accuracy. Alongside the heavyweight nationals, the specialist periodical, *Business & Assets* and a representative local newspaper, the *Western Mail*, were included.

Table 18.4 shows that the *Financial Times*, *Daily Telegraph* and the *Western Mail* were all important media for the sale of private companies. The *Financial Times* was particularly strong with regard to manufacturing companies, while the *Daily Telegraph* heads the lists for service companies.

When it comes to the size of businesses being sold, the *Financial Times* is the clear leader (see Table 18.5). The average business on offer was priced at £455,027 compared with the *Western Mail* where the asking price was only £68,253.

Dressing to kill

If you are thinking of selling it certainly pays to plan ahead and prepare your business to look its best. Your buyer will be looking, at least, at your last three years' performance, and it is important that your figures for these periods are as good and clean as possible.

323

Table 18.3 *The leading agencies advertising private sales in 1983–1987*

Agency	Number of business sales	% of total business sales
Peat Marwick McLintock	284	4.5
Grant Thornton	204	3.2
Cork Gully	155	2.5
Price Waterhouse	117	1.9
Arthur Andersen	111	1.8
Touche Ross	108	1.7
Arthur Young	94	1.5
Ernst & Whinney	93	1.5
Deloitte, Haskins & Sells	83	1.3
Spicer, Pegler & Partners	67	1.1
Robson Rhodes	59	0.9
Stoy Hayward	55	0.9
Edward Symmons & Partners (a)	46	0.7
Henry Butcher Business Brokerage (a)	46	0.7
Binder Hamlyn	37	0.6
Coopers & Lybrand	37	0.6
Humberts Chartered Surveyors (a)	37	0.6
Christie & Co (a)	35	0.6
A P Locke & D R F Sapte	32	0.5
Levy Gee & Partners (a)	26	0.4

(a) Essentially dealing in real estate.

Table 18.4 *Industrial category of private business sales by different data sources, June and November 1987*

Standard industrial category	Data Source									
	Financial Times		Daily Telegraph		The Times		Business & Assets		Western Mail	
	No	%	No	%	No	%	No	%	No	%
Primary	12	3.9	1	0.4	1	1.5	2	3.4	24	8.7
Manufacturing	112	36.0	7	2.5	13	19.7	26	44.8	7	2.5
Construction	13	4.2	5	1.8	1	1.5	0	0.0	3	1.1
Services	168	54.0	270	95.4	49	74.2	30	51.7	241	87.6
Not known	6	1.9	0	0.0	2	3.0	0	0.0	0	0.0

Table 18.5 *Selling price (£s) of private business sales by different data sources, June and November 1987*

Data	Selling price					
	Mean £	Standard deviation £	Minimum £	Maximum £	Number valid cases	% of valid cases
Financial Times	455,027	526,780	3,500	3,000,000	55	17.7
Daily Telegraph	288,988	284,692	20,000	2,000,000	225	79.5
The Times	174,513	208,048	10,500	1,100,000	36	54.5
Business & Assets	230,667	164,020	50,000	450,000	6	10.3
Western Mail	68,253	70,957	1,875	600,000	172	62.5

Taking the latter point first, private businesses do tend to run expenses through the business that might be frowned upon under different ownership. One firm, for example, had its sale delayed for three years while the chairman's yacht was worked out of 'work in progress'. There can also be problems when personal assets are tucked away in the company, or where staff have been paid rather informally, free of tax. The liability rests with the company, and if the practice has continued for many years the financial picture can look quite messy.

The years before you sell up can be used to good effect by improving the performance of your business relative to others in your industry. Going down the Profit and Loss Account and Balance Sheet using ratios such as those covered in Chapter 4 will point out areas for improvement. Once the business is firmly planted on an upward trend, your future projections will look that much more plausible to a potential buyer. You should certainly have a business plan and strategic projections for at least five years. This will underpin the strength of your negotiations by demonstrating your management skills in putting together the plan, and show that you believe the company has a healthy future.

Some entrepreneurs may wonder if such an effort is worthwhile. Perhaps the following example will show how financial planning can lead to capital appreciation for the founder.

A 34-year old owner–manager built up a regional service business in the United States, that had a 40 per cent compounded annual growth rate for the five most recent years. He employed an experienced CPA (Chartered Accountant) as his chief financial officer. This person developed budgets for one- and three-year periods and a detailed business plan charting the company's growth over the next five years. The owner's objective stated to his directors was to be ready to sell his business when the right offer came along.

A UK company interested in acquiring a leading service company in the region and finding a manager with the potential for national leadership carefully analysed the company and came away impressed with management's dedication to running its business in a highly professional manner. Because the previous year's after-tax profits had been $500,000 on sales of $10m, the UK company offered $4.5m on purchase, and $4.5m on attainment of certain profit objectives (well within the growth trend). The transaction closed on these terms.

The $9m offering price, representing 18 times net earnings, was 50 per cent higher than the industry norm and clearly justified the owner's careful job of packaging his business for sale.

Valuing the business

There are no mathematical or accountancy based formulae that will produce the correct value for your business. There are some principles that can help, but the figure you end up with will in all probability have more to do with your negotiating skills, than with audited accounts.

Robert Wright, a Cranfield MBA who started up his venture, Connectair, immediately after completing his MBA in 1985, is a suitable cautionary tale. He sold out to Harry Goodman late of International Leisure fame in 1989 for around £7m. Not bad for just under five years' work. However, negotiations with Goodman took up nearly a year, and his opening offer was under £1m.

The starting point has to be how much you want to make from the sale. If you are planning to retire you will be unpleasantly surprised to discover exactly how much cash you need now to produce anything resembling a decent real salary for the next 20 years. If inflation runs its historic course you can expect the value of your nest-egg to halve every seven years.

The next task is to revalue your assets for sale rather than their continued use in the business. It seems incredible, but companies still leave assets at book value when planning to sell up. Quite recently there was widespread publicity about the sale of a major advertising agency where the buyer found he was able to recoup a large chunk of the sale price by selling off an under-valued office building in Tokyo. Good news for the buyer, galling for the seller.

Finding a formula

It will always be helpful to develop some logic for setting the selling price. The net present value technique involves using a formula with logic behind it, which can provide the basis for a rational rather than a purely emotional discussion with prospective buyers.

The formula used to calculate it is quite simple, but the factors used in arriving at the valuation are somewhat subjective. A simple valuation of a company by way of an example is shown on pages 300–1.

Scrutiny, rarity and uniqueness

There is much anecdotal evidence to demonstrate that purchasers are prepared to pay more than a financial valuation alone would support, when suitable companies are rare in a given sector.

For example, Laura Ashley paid rather more for Penhaligans, the up-market toiletries business, than they eventually got when they sold the business on a couple of years later, in 1990. But Penhaligans was unique, and in the toiletries sector small retail chains are rare. It also seemed a perfect fit to Ashley's style of business. But when their profits slid in 1990, as did many UK retailers, they had to concentrate on their core business and sell off everything else.

The example given earlier of Thomas Goode's is one where prospective buyers were acquiring a name and a collection of royal warrants as much as an income stream. A private company not under the same compulsion as public companies to achieve immediate earnings growth may be prepared to pay more for these intangible benefits.

Afterwards

What happens afterwards rather depends on your goals in selling up. If you are retiring then your plans should be well laid beforehand. If you are staying on as a member of a larger group, as Technophone's Nils Martensson did, then you need to be prepared for corporate rather than entrepreneurial life. This can be hard, and few people make the transition successfully.

If you are walking away with a large cheque, as Robert Wright did, then your experiences may bear a close resemblance to a bereavement. He, and many others who have sold up, have taken years to find the right opportunity to get back into business. What they have found helpful is to set themselves up as a sort of one-man venture capital and management consultancy business. By putting the word out that they are interested in buying or backing ventures in the field they understand best, they receive a steady stream of proposals and presentations, from which they hope to fund their next venture.

Professional advice

Nothing said in this chapter should be construed as a substitute for taking professional advice. Most people only sell a business once in their lives. The best professional advisers in the field sell a dozen or so each year. A good tax and pension strategy can double the end value you receive and legal advice on warranties can make sure you get to keep the money.

You could do worse than put yourself in your potential buyer's mind by re-reading Chapter 11, but reversing roles.

Bibliography

Barrow, Colin, *Financial Management for the Small Business*, 3rd edition, Kogan Page, London 1995.

Barrow, Colin and Golzen, Godfrey, *Taking Up a Franchise*, 10th edition, Kogan Page, London 1994.

Beckhard, Richard and Harris, Reuben T, *Organizational Transitions*, Addison-Wesley, Wokingham 1987.

Belasco, James A, *Teaching the Elephant to Dance*, Hutchinson, London 1990.

Deal, Terrence E and Kennedy, Allen A, *Corporate Cultures: Rites and Rituals of Corporate Life*, Penguin Books, London 1988.

Fuld, Leonard M, *Monitoring the Competition*, John Wiley, Chichester 1989

Gumbert, David E, editor, *Growing Concerns, Building and Managing the Smaller Business*, John Wiley, Chichester 1989.

Handy, Charles, *The Age of Unreason*, Arrow Books, London 1990.

Johnson, Gerry and Scholes, Kevan, *Exploring Corporate Strategy*, 2nd edition, Prentice-Hall, Hemel Hempstead 1988.

Kanter, Rosabeth Moss, *The Change Masters: Corporate Entrepreneurs at Work*, Unwin Publications, London 1985.

McDonald, Malcolm H B, *Marketing Plans*, 2nd edition, Heinemann, Oxford 1989.

Melkman, Alan, *How to Handle Major Customers Profitably*, Gower Press, Aldershot 1979.

Plant, Roger, *Managing Change and Making it Stick*, Fontana, London 1987.

Rosthorn, J, Haldane, A, Blackwell, E and Wholey, J, *The Small Business Action Kit*, 4th edition, Kogan Page, London 1994.

Siropolis, Nicholas C, *Small Business Management: A Guide to Entrepreneurship*, 3rd edition, Houghton Mifflin, Chichester 1986.

Storey, M John, *Inside America's Fastest Growing Companies*, John Wiley, Chichester 1989.

Warnes, Brian, *The Genghis Khan Guide to Business*, Osmosis Publications, London 1985.

Index

Note: references in italics indicate figures or tables.

Index